The Complex Development of Preservice and Inservice Teacher Identities

This book is part of the Peter Lang Education list.
Every volume is peer reviewed and meets
the highest quality standards for content and production.

PETER LANG
New York • Bern • Berlin
Brussels • Vienna • Oxford • Warsaw

Thomas P. Crumpler
and Lara J. Handsfield

The Complex Development of Preservice and Inservice Teacher Identities

Foreword by Brian Edmiston

PETER LANG
New York • Bern • Berlin
Brussels • Vienna • Oxford • Warsaw

Library of Congress Cataloging-in-Publication Data

Names: Crumpler, Thomas P., author.
Title: The Complex Development of Preservice and Inservice Teacher
Identities / Thomas P. Crumpler and Lara J. Handsfield.
Description: New York: Peter Lang, 2020.
Includes bibliographical references and index.
Identifiers: LCCN 2019033974 | ISBN 978-1-4331-7313-4 (hardback: alk. paper)
ISBN 978-1-4331-7314-1 (paperback: alk. paper) | ISBN 978-1-4331-5588-8 (ebook pdf)
ISBN 978-1-4331-5589-5 (epub) | ISBN 978-1-4331-5590-1 (mobi)
Subjects: LCSH: Teachers—Training of. | Student teachers—Training of. |
Teachers—Psychology. | Student teachers—Psychology. |
Identity (Psychology)
Classification: LCC LB1707 .C78 | DDC 370.71/1—dc23
LC record available at https://lccn.loc.gov/2019033974
DOI 10.3726/b16104

Bibliographic information published by **Die Deutsche Nationalbibliothek**.
Die Deutsche Nationalbibliothek lists this publication in the "Deutsche
Nationalbibliografie"; detailed bibliographic data are available
on the Internet at http://dnb.d-nb.de/.

The paper in this book meets the guidelines for permanence and durability
of the Committee on Production Guidelines for Book Longevity
of the Council of Library Resources.

© 2020 Peter Lang Publishing, Inc., New York
29 Broadway, 18th floor, New York, NY 10006
www.peterlang.com

All rights reserved.
Reprint or reproduction, even partially, in all forms such as microfilm,
xerography, microfiche, microcard, and offset strictly prohibited.

Printed in the United States of America

We dedicate this book to public school teachers for their tireless work and daily commitment to the students they teach.

CONTENTS

List of Figures ix
List of Tables xi
Foreword by Brian Edmiston xiii
Acknowledgments xix

Introduction 1
Chapter 1. The Complexities of Teacher Identity 11
Chapter 2. Setting the Stage: Scenes of Inquiry in Pre- and Inservice Teacher Development 31

First Interlude—Dylan 51
Chapter 3. Identity as Becoming in Professional Development: Isabel's Multiple Positioning 55
Chapter 4. Mobile Literacies, Scaling Practices, and Mobile Identities 89
Chapter 5. Performing Multiple Identities in Student Teaching 117

Second Interlude—Camille 139
Chapter 6. Exploring Teacher Identity Development Through Study Groups 141

Chapter 7. Reimagining Teacher Identity Research—A Dramatic
Approach 165

Index 187

FIGURES

Figure 3.1: Isabel. 67
Figure 3.2: Literature Discussion Group. 75
Figure 3.3: Isabel and Alejandro. 78

TABLES

Table 2.1:	Transcript Conventions.	45
Table 3.1:	Data Summary.	65
Table 3.2:	"I don't get this word."	66
Table 3.3:	"You have the question."	68
Table 3.4:	Seeing red.	69
Table 3.5:	World of words.	72
Table 3.6:	"Let's wrap it up."	76
Table 3.7:	"Too bad, so sad."	80
Table 4.1:	Bobby and Moises.	97
Table 4.2:	Bobby Stands.	97
Table 4.3:	Paula, Andrés, and Moises.	99
Table 4.4:	Paula, Raúl, and Andrés.	104
Table 4.5:	Paula Addresses the Discussion Group.	107
Table 4.6:	Paula, Luís, Bobby, and Moises.	110
Table 4.7:	Paula, Bobby, and Luís.	111
Table 5.1:	Interview 1, Excerpt 1 (R = Researcher, C = Camille).	126
Table 5.2:	Interview 1, Excerpt 2 (R = Researcher, C = Camille).	128
Table 5.3:	Video Two, Excerpt 1.	131
Table 7.1:	Process Terms as Research Tools.	170

FOREWORD
Brian Edmiston

The Ohio State University

One of the many strengths of this illuminating book is that, as Thomas Crumpler and Lara Handsfield stress in the Introduction, it is a "series of invitations into thinking and re-thinking ... teacher identities and development." I expect that like me you'll feel invited into reconsidering the significance of attending to teacher identity as Tom and Lara share their insights and offer challenging analysis. Each chapter presents rich data that they have gathered in classrooms and study group seminars over a two-year period as they documented their own and their students' teaching. In particular, they focus on facets of how two preservice and two practicing teachers begin to examine and reexamine their teaching as well as the effectiveness of reflective discussions for analysis as part of their teacher education programs. At the same time, the authors present, review, critique, and extend their view of the landscape of research on professional development and teacher identities which they enrich through the prism of the potential of using process drama.

When I was asked to write the Foreword to this book, I was in the midst of analyzing stories written by teachers as part of a teacher inquiry course I was teaching. Like those whom Tom and Lara write about, preservice and practicing teachers on my course were exploring and changing their teacher identities. At the heart of each class was trying out alternative possible ways of interacting with students. Each edged closer to becoming the sort of teacher they wanted to be as we collaboratively dramatized events from narratives they had written outside of class. The most unsettling but productive dialogue in class, and later on line, focused on differently imagining relationships with youngsters each of us found challenging. Asking, "What if I did this rather than that?" became a refrain brought to life by the collaborative power of using dramatic imagination to inquire into our lives as educators. The teachers, each in their own way, became more aware of overlaps and disconnects between their values and how they were acting in their classrooms. As Crumpler and Handsfield analyze, citing Marilyn Cochran-Smith, the teachers could become, "makers of knowledge and more active participants in examining their own identities and begin to dismantle and reimagine the traditional constructions of teacher identity" (p. xx).

Reading *The Complex Development of Preservice and Inservice Teacher Identities* I was struck by the effectiveness of using positioning theory to recognize and understand more of the complexity of developing teacher identities. Though I've been aware for some time of the importance of considering how teachers position students when using drama in education (Edmiston, 2003), on reading this book I could see more dimensions of its wider significance within teacher education and classroom-based research. Understanding how, both as teachers and as researchers, we position, and may reposition, ourselves and our students is pivotal to how we have become the people we are in classrooms (Fecho, 2011). Changing our positioning can be central to how we might transform both our pedagogy and our research. I had previously been inspired by how, in earlier publications, Tom and Lara had been so honest in recognizing how, despite their intention to the contrary, as literacy educators they had been complicit in perpetuating deficit discourses circulating among teachers as they researched the literacy learning of classroom students. Indeed, to illustrate to the teachers on my course how we can't change and grow as educators unless we're honest and detailed about examining our failures, I had referenced their significant research alongside my own work. Imagine my delight on discovering that Tom's and Lara's book not only had built on their previous findings but also had addressed the same issue I have been grappling with: how and why as teacher educators might we use dramatic approaches to support teachers developing their identities, or using Bakhtin's term, their ideological becoming (Edmiston, 2016).

Crumpler and Handsfield turned to a seminal article by Elizabeth Moje and Allan Luke (2009) to provide an organizing framework for their book. Moje and Luke explore the relationship between identity and positioning and other facets of identification along with their significance for literacy educators and researchers as well as for learning and teaching in general. They present and use five metaphors as heuristics to analyze the educational literature on identity stressing that each metaphor carries implications both for how learning, teaching, and research are understood and for the significance of identities in people's lives in and out of classrooms. Whereas in my teacher inquiry course I had relied more on the metaphor of *identity as narrative*, Crumpler and Handsfield focus on the metaphor of *identity as position*. Like them, I've become fascinated by the potential use of process drama in teacher's inquiries into their practice, or what I often refer to as dramatic inquiry (Edmiston, 2014), along with its significance in developing a teacher identity on a trajectory of bringing into being a future closer to a teacher's imagined ideal classroom life.

As Moje and Luke note, narratives can provide the "gel" that holds classroom experiences together (Ibid., p. 249). Positioning theory focuses on the "storylines" of shared narratives within a community, such as a classroom. The "positioning triangle" developed by Harré and Langenhove (1999) stresses the interrelationships between people's social positions, storylines, and acts. In other words, how we act is affected by, and affects, both the story we're narrating together and how we position ourselves relative to everyone else. Nikki Slocum-Bradley (2008) has extended the triangle by proposing a "positioning diamond." Conceptualizing identity in a way that's close to Moje's and Luke's metaphor of *identity as difference*, she argues that position and identity cannot be conflated. For her, a person's identity both restricts and extends their sense of the rights and obligations that flow from their social position and thus the acts that people assume are possible (or not) because of their identification with a group and the unfolding shared storyline.

Why use dramatic approaches in teacher education? Dramatizing narratives allows people "to act as if they possess identities" (Moje & Luke, 2009, p. 249). And as Crumpler and Handsfield show, using a scalar analysis, as students and/or teachers act differently they reposition themselves when they are able to tactically access semiotic resources different from those typically available to them in the classroom, such as movement. Simple acts that are "lower-scaled" such as moving and speaking as if they are someone else, can disrupt dominant "higher-scaled" discourses such as teacher-initiated IRE

(Initiate-Respond-Evaluate) exchanges. At the same time, though students may be open to productive disruption and mobility across established social boundaries, as the authors illustrate, teachers may miss the opportunity to harness young people's energy and imagination. Conversely, when teachers are open to negotiating with students in ways that inevitably disrupt classroom power relationships, they can become more effective at tactically repositioning themselves to use simple dramatic strategies such as creating still images that "show us" people in an imagined world with whom we might dialogue as ourselves or from the positions of characters from a fictional story or of other people in the everyday world. Thus, dramatic imagination extends possibilities for affecting identity development by positioning oneself and others differently, by changing the shared storyline of a narrative, and by creating opportunities for acting and responding with a changed sense of one's possibility as a teacher for making a difference to young people's learning.

Why use dramatic inquiry with classroom teachers? As Crumpler and Handsfield stress, teachers can reimagine how they might have acted differently in the past so as to play out ways they might interact in the future. In doing so, teachers use their agency not only to explore pragmatic teaching possibilities but also to take charge in becoming a different teacher closer to the one they envision and hope to be for their students. Teachers can not only dialogue and inquire about the significance of particular troubling events to them and their students but also extend the meaning they make via dialogue as they interact as if within those events from multiple perspectives beyond typical comfortable positions such as teacher-in-charge. Any dramatization introduces a storyline that parallels the unfolding classroom storyline of teachers-and-students. Any events from a person's journey to become a teacher may come to life in a study group. More of the complexity of such events may be realized when we are open to interacting as if we are students or teachers who are only present in the room via our collective use of dramatic imagination.

In this perceptive book, Crumpler and Handsfield raise important questions about the complexity of developing teacher identity. They close by quoting Cecily O'Neill with whom both Tom and I had the privilege of working closely and benefiting from her wisdom about the power of drama in the classroom. She argued that process drama, "demands that we discover other versions of ourselves in the roles we play or watch other actors playing." For a while, "We slip the bonds of our identities and participate in other forms of existence" (O'Neill, 1995, p. 151). As you read on, may you "slip the bonds" of your identities as teachers and researchers, reimagine your role in teacher education, and try out using drama with students as you apply the complex but accessible ideas laid out in the chapters that follow.

References

Edmiston, B. (2016). Promoting Teachers' Ideological Becoming: Using Dramatic Inquiry in Teacher Education. *Literacy Research: Theory, Method, Practice, 65*, 332–347.
Edmiston, B. (2014). *Transforming Teaching and Learning with Active and Dramatic Approaches: Engaging Students Across the Curriculum.* New York, NY: Routledge.
Edmiston, B. (2003). What's My Position? Role, Frame, and Positioning When Using Process Drama. *Research in Drama Education, 8*(2), 221–229.
Fecho, B. (2011). *Writing in the Dialogical Classroom: Students and Teachers Responding to the Texts of their Lives.* Urbana, IL: National Council of Teachers of English.
Harré, R., & Langenhove, L. (1999). *Positioning Theory: Moral Contexts of Intentional Action.* Oxford, UK: Blackwell.
Moje, E. B., & Luke, A. (2009). Literacy and Identity: Examining the Metaphors in History and Contemporary Research. *Reading Research Quarterly, 44*(4), 415–437.
O'Neill, C. (1995). *Drama Worlds: A Framework for Process Drama.* Portsmouth, NH: Heinemann.
Slocum-Bradley, N. (2008). *Promoting Conflict or Peace through Identity.* Aldershot, UK: Ashgate Publishing.

ACKNOWLEDGMENTS

The research for this book was completed with the generous support of a grant from the Spencer Foundation. We would like to thank all of those who participated in this study, particularly the teachers. Their thoughtfulness, persistent desire to better serve the children and families they work with, and their willingness to engage critically with us and our work contributed to our thinking and our own development as educators in innumerable ways. We would also like to thank former graduate students and colleagues Tami Dean, Dana Karraker, Helen Fisher, and Carolyn Hunt for their contributions and research insights throughout the project. Finally, thanks to our Illinois State University writing group who patiently read early drafts of chapters and offered critical feedback that improved the final version of our book.

INTRODUCTION

Teacher professional identity development is a complex set of processes that brings together personal, historical, and sociocultural experiences, content knowledge, program preparation, and clinical experiences within contexts and discourses of education (Alsup, 2006; Britzman, 2012; Danielewicz, 2001; Marsh, 2003). While researchers have investigated aspects of these processes and demonstrated the need to look beyond skills and generalized best practices to include social processes, there is minimal empirical work that focuses on teacher identity across both short (e.g., a few minutes) and broader (e.g., months years) time scales. In this book, we aim to show how teacher identities are performed and shift at the micro level and across a span of two years and detail how these shifts are situated in school and classroom contexts. We show how teachers tactically position themselves (de Certeau, 1984) as they engage in classroom practices and interactions with students, colleagues, and us as researchers to navigate current political discourses of accountability and standardization.

Understanding how identities are constructed, evolve, and can shift moment-by-moment is essential for teacher preparation and development programs striving to prepare successful teachers. This is particularly critical in contexts characterized by neoliberal reforms that attempt to quantifiably measure successful teaching to the exclusion of other facets of professional growth. Consider, for example, how the Charlotte Danielson (2011) framework has been scaled up for purposes of teacher evaluation in ways that are more attuned to school accountability and less to authentic teacher development and student learning (Clayton, 2017). Such processes of teacher evaluation tend to reinscribe discourses of decontextualized best practices while minimizing the complex and emotional identity work at the heart of teaching (Hunt & Handsfield, 2013). But while teaching is often mundane, everyday work, it is also dramatic—responsive to and infused with shifting scenes, characters, and sets. In the ensuing chapters, we explore possibilities for making identity awareness a core component of teacher development by using process drama as a lens for think about identity work.

Other books have explored how teacher identity and instructional practices develop with respect to discourses of schooling (Alsup, 2006; Marsh, 2003). However, this book is unique for three reasons. First, we bring together analyses of both preservice and inservice teachers. Second, we situate our analyses and discussion of teacher identities within a syncretic frame that combines critical sociocultural theories (Bakhtin, 1981; Lewis, Enciso, & Moje, 2007), poststructuralist sensibilities, and elements of process drama to analyze linguistic, visual, and gestural data (Handsfield, Crumpler, & Dean, 2010). The process drama lens adds an especially innovative facet to the book because it allows us to delve into and re-conceptualize performative intricacies: moments when linguistic, visual, and linguistic data overlap in complex ways as identities are enacted. In doing so, we illustrate how teachers enact professional identities and instructional practices *over and across* different spaces and scales of time. Finally, we offer specific suggestions for both research and practice in teacher development that operationalize the complexities we highlight. These include addressing researcher–participant collaboration and power relationships, and supporting teacher candidates and practicing teachers in understanding their own professional positioning.

Project Backstory and Description

How should we theorize teacher identities? Who are literacy teachers as professionals? Who should they be? How are literacy teachers positioned in their school contexts vis-a-vis curricula and policies? And what are the tactics new literacy teachers use to take up and play with professional identities so that they can be successful with increasingly diverse learners while still navigating standardizing and technocratic policies? How does an expanding definition of literacy shape these processes and negotiations in teaching contexts characterized by high stakes student assessment and teacher evaluation? These questions and others informed a two-year research project that we undertook to examine initial literacy teacher preparation and professional development. This book is the result of that project.

Project Backstory

Our work began in 2006 as a collaborative investigation of how pre- and practicing teachers' discourses of literacy teaching and learning might shift through coursework and professional development, and subsequently into instruction, framed around new literacies and multilingualism in kindergarten through eighth grade classrooms. Our research was richly generative with respect to the sheer variety and quantity of data we produced. These data led us to think deeply about how teachers navigate multiple and oftentimes conflicting demands manifested within district literacy curricula and policies, facilitate student agency and academic success, and construct and perform their professional identities within classrooms.

Our data and our analyses evoke stories of elementary, middle level, and preservice teachers who engaged in conversations about the shifting modalities of literacies, and how to teach effectively in increasingly linguistically diverse classrooms, while also negotiating complex political demands and power relationships that swirl through public schools and teacher education programs. But these stories also reveal how we bumped up against the limits of research methodologies for interpreting literacy teacher development, discourses, and teacher identities. Moje and Luke (2009) argued for theorizing identity around five metaphors to challenge researchers delve more deeply into identity and social practices of literacy. Among these metaphors was "identity as position" (p. 429). Moje and Luke claimed, "Identities are produced in and through not only activity and movement in and across spaces, but, also in the ways people are cast in or called to particular positions in interaction" (p. 431) We agree that understanding how individuals are thrown into or take up positions is pivotal for understanding identity—particularly in teacher education— and our project builds on Moje and Luke's work. However, we also break new theoretical ground in understanding development of teacher identities by bringing a process drama lens to bear on this development.

Process drama uses dramatic structures such as teacher in role, students in role, tableau and others to activate imaginations and explore interpretive possibilities (Edmiston, 2014; O'Neil, 1995). In our own work (e.g., Crumpler, Handsfield, & Dean, 2011), we have used this lens to investigate how researchers might carry out different researcher/participant roles, replay problematic moments of data collection, and potentially reposition participants in more agentive ways during data collection. Process drama allows us to theorize how we might perform research differently and delve more deeply into the literate practices of teacher identity.

As a result, in this book we call for rethinking how teachers' professional identities are constructed and reconstructed moment by moment, across multiple contexts, and across multiple timescales (Lemke, 2000). This rethinking informed our data analysis throughout the project. As our understanding of teacher identity deepened, we began to see the preservice and inservice teachers who participated in our research as not only being positioned by dominant curricular discourses and institutional structures, but also tactically wielding multiple discourses and structures to construct and reconstruct professional identities. We were particularly struck by how these tactical negotiations occurred within and across small scales of time and how their identity performances were dialogic (Bakhtin, 1981) and shifted as teachers rehearsed identities (Cazden, 1995) and positioned themselves vis-à-vis different school contexts and different research activities. This book explores these intricacies of the ongoing process of becoming literacy teachers. We believe that discursive positioning and repositioning is central to what preservice and inservice teachers do as they navigate shifting political terrain in their work.

This book is designed and written for researchers and educators who want think more deeply about studying teacher identity and explore the possibilities of identity work as a feature of their preparation programs. It is also targeted for educators who are working with classroom teachers and desire to facilitate reflective conversations about identities and their relationships to instruction using a process drama frame. Innovative in its conceptualization and approach to examining teacher identity, informed by salient research and careful data analysis, and supported by significant findings, we believe this book is an important resource for studying the complexities of teacher identity.

Project Description

Literacy professionals' curricula, professional expectations and indeed the nature of what counts as literacy are in flux. Teachers work in increasingly culturally and linguistically diverse classrooms where shifts in technologies and popular culture compel them to rethink their literacy instruction. Designing professional development to respond to this fluctuation is an ongoing challenge. We wondered how these changes were impacting teachers and teaching practices. To address this and other questions we developed a two-year project in which we examined multilingualism and multiliteracies (New London Group, 1996) as a framework for facilitating development of K-8 preservice and inservice teachers. Our overarching goal was to better understand how this frame might support teachers as they contended with shifts in literacy practices informed by increased linguistic and cultural diversity as well as an influx of multimodal technologies. We understand these shifts in practice as historically and culturally situated and tied to specific ideologies and power relationships. For example, K-8 learners' knowledge multiple languages, popular culture texts such as video games and graphic novels, and the internet are part and parcel of their literacy identities. Teachers' recognition of these funds of knowledge expands traditional notions of literacy and necessitates new instructional choices. We also were curious about what discourses of language and literacy teachers might generate during professional development opportunities that were focused around these same concepts.

We designed a three-phase research project with preservice and inservice teachers. Phase one involved redesigning the introductory literacy methods course in our own elementary education program so that it centered around topics of linguistic diversity and multiliteracies (New London Group, 1996). Also during phase one, we designed and facilitated a study group for inservice teachers focused on literacy for linguistically diverse learners.

Phase two included a second study group, also designed and facilitated by us. This study group focused on multimodal literacies and language arts instruction, and was unique in that it brought together both prospective teachers who participated in phase one and some of the same inservice teachers who had participated in the first study group. Finally, phase three included observations of a small group of pre- and inservice teachers as they endeavored to integrate new teaching practices into literacy instruction based on their coursework and study group engagements. At the beginning of this phase, participants were asked to generate a small number of pedagogical goals for their teaching (or student teaching, for prospective teachers). We asked them to make these goals "doable" with respect to the material and political limitations and affordances of their classrooms and schools. We then conducted classroom observations as they were engaged in literacy instruction meant to address their goals. We devote Chapter 2 to a fuller explication of our research project, including our research activities and how we went about generating and analyzing data.

Throughout and across the three phases of this project, our conversations about what we were learning about literacy instruction and the development of literacy teachers simultaneously expanded and deepened. At the end of the project, we recognized that our shifts in understanding of teacher identity were anchored in the daily practices and choices preservice and inservice teachers make as they teach lessons, interact with colleagues, help students comprehend texts, and go about their work in schools and classrooms. The challenges that teachers at all stages of their careers face as they respond to new standards, assessments, and implement curricula that diminish their professional judgments are daunting. As former classroom teachers ourselves, our respect and admiration for their continual efforts on behalf of their students every day is central to this book.

Introduction to the Chapters

In addition to this introduction, this book includes seven chapters, as well as two narrative interludes. This structure creates three sections of the book. Section one includes the introduction, Chapters 1 and 2. Interlude one is placed here. Section two is comprised of Chapters 3, 4 and 5. Interlude two is placed here. The last section includes Chapters 6 and 7.

In Chapter 1, we review and critique research related to teacher identities and introduce a process drama frame that underpins the book. Our intention is not to provide a comprehensive review of scholarship; rather, we distill foundational and current scholarship and theory to provide readers with an overview of the landscape on this topic and to situate our own research project and the chapters that follow. In this chapter, we also describe our own theoretical understandings regarding teacher identity development and discursive positioning, and how our understandings have evolved over the course of our research. In doing so, we set the stage for our more detailed theoretical explorations in later chapters.

In Chapter 2 we describe our research project in detail. We first explain the genesis of the project with respect to broader trends or "turns" in the fields of literacy research and teacher education. We then describe the study contexts (towns, districts, schools) and participants, as well as our research activities, including our data collection and analysis procedures. In this chapter, we also introduce microethnographic discourse analysis (Bloome et al., 2005) and analyses of body movements as primary analytic tools for our research.

In Chapter 3 we zoom in to examine spatial aspects of teacher identities and positioning. To do this, we tell the story of a fourth-grade teacher, Isabel, and her work with her bilingual students. We explore how the traditional categories of "novice" and "experienced" teachers are misleading dichotomies, and showcase how Isabel tactically refashioned her own professional identities by positioning herself in tactical ways across different ideological landscapes of language and literacy. Further, we highlight how a group of Isabel's students negotiated social and academic identities, and ideologies of language and literacy learning during a literature discussion group.

Chapter 4 spotlights Paula, a third-grade bilingual teacher and colleague of Isabel's, as she integrated technology into her writing instruction. In doing so, we illustrate how Paula's positioning can be understood with respect to the concept of scaling practices and metaphors of mobility and how these concepts inform teacher education and the negotiation of identities across time.

Camille, a preservice teacher, is the focus of Chapter 5. We look carefully how Camille tactically recruited her identity as a mother in her methods courses and through her student teaching to position herself in advantageous ways. We illustrate how she positioned herself within immediate, or local, timescales, and across longer timescales as she negotiated the ideologically complex political contexts of teacher preparation and student teaching in her clinical placement.

Chapter 6 focuses on using process drama with teacher study groups (Courtney, 1990; Edmiston, 2014; O'Neill, 1995). We begin by reviewing scholarship on study groups as a professional development structure and argue that often, professional development does not support teacher agency and autonomy. We demonstrate how using process drama tools can foster systematic inquiry about identity and also open spaces for teachers to consider how their own and others' identities are forged in classroom and professional interactions.

We conclude with Chapter 7, in which we argue for a dramatic approach to researching teacher identities with teacher candidates and inservice teachers. We also describe how new instructional practices that are explicitly performative in their orientation can enrich preservice teacher education and inservice teacher development.

In the first interlude, we revisit a preservice teacher (Dylan), and analyze how he negotiates multiple ideologies and discourses in his literacy memoir. His memoir shows how popular culture shapes his sense of literacy instruction. In the second interlude, we return to the classroom of one of our focal participants, Camille, re-story a moment in an instructional sequence, and ask, what if Camille had followed the excitement displayed by students at that moment of teaching? We use the imaginary to inform the real (Booth, 1985), and recruit the power of pretending to consider how an instructional sequence could be performed differently. Both interludes are interruptive spaces within the text that invite readers to pause and imagine other potential scenes of meaning.

Our own thinking about literacy teacher education and professional development, and teacher identity construction shifted over the course of our two-year study, and our ideas continue to shift through the writing of this book. It is our hope that this book not be read as a set of static determinations regarding processes of teacher identities and development, but rather as a series of invitations into thinking and rethinking such phenomena. We hope that readers will use the ensuing chapters as tools for engaging with and moving beyond these ideas presented within them.

References

Alsup, J. (2006). *Teacher identity discourses: Negotiating personal and professional spaces*. New York, NY: Routledge.

Bakhtin, M. M. (1981). *The dialogic imagination* (Michael Holquist, Ed. & Caryl Emerson and Michael Holquist, Trans.). Austin, TX: University of Texas Press

Bakhtin, M. M. (1984). *Problems of Dostoevsky's Poetics* (Caryl Emerson, Trans., p. 17). Minneapolis, MN.

Bloome, D., Carter, S. P., Christian, B. M., Otto, S., & Shuart-Faris, N. (2005). *Discourse analysis and the study of classroom language and literacy events: A microethnographic perspective*. New York, NY: Routledge.

Booth, D. (1985). "Imaginary gardens with real toads": Reading and drama in education. *Theory into Practice, 24*(3), 193–198.

Britzman, D. P. (2012). *Practice makes practice: A critical study of learning to teach*. Albany, NY: Suny Press.

Cazden, C. B. (1995). New ideas for research on classroom discourse. *TESOL Quarterly, 29*(2), 384–387.

Clayton, C. (2017). Raising the stakes: Objectifying teaching in the edTPA and Danielson rubrics. In Julie H. Carter & Hilary A. Lochte (Eds.), *Teacher performance assessment and accountability reforms* (pp. 79–105). New York, NY: Palgrave Macmillan.

Courtney, R. (1990). *Drama and intelligence: A cognitive theory*. Montreal, QC: McGill-Queen's University Press.

Crumpler, T., Handsfield, L., & Dean, T. (2011). Constructing difference differently in language and literacy professional development. *Research in the Teaching of English, 46*(1), 55–91.

Danielewicz, J. (2001). *Teaching selves. Identity, pedagogy, and teacher education*. Albany, NY: State University of New York Press.

Danielson, C. (2011). *Enhancing professional practice: A framework for teaching*. Alexandria, VA: ASCD.

de Certeau, M. (1984). *The practice of everyday life* (Steven Rendall, Trans.). Berkeley, CA: University of California Press.

Edmiston, B. (2014). *Transforming teaching and learning with active and dramatic approaches: Engaging students across the curriculum*. New York, NY: Routledge.

Handsfield, L. J., Crumpler, T. P., & Dean, T. R. (2010). Tactical negotiations and creative adaptations: The discursive production of literacy curriculum and teacher identities across space-times. *Reading Research Quarterly, 45*(4), 405–431.

Hunt, C. S., & Handsfield, L. J. (2013). The emotional landscapes of literacy coaching: Issues of identity, power, and positioning. *Journal of Literacy Research, 45*(1), 47–86.

Lemke, J. L. (2000). Across the scales of time: Artifacts, activities, and meanings in ecosocial systems. *Mind, Culture, and Activity, 7*(4), 273–290.

Lewis, C., Enciso, P., & Moje, E. B. (2007). *Reframing sociocultural research on literacy: Identity, agency, and power*, Mahwah, NJ: Lawrence Erlbaum.

Marsh, M. M. (2003). *The social fashioning of teacher identities. Rethinking childhood*. New York, NY: Peter Lang.

Moje, E. B., & Luke, A. (2009). Literacy and identity: Examining the metaphors in history and contemporary research. *Reading Research Quarterly, 44*(4), 415–437.

The New London Group. (1996). A pedagogy of multiliteracies: Designing social futures. *Harvard Educational Review, 66*(1), 60–93.

O'Neill, C. (1995). *Drama worlds: A framework for process drama*. Portsmouth, NH: Heinemann.

· 1 ·
THE COMPLEXITIES OF TEACHER IDENTITY

Introduction

CAMILLE:	All right
	Now	you guys have a <u>mission</u>		
STUDENTS:	[Ooh Aah]
CAMILLE:	Now	First I'm going to show you some <u>examples</u>
	So don't <u>panic</u> if you don't know what to do
	We're going to write down two or three sentences
	from your manuals	
	that have pronouns in 'em↓
	OKAY↑ (Transcript from Camille's student teaching)

Camille was a returning student in elementary education pursuing a teaching license after working in another job and choosing to start a family. She was trying to bring an aspect of popular culture into the classroom, in particular video games, which she had read and talked about in study groups that were a facet of the larger project that informs this book. The moment captured in this brief interaction between Camille as a student teacher and her students was part of a larger instructional sequence in which she used video game manuals to teach pronouns.

On the surface, this exchange simply looks like the beginning of an instructional task in which a student teacher is providing directions to a group of elementary students; and, this is indeed what she was doing. However, we believe that much more is happening on a variety of levels simultaneously in this moment. With the short phrase, "All right. Now you guys have a mission," Camille jumps to a new instructional space—a potential mission with a new instructional worry—who might panic? Her? The students? Both students and Camille as they take up this new learning endeavor? She also initiates a new temporal sequence, "First I'm going to show you some examples" to help the students prepare for the mission, shifting from "clock time" to "narrative time" (Mishler, 2006, p. 30) because this mission carries with it an implicit narrative.

This moment of interaction lasted less than twenty seconds. However, in this interaction with students, Camille is constructing and reconstructing her identity as a teacher through blending popular culture with discourses of schooling at a particular moment in an elementary classroom. Camille forges her teacher identity while at the same time moving into a new instructional sequence. We view this type of sequence with the students in the transcript data above as moving to a new timescale of instruction—a mission in which there is a possibility for a new narrative that the students will have a role in creating. Moments like this one are part of teaching, and central to understanding teacher identities.

We understand teacher identities as constructed in the nexuses of classroom practice, discourses of schooling, teacher preparation programs, and personal histories. Identities are dynamic, performative, shift moment by moment, and are developed over longer timescales (Beauchamp & Thomas, 2009). We have drawn on Bakhtin's concept of chronotope (1981) in our own research on teacher identities (Crumpler, Handsfield, & Dean, 2011; Handsfield, Crumpler, & Dean, 2010; Handsfield, 2012) to better understand how space and time converge as teachers negotiate teaching, learning, and professional development. In the next section, we introduce Bakhtin's notion of chronotopes—literally timespaces—as well as other scholarship that has informed our own thinking regarding teachers' identity work.

Chronotopes and a Dramatic View of Teacher Identities

Bakhtin (1986) theorized combining space and time in language or other sign systems to create meaning, and labeled them chronotopes. More recently

Lemke (2000) wondered how seemingly isolated moments of human experience could "add up" (p. 273) to larger meaning in a life as he conceptualized roles of different timescales within the complexities of social relations. Bakhtin (1981) appropriated the term "chronotope" from Einstein and used it to define the "intrinsic interconnectedness of temporal and spatial relationships" (p. 84). His use was literary—and his purpose was to theorize how "time thickens, takes on flesh, becomes artistically visible" and how "space becomes charged and responsive to the movements of time, plot and history" (p. 84). However, scholars have also applied the concept of chronotope to literacy research to explore "ideological becoming" (Ball & Freedman, 2004, p. 3), or how identities both construct and are responsive to time, plot, and history. We understand thickening and charging of chronotopes as the "ground for activity" (Morson & Emerson, 1990, p. 369) or a dialogic basis that makes narrative and identity construction possible. Chronotopes are not neutral and vary in qualities. In other words, there are many different chronotopes, and as grounds for activity, different social relations and ways of becoming are possible.

To study teacher identity is to enter into such complexities. These complexities include questions about how professional identities are formed; the roles of context in shaping identities; how power informs identities; and, how identities are constructed moment by moment and across longer scales of time (Lemke, 2000; Wortham, 2006). We recognize that all human activity unfolds across different contexts and timescales: moments, hours, days, years, and is realized in social interactions within communities large and small. Identity is also linked to timescales (Canagarajah & De Costa, 2016). To recognize how identity construction unfolds in this way is to play with identities and thus to play with time. Playing with time is a tactical, innovative way to reimagine the work of preparing teachers and understanding identity. To situate these innovations, we draw in part on Moje and Luke (2009), who argued for theorizing identity around five metaphors to challenge researchers to delve more deeply into identity and social practices of literacy. Among these metaphors is "identity as position" (p. 431). Moje and Luke claimed, "Identities are produced in and through not only activity and movement in and across spaces, but, also in the ways people are cast in or called to particular positions in interaction" (p. 432).

Process Drama

We agree that understanding how individuals are thrown into or take up positions is pivotal for understanding identity—particularly in teacher education.

However, in this book we break new theoretical ground by bringing a process drama lens to bear on teacher identity development. Process drama uses dramatic structures such as teacher in role, students in role, tableau and others to activate imaginations and explore interpretive possibilities (Edmiston, 2014; O'Neil, 1995). In some of our previous work (Crumpler, Handsfield, & Dean, 2011), we have used this lens to investigate how researchers might carry out different researcher/participant roles, replay problematic moments of data collection, and potentially reposition participants in more active roles of data collection. Process drama allows us theorize how we might perform research differently and delve more deeply into the literate practices of teacher identity by asking "what if" and creating spaces for exploring tensions between what is and what could be (Edmiston, 2003):

- What if we actively engaged preservice and inservice teachers in serious dialogues about construction of teacher identities in preparation programs?
- What if we created social histories with groups of teachers in professional development contexts to explore genealogies of educational issues?
- What if we used dramatic structures to replay moments of tension in classroom research in which comments were made that reinforced deficit discourses, and created "research interludes" to explore ways to recast those discourses?

These are questions we can ask from a process drama framework.

The basis for this book is a two-year long qualitative research project in which we investigated how a multiliteracies framework was taken up preservice and inservice teachers. Developing a dramatic frame to our analyses helped deepened our understandings of teacher identities because we recognized that through drama, we could potentially replay moments in which identities were being constructed, revisit those moments, and re-analyze those moments in terms of other possible interpretations. Specifically, a dramatic understanding helped us see the preservice and inservice teachers, as well as ourselves, as tactically wielding multiple discourses of literacy and teaching to construct identities within small scales of time. Our findings are multifaceted and show how teachers' identity performances dialogic (Bakhtin, 1984) and dynamic—shifting as teachers rehearse identities (Courtney, 1995) and position themselves vis-à-vis different and oftentimes conflicting ideologies of schooling. As such, discursive positioning and repositioning are central to what preservice and inservice teachers do as they navigate the political climate, which has turned toward high stakes accountability in the teaching profession. Overall, we are calling for rethinking how teachers' professional identities are performed—constructed and reconstructed—moment by moment, across multiple contexts, and across multiple timescales.

Chronotopes and Scale

Recently, new understandings of teacher identity have emerged as scholars have built upon Bakhtin's chronotopic view of identity to theorize change across timescales and investigate these new constructs with teachers in classrooms (Buchholz, 2016; Compton-Lilly & Halverson, 2014). To further ground this book theoretically, we describe how others have built on the notion of chronotopes with respect to scale—both timescales (Lemke, 2000) and sociolinguistic scales (Blommaert, 2010, 2015; Canagarajah & DeCosta, 2016; Lempert, 2012). Next, we review other scholars in literacy who utilize these frames to examine literacy education (Buchholz, 2016; Compton-Lilly & Halverson, 2014; Wortham, 2006) and follow with a review scholarship in teacher identity (e.g., Beauchamp & Thomas, 2009; Beijaard, Meijer, & Verloop, 2004; Izadinia, 2013). Finally, we expand our argument for integrating process drama into re-envisioning teacher identity based on this body of scholarship.

Timescales

Although Bakhtin does not refer to timescales specifically, he claimed that chronotopes are "where the knots of narrative are tied and untied" (1984, p. 250). We understand this tying and untying as similar to jumps in timescales; and, for example when Camille moves from the prosaic instruction of pronouns using video game manuals to a "mission," she is untying a knot of instruction and lacing it to a new space where other temporal possibilities for learning and social relations await the students. We believe that teachers and preservice teachers can learn to notice opportunities for shifting across timescales with their students and that researchers can gain insights into the complexities of teacher identity through a framework informed by process drama. This is a central argument of this book. However, first we want to think more about timescales.

Lemke (2000) explores the complexity and puzzles of timescales on a human activity level. He suggested that "every process, action, social practice, or activity occurs on some timescale" (p. 275) and that in complex systems such as classrooms "on more than one timescale" (p. 275). Lemke considers timescales in classrooms within other "adjacent" timescales such as a single lesson, a school day, educational system change, and world system change to illustrate interactions between higher and lower timescales (p. 277). He argues that timescales are nested so that "the processes and the next lower timescale make possible the repeatable patternings of the next longer scale" (p. 276). For example, repeated lessons comprise the school day, and days of instruction become units of study.

However, a timescale like educational change already provides a longer context that informs how social practices are privileged in teacher education programs, which pedagogies are highlighted, and which are marginalized. In the research project, Camille was in a literacy methods course and a study group of inservice teachers who read and thought about how popular culture could be taken up in literacy instruction prior to her student teaching. The group interacted within the timescale of our research study, where we privileged discourses about popular culture and multiliteracies. Camille planned lessons that used the popular culture for instruction within the community of her classroom during student teaching. Her instructional practices were informed by shifting notions of what counts as literacy, a longer context already running at a higher scale.

Sociolinguistic Scales

Blommaert (2010, 2015) argues for the importance of chronotopes and timescales to study language in increasingly complex global contexts. He defines chronotopes as "invokable chunks of history that organize the indexical order of discourse" (2015, p. 105), and reminds us that for Bakhtin, history is a "spatiotemporal concept" (110). For Blommaert, scale develops in timespace; it is not simply a spatial metaphor but is also a social one involving human interactions (2010). In a sociolinguistic analysis exploring how language shifts within discourses of globalization, Blommaert (2010), building on Bakhtin and others, describes how language practices within social relations allow for "jumping from one scale to another" (p. 33) (also see Lempert, 2012) to index higher levels of meaning. For example, Camille's shift from the study of pronouns points toward a shared experience of a "mission" constitutes a jump to a new scale of shared meaning, embedded in discourses of adventure, such as that found in many video games, that elicits a response of excitement from the students. This moment is loaded with instructional potential, as well as potential for alternative and multifaceted meaning making and within it, complex teacher identities are being fashioned.

Our work in teacher identity follows Blommaert's argument that what is most generative about the chronotope as Bakhtin theorized it is "its connection to historical and momentary agency" (2015, p. 110). In other words, other histories converge in current moments and meaning making processes of the here and now. For example, Camille tells the students "don't panic" if they don't understand what to do after she has provided examples to facilitate the mission. The phase "don't panic" indexes her momentary agency as a preservice teacher attempting to reassure students about the mission, while other timescales—her experiences as a mother and knowledge of popular culture from interacting in the study group—converge to produce a specific identity in which she positions herself as a particular type of teacher. In that moment, she is a teacher who has piqued student enthusiasm with the promise of a mission, but worries that some might panic and explains they will write down sentences from video game manuals. The action of writing sentences returns to a timescale of traditional classroom instruction, which has spanned decades, copying from another text. Camille is rehearsing and performing possibilities while working in her cooperating teacher's (CT) classroom—and she co-creates this moment with her CT, the students, and all the histories that they bring to this classroom.

Scaling Practices as Strategies and Tactics

De Certeau (1984) also theorized about everyday practices in cultural production, tying these practices to power and space by distinguishing between strategies and tactics. Strategies are the practices of an institution or bureaucracy that order or manage social spaces. A strategy proposes a place that can be delimited as its own and serves as the foundation from which relations with other subjects and places can be managed (de Certeau, 1984). Similar to Foucault's (1977) panopticon, strategies instill a "conscious and permanent visibility that assures the automatic functioning of power" (p. 201).

Tactics, however, are calculated actions used by the less powerful—those without a space of their own. A tactic "... must vigilantly make use of the cracks that particular conjunctions open in the surveillance of the proprietary powers. It poaches in them. It creates surprises in them. It can be where it is least expected" (de Certeau, 1984, p. 37). Thus, in addition to strategically restricting access to semiotic resources, scaling practices may be tactical as people recontextualize semiotic resources across chronotopes, opening up space for alternative practices and identities (Collins & Blot, 2003; Handsfield & Crumpler, 2013; Handsfield, Crumpler, & Dean, 2010; Hunt, Crumpler, & Handsfield, 2016).

De Certeau's theorization of the practice of everyday life draws our attention to power as a microscopic function. The idea here is that even when literacy instructional practices or curricular models seem fairly static or rigid, when we zoom in to examine fine-grained, moment-by-moment interactions and practices, mobility becomes not only apparent, but the modus operandi. Examining mobilities at a micro-level illustrates the dynamic and unstable aspects of broader ideologies and power structures. Indeed, the whole system may jiggle. Even with regard to materiality, solids are composed of molecules on the move. De Certeau (1984) refers to this jiggling as a "mobile infinity of tactics" (de Certeau, 1984).

Identity work is complex work indeed. In the next section, we review recent research that has grappled with timespace in literacy learning.

Chronotope and Scales in Literacy Research

Recently, literacy researchers like Ball and Freedman (2004), Buchholz (2016), Compton-Lilly and Halverson (2014), and Wortham (2006) have examined how these complexities of timespace inform teacher identities. In this section, we briefly review scholarship by each author in terms of how their ideas have informed our ideas in this book.

Ball and Freedman (2004) ground their study of language and literacy in a Bakhtinian "ideological becoming, how we develop our way our way of viewing the world, our system of ideas" (p. 6), and link becoming in classrooms to tensions between "authoritative discourse and internally persuasive discourse" (p. 7). Authoritative discourse is what Bakhtin calls "the word of the fathers" (1981, p. 342) while internally persuasive discourses are discourses of the people we encounter daily in our lives in social interaction. Ball and Freedman (2004) argue that tensions and struggles between these two discourses that are central to ideological becoming. Others have built on this theoretical framing to examine literacy coaches' negotiations of authoritative discoruses (Hunt, 2018). We build on these arguments, contending that becoming is identity work is performed moment by moment across multiple space-times. Camille's discourse as a mother is important to her development as a teacher, and we explore this facet in more detail later in this book.

Wortham's (2006) study details how two students' identities developed over an academic year in the contexts of classroom interactions with teachers, peers, and curricula. Wortham makes a case for the necessity of examining the interplay of learning and identity over longer spans of time and argued for the importance of "cross-timescale relations" (p. 90) to understand social identification. Wortham recognized how longer timescales like race and gender were "mediated" by shorter timescales in classroom interactions. His work informs our understanding of how Camille's identity as a teacher developed over the two years she participated in our study. However, we also argue that teacher identities also shift in moment-by-moment performances and that understanding this development requires focusing on both timescales.

Compton-Lilly and Halverson (2014) review how timespace has been taken up in literacy research over the last century. Regarding the use of the concept of chronotope in literacy research, they argue that the "chronotope is an explanatory construct that invites educators to explore how time and space intersect in daily experiences and how those experiences are taken up, made sense of, and ultimately matter to teachers' and students' lives" (p. 4). In the introduction, Compton-Lilly (2014) and Halverson contend that timespaces are not "flat" like traditional conceptions of time, but have dimensionality that shapes classroom contexts and interactions on a daily basis. Our book follows their argument in that we examine daily experiences of teachers to discover space-time intersections and retheorize them from a process drama perspective.

Buchholz (2016)'s work investigated "the social construction of temporality in the classroom" (p. 125) over a four-year period. She suggested that space-time relationships are produced through instructional interactions among "intersecting discourses, historical bodies, and artifacts" (p. 125) in a moment of instruction. Camille as historical body, a returning teacher moving through the classroom with the students, using artifacts such as the Whiteboard, negotiating discourses of popular culture as a student teacher, all are aspects of her developing identity. Similar, Paula's and Isabel's histories as bilingual White women, their different professional histories, and their use of a variety of material resources all impact and reflect their mobile professional identities. We are interested in these intersections and how, as educators, we might examine them as aspects of teacher preparation and development to gain insights into how identity work is knotted with content knowledge learning in moment-to-moment interactions and across larger time scales. To frame this aspect of the book, we review scholarship on teacher identities in the next section.

Research on Teacher Identities

Researchers have brought a variety of theoretical perspectives to the study of teacher identity construction or development. Britzman (2007) draws on psychoanalytic theory to challenge a traditional myth of teacher development, viewing it as much more "uneven." Rutherford, Conway and Murphy (2015) use Foucault's work on disciplining the body to examine compliance in teacher identity. Hobson and McIntrye (2016) situate their research in third space theory to explore relationship between identity and resilience, while Lasky (2005) brings sociocultural theory to investigate relationships among teacher identity, agency, and context. Varghese, Morgan, Johnston, and Johnston (2005) analyzed teacher identity from multiple perspectives—situated learning theory, social identity theory, and image-text theory to demonstrate its complexity. Finally, Zembylas (2003) synthesized scholarship in postructuralist theory to consider the role of emotions in teacher identity.

Clearly, how to best understand teacher identity has long interested researchers in the field. Further, recent reviews of scholarship on teacher identity (Beauchamp & Thomas, 2009; Beijaard, Meijer, & Verloop, 2004; Izadinia, 2013) have suggested a lack of consensus about what we mean by teacher identity, and argued that a better understanding could inform teacher education as a whole and preservice teacher development in particular. Following others who have conceptualized identity as dynamic rather than static, this book argues for rethinking teacher identity as not inexorably tied to dichotomous categories like preservice or inservice, but as multiple, fluid and shifting within social and professional contexts.

Our study built on the research of previous scholars of teacher identity (Alsup, 2006; Danielewicz, 2014; Marsh, 2003) and recent scholarship in literacy studies (Hall, Johnson, Juzwik, Wortham, and Mosely, 2010; Hunt, 2018). Together the work by these researchers helped us understand teacher identity as fluid rather than static and recognize that teacher identity development does impact student learning in complex ways. However, we often noted that teacher identity was still categorized into pre-and inservice, experienced and apprentice, immature and mature and other binaries that may limit how we conceptualize teacher identity and therefore limit a more complete understanding of its complexities. Moreover, the work on teacher identities has yet to take up understandings of timescales and sociolinguistic scales. To push teacher identity development in new directions, we draw on scholarship in process drama to reimagine its conceptual and pedagogical possibilities. Next we review scholarship on drama and teacher identities. We then conclude this chapter by discussing positionality and new possibilities for exploring teacher identity through a process drama frame.

Drama and Teacher Identities Across Timespaces

In a late essay, Bakhtin (1986) problematized that nature of text and language, asking, "Does the author not always stand *outside* the language for the work of art? Is not any writer (even a pure lyricist) always a 'dramaturge' (see endnote) in the sense that he directs all words to others voices, including to the image of the author (and to other authorial masks)" (p. 110)? Bakhtin theorized that it is this "outsidedness" that is central to a dialogic understanding of language, and as speakers we enter the viewpoints of others and allow their views to mix with ours (Edmiston, 2013). We have argued that teacher identites are constructed in a nexus of programmatic discourses, discourses of popular culture, classroom practices, and personal histories teachers of inservice and teacher interns. To extend Bakhtin's metaphor, we conceptualize teacher identity work as dramaturgic because as professionals they participate in a variety of "drama worlds" (O'Neill, 1995) that are spontaneous, structured, and offer multiple possibilities for growth and development of agency (O'Neill, 1995, xviii). We believe a process drama can help preservice and inservice teachers take a critical look at identity development and offer new directions for conducting research on teacher identities. We will return to these two arguments later in the book. However, in the last section of this chapter, we more fully explain our process drama frame, how it connects to understandings of timescales and sociolinguistic scales, and argue for its potential for understanding teacher identity construction.

Process Drama and Possibilities for Teacher Identity Development

Process drama draws on using structures and elements, theater, story drama, readers' theater, and other sources to activate learning (O'Neill & Lambert, 1982). In process drama with learners, teachers use pretext, working in role, tableau, debriefing, and other concepts to create drama worlds in which the imaginary is used to examine the real (O'Neill, 1995). Examinations of this nature position the teacher as a co-learner with students and a participant in the drama created with students. In approaches to literacy instruction, process drama can become a way to explore the construction of meaning, relationships of power in texts, and deconstruct those relationships to recognize alternative interpretive possibilities (Edmiston, 2013; O'Neill, 1995; O'Toole, 1992). For example, in work exploring how process drama can serve as pedagogical practices to foster multiliteracies (Crumpler, 2006), middle school students generated tableaus (silent frozen moments) to examine multiple interpretations of the character of Scout in *To Kill a Mockingbird* (1960) and were able to deepen their understanding about the novel as a whole (Haling & Crumpler, 2011). Other drama theorists (Bolton, 1999) have argued for extending the concept of *process* to include what he calls the work of "making" (p. 271), which he contends is central to larger processes of dramatic work that enact learning. This extension also emphasizes that a product must be an outcome of a process, and that products can be reflected upon after the drama is concluded. Bolton's notion of making spurs our thinking about ways to reflect on outcomes and use process drama tools to imaginatively revisit key moments in learning processes and speculate about other possible outcomes.

The power of process drama comes from tensions between improvisation and structures; setting limitations and encouraging freedom of expression; recognizing potential controversial topics and using dramatic structures to confront them; and, directing development while allowing it to shift organically. O'Neill (1995) puts it this way:

> Although process drama is essentially improvised, it is not a matter of casting off all forms and limitations in order to be free and spontaneous. We use these forms and constraints in order to transcend them. The solution is to a create a dramatic moment that is so intriguing and tantalizing that it inevitably leads us on to the next moment. Each moment begins to grow and evolve its own structure, its own imagined world, with its own identity. (p. 151)

In our framework for understanding teaching identities, we emphasize how process drama allows possibilities for investigating moments of identity construction so that an understanding of teacher identity grows and evolves, and insights into its significance for professional development become clearer. In this next section, we discuss playing with time, the roles of affective elements or feelings, and positionality in this framework. We conclude this chapter by building on Moje and Luke's (2009) metaphor of positionality as identity by using process drama and introduce the concept of shape shifting (Davis, Sumara, & Luce-Kapler, 2013; Gee, 2006) to extend the metaphor in new ways to better understand complexities of teacher identities.

Process Drama and Playing With Time

Conceptualizing process drama as a framework for investigating teacher identity opens possibilities for studying how moments of identity progress, circle back, crack and reform, and change across longer timescales. A process drama framework provides a way to replay moments of discomfort and revisit instances of deeper understanding and thus "play with time." O'Toole (1992) recognized the potential of processes of drama for creating social histories, revisiting pasts, examining futures, and replaying moments in the present. Building on his work, it is possible to stop during moments of discomfort or controversy during a discussion with preservice or inservice teachers and replay them. Replaying them means that a researcher or facilitator skillfully interrupts a moment, and recasts the group into other roles to explore how the discussion could take a different direction. In our work, we argue for process drama as a research tool to reimagine how comments suggesting a deficit view of emergent bilingual (EB) students could be momentarily frozen and then reexamined by working in role. We developed the concept of "research interludes" in which inservice teachers would be invited to replay a section of a group discussion and recast a member of the discussion as an EB learner (Crumpler, Handsfield, & Dean, 2011). This practice can create possibilities for examining what happened in an interaction, what could have happened, and create additional data to explore different ways to respond to the same situation.

More recently, Edmiston (2013) developed "dramatic dialogic inquiry" (pp. 39–40) as a mode of active learning for groups of learners to investigate issues and topics by "dramatizing their inquiry" (p. 39) in which "learners collaboratively explore the meaning and co-author understanding about topics and narratives (p. 40). This mode of inquiry is based on a group of learners having a shared goal and using dramatic structures to inquire into that goal. Edmiston explains that "learners make meaning about real and imagined worlds" (p. 40). In other words, dialogic relationships are created between the real and the imaginary worlds as participants use process drama to explore both. This exploration involves asking, "what if," and being open to new possibilities (Edmiston, 2003). Groups of teachers and teacher interns can be invited to notice multiple discourses informing their own teacher identities and use the structure of working in role to imaginatively travel back to moments in their personal or programmatic pasts and reexamine them. This is, however, emotional labor.

Process Drama and Emotions

Courtney (1990) argues for the power of emotions in dramatic work because "through drama, our feelings evolve into what we see and believe; we feel there is perceptual continuity; ... we socially construct reality" (p. 33). In a time of scripted curricula, and an overemphasis on constructs like "best practices" or "high leveraged teaching," teaching can become overly technocratic and the dynamic, dialogic nature of teaching can be compromised (Aukerman, 2013). Consequently, views of teachers' identity development may become static and the affective facets of teaching marginalized.

A process drama framework opens opportunities to examine and theorize about how feelings inform teacher identity development (Courtney, 1990). A process drama framework is also a catalyst for examining emotions and their roles in identity development. O'Neil (1995) argues for the importance of building "drama worlds," interactions of the fictional and the real. He explains, "Dramatic worlds generated in process drama are likely to be both impressionistic and fragmented, but will still be capable of generating satisfactory experiences for participants" (xviii). These worlds are liminal spaces where feelings are brought into play to explore and examine issues of professionalism, the challenges new teachers face as they enter classrooms, the challenges veteran teachers face as they adjust to shifting demands for accountability, and other discourses that inform teachers' work.

Other scholars in literacy have examined the roles emotions play in constructions of teacher identities (Hunt, 2016; Hunt & Handsfield, 2013; Zembylas, 2003). Zembylas brought a poststructuralist lens to studying teacher identities and argued that emotion was key to teacher identity development and that emotion had to be understood in relationship to agency and power. Hunt's research investigated how emotions played into the identities of literacy coaches. She also recognized the roles of power and positioning in coaches' avoidance of emotions in coaching interactions. Together, these studies indicate the importance of positionality and emotions for understanding the complexities of teacher identity work.

Positionality Across Space and Time as Shape Shifting

Harré and Langenhove (1998) recognized the inherent positioning involved in any social situation and argued that positioning has consequences for how meaning is constructed. Teachers shift positions in classrooms many times during a day of instruction, and even in one lesson, from instructional leader to co-learner, from counselor to arbitrator, and myriad others as they deliver instruction and respond to students. From a process drama perspective, positioning and repositioning is part and parcel of engaging participants in imaginative work. For example, participants using drama to examine a literary text might be positioned as critics as a way to create sense of expertise in a discussion.

Berry (2002) described how elements of process drama can be viewed as catalysts for curricular change, equates repositioning with "re-authoring," and argues that dramatic forms can provide tactics to resist construction of "dominant imaginations" (p. 119). In other words, working in role, tableau and other process drama approaches reposition participants to speak as someone other than themselves and interrogate those roles. Our research (Crumpler, Handsfield, & Dean, 2011) suggested the potential for using dramatic positioning to examine how teacher identities are constructed and reconstructed moment by moment. Returning to the exchange between Camille and her students that began this chapter, we notice how Camille begins by positioning herself as a facilitator of a new "mission" with the students and then a few lines later repositions herself in a more traditional role as a teacher assuring the students "don't panic if you don't what to do." These shifts of identity on a micro-level illustrate the positioning and repositioning we believe both preservice and inservice teachers perform in their everyday classroom practices.

A process drama framework can help both groups become more aware of how identities are dynamic and performed in contexts of multiple discourses that inform literacy and teacher development. Further, this framework can provide ways for preservice and inservice teachers to move beyond awareness and see positionality as a pedagogical tool to improve teaching practices. Understanding positionality this way, teachers could self-fashion their identities and become "shape shifters" (Gee, 2006; Greenblatt, 1980). Greenblatt draws on anthropological and literary theory to argue that renaissance authors "self-fashioned" (p. 6) identities from language and cultural symbols available within contexts of cultural practices. Gee (2006) builds on Greenblatt and other scholars to contend that adolescents fashion and refashion their identities and become shapeshifters in response to the "changing nature of skills technology, and knowledge at an ever-faster pace" (p. 167).

In mythology, shape shifting meant that a creature could entirely change its physical shape and become something different, and this notion is seen in popular culture texts like comics and films, in which a human shifts into another entity, usually with super powers. However, in this book we understand shape shifting as teachers' abilities to refashion their identities in response to changing expectations, accountability, and curriculum at a rapid pace to meet the strengths and needs of the students they teach. While teachers are not shifting their physical shapes, we argue that by shifting their identities within classrooms they shift the shapes and potentials of instruction. Gee (2006) claims that shape shifting of identities is tied to social class, and individuals with more social capital can shape shift more easily that those who have less in a given context. We extend this concept in our book by showing that a process drama framework provides insights into how teacher identities are forged in moments and across timescales, and that becoming aware of these processes helps build capital to self-fashion successful professional identities.

Bakhtin (1986) contended that "there is neither a first or last word and there are no limits to the dialogic context" and a discourse exists within a "boundless past and a boundless future" (1986, p. 170). He was theorizing about the nature of language, but teacher identity is also dialogic. Teacher identities' boundless pasts are the traditional positions of nurturer and disciplinarian, mentor and mentee, apprentice and expert, and other binary roles historically and currently ascribed to preservice and inservice teachers. Teacher identities' boundless futures are the identities that teachers could take on and self-fashion to push beyond traditional binaries and become catalysts for new learning opportunities in classrooms where the demarcations are less fixed, and the ability to shape shift is an affordance to work effectively with all students. Exploring and understanding teacher identities by working in role, using tableau, research interludes, tapping in, and other structures of process drama will help make these futures possible for teachers.

In Chapter 2, we detail the design of our research study. A concept central to our design was the performance of identity. Process drama helped us think more deeply about how the nuances of teacher identities were performed by preservice and inservice teachers, consider how imaginative play could help make those nuances more visible and apply process drama as a tool for research on identity with both groups.

Note

1. Dramaturge is a dramatist, a literary editor on the staff of a theatre who liaises with authors and edits texts.

References

Alsup, J. (2006). *Teacher identity discourses: Negotiating personal and professional spaces*. New York, NY: Routledge.

Aukerman, M. (2013). Rereading comprehension pedagogies: Toward a dialogic teaching ethic that honors student sense making. *Dialogic Pedagogy, 1*, A1–A30.

Bakhtin, M. M. (1986). *Speech genres and other late essays* (Caryl Emerson & Michael Holquist, Eds. & Vern W. McGee, Trans.). Austin, TX: University of Texas Press.

Bakhtin, M. M. (1984). *Problems of Dostoevsky's Poetics* (Caryl Emerson, Trans., p. 17). Minneapolis, MN.

Bakhtin, M. M. (1981). *The dialogic imagination: Four essays* (M. Holquist, Ed. & C. Emerson & M. Holquist, Trans.). Austin, TX: University of Texas Press.

Ball, A. F., Freedman, S. W., & Pea, R. (Eds.). (2004). *Bakhtinian perspectives on language, literacy, and learning*. Cambridge, UK: Cambridge University Press.

Beauchamp, C., & Thomas, L. (2009). Understanding teacher identity: An overview of issues in the literature and implications for teacher education. *Cambridge Journal of Education, 39*(2), 175–189.

Beijaard, D., Meijer, P. C., & Verloop, N. (2004). Reconsidering research on teachers' professional identity. *Teaching and Teacher Education, 20*(2), 107–128.

Berry, K. S. (2002). *The dramatic arts and cultural studies: Educating against the grain*. New York, NY: Routledge.

Blommaert, J. (2010). *The sociolinguistics of globalization*. Cambridge, UK: Cambridge University Press.

Blommaert, J. (2015). Chronotopes, scales, and complexity in the study of language in society. *Annual Review of Anthropology, 44*, 105–116.

Bolton, G. M. (1999). *Acting in classroom drama: A critical analysis*. Calendar Islands Publishers.

Buchholz, B. A. (2016). Dangling literate identities in imagined futures: Literacy, time, and development in a K–6 classroom. *Literacy Research: Theory, Method, and Practice, 65*(1), 124–140.

Britzman, D. P. (2007). Teacher education as uneven development: Toward a psychology of uncertainty. *International Journal of Leadership in Education, 10*(1), 1–12.

Canagarajah, S., & De Costa, P. I. (2016). Introduction: Scales analysis, and its uses and prospects in educational linguistics. *Linguistics and Education, 34*, 1–10.

Collins, J., & Blot, R. (2003). *Literacy and literacies*. New York, NY: Cambridge University Press.

Compton-Lilly, C., & Halverson, E. (Eds.). (2014). *Time and space in literacy research*. New York, NY: Routledge.

Courtney, R. (1990). Drama and intelligence: A cognitive theory. McGill-Queen's Press-MQUP.

Courtney, R. (1995). *Drama and feeling an aesthetic theory*. Montreal, QC: McGill-Queen's University Press.

Crumpler, T. P. (2006). Educational drama as response to literature: Possibilities for young learners. In *Process drama and multiple literacies: Addressing social, cultural, and ethical issues* (pp. 1–14), Portsmouth, NH: Heinemann.

Crumpler, T. Handsfield, L., & Dean, T. (2011). Constructing difference differently in language and literacy professional development. *Research in the Teaching of English, 46*(1), 55–91. (Research supported by Spencer Foundation.)

Danielewicz, J. (2014). *Teaching selves: Identity, pedagogy, and teacher education*. Albany, NY: Suny Press.

Davis, B., Sumara, D. J., & Luce-Kapler, R. (2013). *Engaging minds: Changing teaching in complex times*. New York, NY: Routledge.

de Certeau, M. (1984). *The practice of everyday life* (Steven Rendall, Trans.). Berkeley, CA: University of California Press.

Edmiston, B. (2013). *Transforming teaching and learning with active and dramatic approaches: Engaging students across the curriculum*. New York, NY: Routledge.

Edmiston, B. (2003). What's my position? Role, frame and positioning when using process drama. *Research in Drama Education, 8*(2), 221–230.

Foucault, M. (1977). *Discipline and punishment: The birth of the prison*. London, England: Allen Lane.

Gee, J. P. (2006). Self-fashioning and shape-shifting: Language, identity, and social class. *Reconceptualizing the Literacies in Adolescents' Lives, 2*, 165–185.

Greenblatt, S. (1980). *Renaissance self-fashioning, from More to Shakespeare*. Chicago, IL: University of Chicago Press.

Haling, L., & Crumpler, T. P. (2011). Readers, texts, and contexts in the middle: Re-imagining literature education for young adolescents. In *Handbook of research on children's and young adult literature* (pp. 75–87). New York, NY: Routledge.

Hall, L. A., Johnson, A. S., Juzwik, M. M., Wortham, S. E., & Mosley, M. (2010). Teacher identity in the context of literacy teaching: Three explorations of classroom positioning and interaction in secondary schools. *Teaching and Teacher Education, 26*(2), 234–243.

Handsfield, L. J. (2012). Mediating learning and negotiating curricular ideologies in a fourth grade bilingual classroom. In *Teachers' roles in second language learning: Classroom applications of sociocultural theory* (pp. 41–61). Charlotte, NC: Information Age Publishing.

Handsfield, L. J., & Crumpler, T. P. (2013). "Dude, it's not a appropriate word": Negotiating word meanings, language ideologies, and identities in a literature discussion group. *Linguistics and Education, 24*(2), 112–130.

Handsfield, L. J., Crumpler, T. P., & Dean, T. R. (2010). Tactical negotiations and creative adaptations: the discursive production of literacy curriculum and teacher identities across space-times. *Reading Research Quarterly, 45*(4), 405–431.

Harré, R., & Van Langenhove, L. (Eds.). (1998). *Positioning theory: Moral contexts of international action*. Oxford, UK: Wiley-Blackwell.

Hunt, C. S. (2018). Toward dialogic professional learning: Negotiating authoritative discourses within literacy coaching interaction. *Research in the Teaching of English, 52*(3), 263–287.

Hunt, C. S. (2016). Getting to the heart of the matter: Discursive negotiations of emotions within literacy coaching interactions. *Teaching and Teacher Education, 60,* 331–343.

Hunt, C. S., Crumpler, T. P., & Handsfield, L. J. (2016). "Do you want an idea of what they're doing?" Transgressive data generation and analysis within a bilingual writers workshop. *International Journal of Qualitative Studies in Education, 29*(3), 399–425.

Hunt, C. S. & Handsfield, L. J. (2013). The emotional landscapes of literacy coaching: Issues of identity, power, and positioning. *Journal of Literacy Research, 45*(1), 47–86.

Izadinia, M. (2013). A review of research on student teachers' professional identity. *British Educational Research Journal, 39*(4), 694–713.

Lasky, S. (2005). A sociocultural approach to understanding teacher identity, agency and professional vulnerability in a context of secondary school reform. *Teaching and teacher education, 21*(8), 899–916.

Lemke, J. L. (2000). Across the scales of time: Artifacts, activities, and meanings in ecosocial systems. *Mind, Culture, and Activity, 7*(4), 273–290.

Lempert, M. (2012). Interaction rescaled: How monastic debate became a diasporic pedagogy. *Anthropology & Education Quarterly, 43*(2), 138–156.

Marsh, M. M. (2003). *The Social Fashioning of Teacher Identities. Rethinking Childhood.* New York, NY: Peter Lang.

McIntyre, J., & Hobson, A. J. (2016). Supporting beginner teacher identity development: external mentors and the third space. *Research Papers in Education, 31*(2), 133–158.

Mishler, E. G. (2006). Narrative and identity: The double arrow of time. In A. De Fina, D. Schiffrin, & M. Bamberg (Eds.), *Discourse and identity* (pp. 30–47). Cambridge, UK: Cambridge University Press.

Moje, E. B., & Luke, A. (2009). Literacy and identity: Examining the metaphors in history and contemporary research. *Reading Research Quarterly, 44*(4), 415–437.

Morson, G. S., & Emerson, C. (1990). *Mikhail Bakhtin: Creation of a prosaics.* Palo Alto, CA: Stanford University Press.

O'Neill. C. (1995). *Drama worlds: A framework for process drama.* Portsmouth, NH: Heinemann.

O'Neill, C., & Lambert, A. (1982). *Drama structures: A practical handbook for teachers.* London, England: Nelson Thornes.

O'Toole, J. (1992). *The process of drama: Negotiating art and meaning.* London, England: Routledge.

Rutherford, V., Conway, P. F., & Murphy, R. (2015). Looking like a teacher: fashioning an embodied identity through dressage. *Teaching Education, 26*(3), 325–339.

Varghese, M., Morgan, B., Johnston, B., & Johnson, K. A. (2005). Theorizing language teacher identity: Three perspectives and beyond. *Journal of language, Identity, and Education, 4*(1), 21–44.

Wortham, S. (2006). *Learning identity: The joint emergence of social identification and academic learning.* Cambridge, UK: Cambridge University Press.

Zembylas, M. (2003). Emotions and teacher identity: A poststructural perspective. *Teachers and Teaching, 9*(3), 213–238.

· 2 ·
SETTING THE STAGE

Scenes of Inquiry in Pre- and Inservice Teacher Development

H: when I first started teaching
it was 'the red birds and blue birds'
and the other kids were filling in worksheets
and now I think the biggest difference
is we want the other kids doing something more meaningful
than filling out, like, worksheets
P: Um huh
H: Then you come up with the trick
of so 'okay how do I differentiate for all those kids sitting at centers'
or- you know and that to me is the way it should be

(Prairie Center Study Group Meeting October, 2007).

The brief interaction above is from a transcript of a study group meeting at Prairie Center Elementary School. What we find particularly notable about this short excerpt is how it illustrates H's awareness of shifting temporal and political contexts or expectations for literacy instruction, as well as a tacit assumption that professional development involves learning "tricks of the trade." The notion of learning new tricks suggests a view of professional learning in response to shifting pedagogical terrain as either acquiring particular methods or techniques, also denoted by the somewhat common reference to a teacher's "bag of tricks," or even a more elusive instructional magic—pedagogies that are not necessarily easy to simply pull out of a hat and implement. The excerpt also involves H discursively positioning herself as changed in response to shifting pedagogical expectations, from static ability grouping to fluid differentiation. In short, we see H engaging in a discursive coconstruction of both shifting chronotopes—space-times—and her shifting professional identities.

In Chapter 1 we articulated our own theoretical commitments as they inform our understandings of teacher identities. The discursive and embodied negotiation and construction of professional identities and chronotopes of literacy teaching and learning, such as H's above, however, are not simply phenomena we have observed and noted in our research participants, but also in ourselves—in our own research processes. Throughout our study, we were very aware of context and our own positioning in concert with our participants. This involved, among other things, not wanting to be read as expert researchers with the pedagogical answers, or as purveyors of new "tricks" of the trade. Overall, just as H alludes to multiple tensions with respect to her teaching context and her own positioning vis-à-vis language and literacy instruction, our study was also rife with historical and political tensions. In this chapter, we explain how our research focus and methodologies, including our own positionality as researchers, were similarly shaped and were shaped by shifting demographic, social, and political contexts.

We begin by setting the stage, describing the scenes of our inquiry according to three related "turns" in literacy and teacher education research: (1) The discursive turn in language and literacy research (Rex et al., 2010), (2) the digital turn in New Literacy Studies (Mills, 2010), and (3) the practice turn in teacher education (Jenset, Klette, & Hammerness, 2018). We then describe our research activities, participants, setting, and methods for data generation and analysis.

Turn, Turn, Turn

The song "Turn! Turn, Turn," made popular by the Byrds (1965; based on Ecclesiastes 3:1–8), emphasizes a cycle of time and purpose underpinning changes in the world around us and in ourselves. This is no less the case for research methodologies and theories, which similarly shift along with the ebbs and flows of space and time. A variety of theoretical "turns"—shifts in epistemological and methodological framing—have been noted in the field of education and have influenced our work. These include including the "linguistic" turn and the "social turn" (Moje & Luke, 2009). However, the discursive, digital, and practice turns were particularly important in shaping how and why we designed our research project.

The Discursive Turn

While several language and literacy researchers allude to the discursive turn (e.g., Macías, 2016; Rex et al., 2010), few define it. We understand this term as related to a sociocultural turn, with increased attention paid to how language and literacy practices, as well as identities, are discursively coconstructed; that is, how they are simultaneously productive of and structured by ideologies of language and literacy within relations of power (Handsfield & Valente, 2016; Lewis, Enciso, & Moje, 2007; Street, 1995, 2013). This turn has brought a heightened awareness of the social and political contexts of language, literacy, and teaching, and of identity and how power relationships operate within researcher–participant relationships.

The focus on language and literacy as discursively constructed has been accompanied by increased methodological emphasis on dialogue and interaction, including discourse analytic methods. This has meant a focus on research participants' language use and positioning, as well as an acknowledgement of researchers as coparticipants within processes of data generation (Hunt, Crumpler, & Handsfield, 2016).

Pedagogically, this turn has brought about emphases on dialogic and collaborative instructional approaches. Such approaches sit well with Vygotskian theories regarding semiotic mediation, but also move beyond basic linguistic modeling to involve opportunities for extended academic and social discourse. Examples of such approaches include small group inquiry projects and project-based learning, literature discussion groups or literature circles, reading and writing workshop, and process drama, among others.

The discursive turn is also reflected in research on professional development, including models that nurture sustained critical and dialogic engagement around pedagogically sophisticated ideas and assumptions (Pella, 2015; Phillips, McNaughton, & MacDonald, 2004; Richardson & Placier, 2001; Roskos & Bain, 1998). Teacher study groups, for example, has been forwarded and utilized in many contexts as a dialogic model or structure for promoting transformative professional development, as have inquiry-based and dialogic approaches to literacy coaching (Hunt & Handsfield, 2013;

International Literacy Association, 2018; MacPhee, 2013). And research on preservice teacher education has long suggested the value of dialogic and critical approaches (Johnson, 2002; King, 1991; Ladson-Billings, 2001; Whang & Waters, 2001).

However, this turn itself has continued to evolve such that the very notion of discourse itself has broadened. Rather than simply focusing on utterances or print texts, discourse is more typically understood with respect to a broader array of semiotics (Blommaert, 2010), including visual modes (Kress & van Leeuwen, 1996), gesture and gaze (Leander, 2002), material objects (Beucher, Handsield, & Hunt, 2019; Boomer, 2003; Kress, 2011), and larger body movements across classroom spaces (Handsfield & Crumpler, 2013; Handsfield, Crumpler, & Dean, 2010; Hunt, Crumpler, & Handsfield, 2016).

Methodologically, this broader understanding of discourse has contributed to further analytical attention to this wider array of semiotics (Rex, Green, Dixson, & Santa Barbara Classroom Discourse Group, 1998). Among other things, thiss has meant a surge in data generation approaches involving video recording (Baker, Green, & Skuskauskaite, 2008). As we describe later in this chapter, this expansion of meaning making resources with respect to data generation and analysis may offer richer and alternative accountings of phenomena such as instructional decision making and identity development, but at the same time complicates how we attribute issues of agency and power within such research practices (Hunt, Crumpler, & Handsfield, 2016).

The Digital Turn

Mills (2010) describes the increased emphasis win New Literacy Studies (Gee, 1996; Street, 1995) on digital literacy practices and literacy practices in digital contexts, including work, peer groups, and classrooms, a "digital turn." Two seminal pieces of research within this area are the New London Group's (1996) manifesto titled "A Pedagogy of Multiliteracies" and Lankshear and Knobel's (2003) book titled "New Literacies." Both of these works, among others, argue for the need to shift not only literacy instructional practices based on changing language and literacy practices and tools, but also basic assumptions regarding power relationships between teacher and student, as well as readers (text consumers) and writers (text producers).

Moreover, for almost two decades now, literacy researchers have called for attention to proliferating literacy practices and linguistic diversification in literacy teacher education and professional development. However, while various professional development programs aim to meet these criteria, at the time that we designed our study, virtually no research had systematically examined multiliteracies (including increased multilingualism) or the digital turn as a framework for teacher development, or how this framework may facilitate pedagogical change. This is despite claims made at the time regarding the need to integrate digital and multimodal literacy practices into classrooms. In other words, calls were made for a digital turn in literacy teacher preparation and development without a real understanding of how this turn might unfold in different contexts of practice.

The Practice Turn

The first two decades of the 21st century have seen a significant shift in teacher education policy toward more practice-based models of teacher preparation in order to break down the infamous theory-practice divide within the field, to bolster teacher retention (Feiman-Nemser, Tamir, & Hammerness, 2014), and to enhance new teachers' pedagogical skills (Brouwer & Korthagen, 2005). This trend has occurred not just in the U.S., but globally (Darling-Hammond et al., 2017; Jenset, Klette, & Hammerness, 2018). The practice turn has taken a variety of forms in terms of teacher preparation program design and implementation, from additional or extended clinical placements to residencies and partnerships with schools and districts (Jenset, Klette, & Hammerness, 2018; Zeichner, 2010). Further, the practice turn has arguably stemmed from a challenge to university-based teacher education programs from advocates of alternative certification routes, such as Teach for America.

In teacher professional development, the practice turn aligns with professional learning that is classroom-centered, ongoing (rather than one-shot workshops), dialogic, and inquiry based. Teachers may be involved in study groups or professional learning communities that engage in pedagogical design and experimentation along with continued reflection on practice (Handsfield & Valente, 2016; Pella, 2015; Riley, 2015). In many ways this practice turn reflects more practice-based theories of language and literacy teaching and learning, including the work of de Certeau (1984) and Pierre Bourdieu (1992, 1998), who critiqued a "scholastic view" of the world that was removed from real social practices. Notably, these theories also seek to understand how dominant discourses and storylines flow as a function of power in everyday practices.

The social and political contexts of this turn influenced our design of this study, in particular our integration of pre- and inservice teachers within one of our study groups and our decision to extend the research into participants' classrooms (Jacobs, 2007). While we would not characterize our project as action research (Kemmis & McTaggart, 2000; Noffke, 1997), or as participatory action research (Kinloch, 2010; Morrell, 2008), we were influenced by naturalistic and classroom-based research models—research that carries ecological validity (Pennycook, 2001) in that it is grounded in teachers' and students' everyday practices and the messy contingencies of classroom life.

Study Design and Methodology

We designed our study within and in response to the social and political contexts described above. We sought to answer the following three research questions: (1) How does a new literacies framework for teacher development facilitate responsive and innovative instructional pedagogies? (2) What language and literacy discourses do teachers articulate during study groups focusing on multilingualism and multiliteracies and during literacy instruction? And (3) what language and literacy discourses do preservice teachers articulate as they move from methods coursework, through collegial professional development, into instructional practice?

Building on the digital and practice turns, we were interested in how teacher development centered on the concepts of multilingualism and multiliteracies might support teachers in responding pedagogically to changes in everyday literacy practices that accompany increased linguistic and cultural diversity and the proliferation of multimodal and mass communications technologies. And connecting to the discursive turn, we also wanted to know what language and literacy discourses teachers might articulate both during professional development activities centered on these themes and as they attempted to shift their classroom practices.

Research Settings

To conduct this study, we collaborated with local school districts and our own university's elementary education program. For the inservice teacher development component of our study, we collaborated with one of the school districts within which the university was situated. Broadacre was a small Midwestern city located approximately two hours from a major urban center. In addition to being surrounded by smaller farming communities, major employers in Broadacre included the headquarters for two large national corporations, as well as major hospitals and a large state university.

The district drew its student population from the wider county in which it was situated. Whereas in the decades preceding our study the student population was comprised almost entirely of monolingual White native English-speaking students, in the few years prior to our work with the district, the county experienced a rapid and significant increase in the immigrant population (just over 50 % growth within three years). According to District Report Cards, between 2002 and 2005, the percentage of its students qualifying for language services more than doubled—growing from 0.9 % to 1.9 % of the K-12 student population.

This new immigrant population was largely Spanish-speaking but also included families from both Asian and African countries. These families were generally of low socioeconomic status, and family members typically worked in manual labor or the hospitality industry, as well as in other types of traditionally lower status and lower paying jobs. However, the community also witnessed an amplification of available consumer goods, services, and media, such as Spanish language radio, Indian and Mexican grocers, and new ethnic restaurants.

Despite the increase in wealth of community goods and resources, the district's response to this increased multilingualism and multiculturalism was centered on language support through the development of an English as a Second Lanugage (ESL) program at one elementary school—Prairie Center—and one middle school—Blue Field Junior High—, and a Spanish–English transitional bilingual education (TBE) program at one elementary school—Southend. The bilingual program was still quite new at the time of our study, and many of the teachers seemed to embrace it. For example, several teachers and the principal formed a cohort to complete their ESL certification in order to prepare for working with EB students. However, according to some of the teachers in our study, once the bilingual program was established and functioning, support from the district waned, and teachers and families within the program felt minimally supported.

The vast majority of teachers in the district spoke only English and had minimal professional development or teacher education focused specifically on working with multilingual students. They were largely unsure how to effectively communicate with their multilingual students and families, or how to best design and carry out literacy instruction in multilingual classrooms. This issue was compounded by curricular changes that were occurring simultaneously in the district, which involved moving away from a basal reading series and toward reading and writing workshop, and the recession of the late 2000s, which depleted the district's professional development funds.

The preservice teacher preparation component of phase one took place in an elementary teacher preparation program at a large state university in Broadacre. Two literacy methods courses were required of teacher candidates in the program—one in fall and another in the spring of teacher candidates' third year. A three-week clinical experience followed the next fall, and student teaching occurred the following spring during candidates' final year in the program.

One of the teacher candidates in phase three—Camille—student taught in an all-English third-grade classroom at a small rural elementary school approximately an hour's drive from Broadacre. This school—Central Harvest—served a predominantly White and economically diverse student population. The other taught in a school within the same district as the practicing teachers. This school served the small town of Lakeville, which was located east of Broadacre. Lakeville's primary industry was agriculture, although a local hospital was also a major employer.

Research Activities and Participants

Research activities occurred in three different phases between August 2006 and June 2008. Phase one included teaching an adapted literacy methods course for preservice teachers and facilitating a study group for practicing teachers on literacy for linguistically diverse learners. In phase two we brought together participating preservice and inservice teachers into a second integrated study group on multimodality and literacy instruction. Finally, in spring 2008 (phase three), we followed a subset of preservice and practicing teachers who participated in both phases one and two into their classrooms (or their student teaching contexts for preservice teachers) to document their literacy instruction.

Phase one. In phase one (fall 2006) we carried out teacher development activities for preservice and inservice teachers in parallel. This included four sections of an altered literacy methods course for preservice teachers, two of which were taught by Lara, and two of which were taught by collaborating clinical faculty at our university. This course was the first of the two required literacy methods courses, and was broad in scope, addressing language and literacy development, children's and young adult literature, as well as literacy instructional routines and approaches. A primary focus of the redesigned course was to center ideas of multimodality and multiliteracies, as well as to reframe multilingualism as a mainstream phenomenon. These concepts were infused throughout the course, rather than presented in isolation.

Simultaneously, we designed and facilitated the first of two study groups in the project, in which we worked with 25 practicing teachers to explore literacy instruction for linguistically diverse learners for practicing teachers. Our goals for this study group were two-fold: (1) to generate a dialogic space in which practicing teachers could explore foundational concepts and pedagogical possibilities for their multilingual students, and (2) to support participating teachers noticing and scrutinizing deficit models of EB students (Kennedy, 2016; Vangrieken, Meredith, Packer, & Kyndt, 2017).

The 25 participating teachers included two bilingual elementary teachers, one bilingual Title 1 elementary teacher, five non-bilingual Title 1 elementary teachers, eight non-bilingual elementary classroom teachers, four non-bilingual middle school teachers), two pull-out ESL teachers, one elementary special education teacher, one elementary Art teacher, and one bilingual social worker. These teachers ranged in age from their mid-20s to their 50s.

The study group was designed with both large and small group meetings. We facilitated four large group meetings with all participants—one in September, two in October, and one in November. These meetings lasted approximately two hours each and were alternately held at three different schools where participating teachers worked. These meetings included whole group discussions about literacy for multilingual students and biliteracy development as well as time for participants to meet in smaller work teams.

The small work teams enabled participants to explore more focused topics of interest related to teaching multilingual students. Each work team consisted of four to six participants and centered around a self-selected professional text. These texts represented a variety of topics, including content learning, writing instruction, reading instruction, and literature-based literacy instruction. While we facilitated the whole group sessions, we only attended teachers' work team meetings when they requested.

Phase two. For phase two of the study, we brought together participating preservice and practicing teachers (15 and 11, respectively) into second study group, which took place in fall 2007. This study group centered more broadly on multilingualism and multiliteracies and integrating multimodal literacies into instruction. Specifically, participants explored intersections among multilingualism, popular culture literacies, their own teaching practices.

New literacy technologies were examined as they related to literacy instruction in K-8 classrooms. This study group was structured in the same way as the first study group, with both large group meetings and smaller work teams. Each work team consisted of a combination of preservice and practicing teachers. Some of the specific topics explored by the work teams included popular culture literacies, integrating digital technologies into literacy instruction, and teaching multimodal writing.

At the end of the study group, participants were asked to generate one to three instructional goals related to their work team topics that were doable in terms of time and resources. These goals then formed the basis for phase three of the study.

Phase three. Teachers who participated in both study groups were invited to participate in this final phase of the study (spring 2008), in which we observed and video-recorded them as they attempted to work their goals into their instruction. The purpose of this third phase was explicitly non-evaluative. That is, the purpose was not to discern whether or not teachers were successful in meeting their goals, but rather what sorts of challenges and successes they experienced in their efforts to adapt their instruction.

Neverteheless, despite our attempts to communicate the non-evaluative nature of phase three, few teachers volunteered for this final portion of the study. For preservice teachers, this was primarily due to the intensity of their student teaching experience, which already involved managing multiple and sometimes competing tensions between their university supervisors, themselves, and their cooperating teachers. Adding on video-recorded lessons and debrief sessions on top of those commitments deterred many from participating. Nevertheless, three preservice teachers agreed to participate, one of whom (Camille) we focus on in depth in this book (Chapter 5).

Three practicing teachers agreed to participate—two novice bilingual elementary teachers (Isabel and Paula; featured in Chapters 3 and 4) and one bilingual social worker. We speculate that the bilingual teachers may have been more apt to participate given that they were already fairly attuned to the importance and benefits of multilingualism prior to joining the study, and thus felt less concerned regarding two university professors coming into their classrooms to document their teaching.

Generating Data On and Off Script

Over the course of the research activities we generated a wealth of data. We took field notes and audio- and video-recorded during both the preservice literacy methods courses and during the whole group study group sessions. In addition, we conducted small group interviews with each of the work teams during both study groups as well as individual interviews and eight to ten video-recorded observations with those who chose to participate in phase three of the study. Finally, we collected classroom and instructional artifacts from phase three in order to further contextualize and understand the challenges and successes that participating teachers experienced as they attempted to adapt their practice.

In interviews, we worked from semi-structured lists of questions that helped focus our discussions on participants' work team investigations, their thoughts about teaching literacy with multilingual students, their perspectives on the district's literacy curriculum, their views on popular culture, technology use, and multimodal texts. We also focused our conversations on debriefing classroom practices that we observed in phase three. But although we entered into these interviews with some specific questions and topics in mind, the interviews were largely conversational, in part due to the rapport that we built with teachers over the course of the two years, but also because we wanted to elicit teachers' narratives, or "small stories" (Bamberg & Georgakopoulou, 2008; Hunt & Handsfield, 2013; Juzwik & Ives, 2010), of practice. This helped us understand teachers' and student teachers' positioning and discourses of language, literacy, and teaching, as well as critically reflect on our own positionality in the construction of our data. As with just about any qualitative research project, the plan that we set out prior to beginning this work was just that—a plan. Once we began video recording, meeting with participants, interacting with them during classes, work teams, and study group meetings, and debriefing instruction, our research needed to respond to how these interactions and events unfolded (Miles, Huberman, & Saldaña, 2014). Indeed, we were sometimes quite surprised by the directions that specific research activities and moments took. For instance, during phase three, as Lara was video recording in Isabel's classroom, the students and Isabel would often approach Lara to chat, and occasionally would look directly into the video camera lens to address the audience. As Lara responded, the presence of the video camera itself, and of us as researchers, became quite pronounced.

Some may challenge such episodes as indications of a less naturalistic scene of data "collection" and of researchers' undue impact on classroom activities. However, we would argue that any time that a researcher (or anyone else) with or without a camera enters into a space of practice, that space inevitably changes with respect to discourses and power relationships, even if in subtle ways. The choices we made in those moments, and that we continue to make as we have analyze and as we write, become part of the data and thus open for analysis and critique—a stance that we take up in the ensuing chapters, and that we have written about elsewhere (e.g., Crumpler, Handsfield, & Dean, 2011; Hunt, Crumpler, & Handsfield, 2016).

Interestingly, while we assumed a stance of supporting broadened understandings of literacy for our participants, we also found our own previous assumptions challenged as we entered classroom spaces to document participants' literacy instruction. While we knew that some of the participating middle level teachers in phases one and two of the project taught in social studies, art, math, etc., our four focal participants for phase three were all elementary preservice and practicing teachers. We thus assumed that we would be observing during literacy blocks or times designated for reading and writing in teachers' schedules. However, both of our practicing teacher participants for phase three—Isabel and Paula—had us observe their literacy instruction across content areas. We observed Paula teaching during both reading and social studies, and we observed Isabel during both writing workshop and science instruction.

Data Analysis

Although this section follows our section on data generation, as is often the case in qualitative research, our analyses occurred alongside our research activities. We wrote research memos after research activities and read through transcripts to inform subsequent activities such as interviews and observations or later work team and study group meetings. Our analytical approach was also multilayered, involving recursive coding (Miles, Huberman, & Saldaña, 2014; Strauss & Corbin, 1990) as well as more focused microethnographic discourse analyses (Bloome et al., 2005) and analyses of body movements across space and time (Handsfield, Crumpler, & Dean, 2010; Handsfield & Crumpler, 2013; Hunt, Crumpler, & Handsfield, 2016).

Recursive coding. We began with a recursive open coding process (Strauss & Corbin, 1990). This involved each of us separately reading and rereading transcripts of both audio and video data, as well as our transcribed field notes, noting patterns, and drawing connections across data sources. As we began to re-read, we revisited our research memos and clarified specifics as needed with our participants. Throughout our initial coding processes, we tried to stay as close to the data as possible, attempting to apply low inference codes—codes that are grounded in specific events (e.g., a lesson or a work team meeting), signs (e.g., a photograph of student work), or particular utterances (e.g., a teacher's exact words an interview or observation) (Carspecken, 1996). Our intention was to consciously try to keep our interpretations in check at this early stage of analysis.

Our coding process continued as we came together to identify similarities and differences in our codes and where we might need to generate additional codes or fold some codes into one another. In a process akin to axial coding (Strauss & Corbin, 1990), we then identified broader sets of ideologies, which we conceptualized as chronotopes, as discussed in the previous chapter. These included standardization, new literacies, writers' workshop, novice teacher status, being a novice teacher, being an expert teacher, popular culture in the classroom, strategic reading, literature discussion, being nontraditional teacher, and TBE. These chronotopes seemed to function and be constructed throughout the study as "formally constitutive" (Bakhtin, 1981, p. 85) categories through which multiple connecting ideologies circulate to shape literacy instruction and identities. These chronotopes should not be viewed as unitary nor stable; rather, they are heteroglossic and dynamic, "responsive to the movements of time, plot and history" (Bakhtin, 1981, p. 84).

Microethnographic discourse analysis. Our microethnographic approach is similar to indexical analysis in its focus on "how language provides cues about relevant context, and how, conversely, readings of context inform the meanings we attribute to utterances" (Collins, 2012, p. 196). However, microethnographic discourse analysis can also be used to make sense of discursive practices beyond utterances, such as how material objects and body movements play into identity construction and power relationships. The idea is that the analytical lens is zoomed in and focused on micro-moments—a few seconds up to several minutes—of an event involving interactions and practices with the purpose of understanding how identities are performed and ideologies are reproduced, challenged, or repurposed through such positioning.

We began by selecting interview and video excerpts based on our initial coding that were multiply coded and excerpts that seemed to speak to multiple chronotopes that we identified. We reasoned that this multiplicity indicated contestation regarding dominant ideologies in discursive practices in the interviews and in the video recordings of teaching. This enabled us to analyze how our participants negotiated competing expectations and power relationships as they crafted their professional identities.

Although microethnographic discourse analysis typically focuses on utterances and paralinguistic cues (e.g., gaze, gesture), we also use it to analyze larger body movements. When we observed participating preservice and practicing teachers in the classroom, they and their students often moved across classroom spaces. In other words, their movements extended well beyond gestures and the physical spaces immediately encompassing a person's torso (McNeill, 2008). Accordingly, we included video stills and descriptions in our microethnographic transcripts to capture these body movements in later chapters.

Goodwin (2007) proposed the notion of participation frameworks to conceptualize how individual people's bodily positioning contributes to emergent stances, or positioning, arguing that embodied actions and participation frameworks are co-constructed, rather than independent from one another. Radinsky et al. (2012) build on Goodwin's work, proposing the idea of representational fields as spaces constructed through embodied actions. More specifically, they identified different kinds of moves within such representational fields: use moves (uses of the representational field) and assembly moves (the making of the representational field). Assembly moves may include access moves and directing moves to gain, deny, invite, and request access to the field as students and teachers engage in classroom events. This framework offers tools for analyzing body movements alongside utterances. However, our approach differs in that we are interested not only in the representational meanings, but also indexical meanings—how participants' body movements alongside utterances shift, or scale, different ideologies of literacy and teaching and power relationships (Blommaert, 2007). For instance, a teacher may shift her stance or lean in toward a particular student and away from another as a way of conferring validity to her ideas or the participation norms during a class discussion. This sort of discursive "move" need not include words to index particular ideologies or power relationships and thus rescale a classrooms interaction. These kinds of questions and issues required fine-grained transcription practices of both audio and video data.

To create the microethnographic transcriptions, we first transcribed the audio and video recordings using transcript conventions adapted from Green and Wallat (1981) (Table 2.1). This involved identifying speaker turns,

Table 2.1: Transcript Conventions.

|	= one second pause
vowel +	= elongated vowel (So++, We+ll)
word	= boundaries of a style or voice change
-	= stops abruptly or speaker is cut off
text	= stress
text ...	= trails off (not cut off, or abrupt
TEXT	= loudly spoken or shout (chapter 3 transcripts)
text	= loudly spoken or shout (chapter 5 transcripts)
↑	= rise in pitch
↓	= drop in pitch
<text>	= spoken quickly, impatiently
(text)	= translation of preceding text
{text}	= double-voicing;[1] when change of voice not introduced by speaker
"text"	= speaker quoting another
Text	= reading text aloud
XXX	= unintelligible speech
[text]	= overlapping speech
US	= unidentified student
P	= unidentified participant

[1] *Double-voicing*: using "someone else's discourse for his own purposes, by inserting a new semantic intention into a discourse which already has, and which retains, an intention of its own. Such a discourse ... must be perceived as belonging to someone else" (Bakhtin, 1984, p. 189).

semantic features of utterances, volume, and other contextualization cues (e.g., falling or rising intonation, stress; Gumperz, 1982). In the right-hand column of the transcripts we include additional descriptions and still images from the video of participants' gazes, gestures, and body movements with respect to other objects and materials in the classrooms (e.g., Paula getting up from desktop computer and navigating around desks to reach a student, or Camille moving toward the whiteboard during a whole class lesson), appear in the right-hand column of the transcripts.

Next, we separated the utterances into message units, which Green and Wallat (1981) described as the smallest units of meaning in conversation. We then used line breaks to demarcate interaction units (IU), which can be thought of as stretches of "conversationally tied message units" (1981, p. 200). To do this, we used contextualization cues from the audio and video files. These cues included changes in speakers' goals, topical shifts in the conversation, changing demands for how students and/or others in the classroom should participate in the activity or discussion at hand, and participants' body movements.

Finally, we examined the transcripts to identify how the participating preservice and inservice teachers recruited different semiotic resources to negotiate competing pedagogical demands in order to position themselves and their students in particular ways. Importantly, this also involved turning the analytical lens onto ourselves as the researchers, which helped us see how our own participation impacted how events unfolded and how the participants and we as researchers were all folded into processes of identity construction.

Our recursive and multilayered analytical processes opened up windows into teachers' identity performances as they were grounded within and responsive to specific contexts of practice and complex and heterotopic ideological landscapes. In the next section of the book, we delve into our analyses and findings, and invite readers to consider along with us the multitude of ways in which three different teachers' professional identities were performed, constructed, and reshaped over scales of space and time. We begin with Chapter 3, in which we zoom into Isabel's classroom and her literacy instruction, exploring how she and her students positioned themselves and each other with respect to different ideologies of language and literacy during a literature discussion group.

References

Baker, W. D., Green, J., & Skukauskaite, A. (2008). Video-enabled ethnographic research: A microethnographic perspective. In G. Walford (Ed.), *How to do educational ethnography*. London, England: Tufnell Press.

Bakhtin, M. M. (1981). *The dialogic imagination: Four essays* (M. Holquist, Ed. & C. Emerson & M. Holquist, Trans.). Austin, TX: University of Texas Press.

Bakhtin, M. (1984). *Problems of Dostoevsky's Poetics* (Caryl Emerson, Trans., p. 17). Minneapolis, MN.

Bamberg, M., & Georgakopoulou, A. (2008). Small stories as a new perspective in narrative and identity analysis. *Text & Talk*, 28(3), 377–396.

Beucher, R., Handsfield, L. J., Hunt, C. S. (2019). What matter matters? Retaining the critical in new materialist literacy research. *Journal of Literacy Research*. https://doi.org/10.1177/1086296X19876971.

Blommaert, J. (2010). *The sociolinguistics of globalization*. Cambridge University Press.

Blommaert, J. (2007). Sociolinguistic scales. *Intercultural pragmatics*, 4(1), 1–19.

Bloome, D., Carter, S. P., Christian, B. M., Otto, S., & Shuart-Faris, N. (2005). *Discourse analysis and the study of classroom language and literacy events: A microethnographic perspective*. Mahwah, NJ: Lawrence Erlbaum.

Bomer, R. (2003). Things that make kids smart: A Vygotskian perspective on concrete tool use in primary literacy classrooms. *Journal of Early Childhood Literacy, 3*(3), 223–247.

Bourdieu, P. (1998). *Practical reason: On the theory of action*. Stanford University Press.

Bourdieu, P., & Wacquant, L. J. (1992). *An invitation to reflexive sociology*. University of Chicago Press.

Brouwer, N., & Korthagen, F. (2005). Can teacher education make a difference? *American Educational Research Journal, 42*(1), 153–224. doi:10.3102/00028312042001153.

Byrds. (1965). Turn! Turn! Turn. Columbia Records.

de Certeau, M. (1984). *The practice of everyday life*. Berkeley, CA: University of California Press.

Carspecken, P. F. (1996). *Critical ethnography in educational research*. New York, NY: Routledge.

Collins, J. (2012). Migration, sociolinguistic scale, and educational reproduction. *Anthropology & Education Quarterly, 43*(2), 192–213.

Crumpler, T. Handsfield, L., & Dean, T. (2011). Constructing difference differently in language and literacy professional development. *Research in the Teaching of English, 46*(1), 55–91.

Darling-Hammond, L., Hyler, M. E., & Gardner, M. (2017). *Effective teacher professional development*. Palo Alto, CA: Learning Policy Institute.

Feiman-Nemser, S., Tamir, E., & Hammerness, K. (2014). *Inspiring teaching: Preparing teachers to succeed in mission-driven schools*. Cambridge, MA: Harvard Education Press.

Gee, J. P. (1996). Discourses and literacies. *Social Linguistics and Literacies: Ideology in Discourses, 2*, 122–148.

Goodwin, C. (2007). Participation, stance and affect in the organization of activities. *Discourse & Society, 18*(1), 53–73.

Green, J., & Wallat, C. (1981). Mapping instructional conversations. In J. L. Green & C. Wallat (Eds.), *Ethnography and language in educational settings* (pp. 161–195). Norwood, MA: Ablex.

Gumperz, J. (1982). *Discourse strategies*. Cambridge, MA: Cambridge University Press.

International Literacy Association. (2018). *Literacy coaching for change: Choices matter [Literacy leadership brief]*. Newark, DE: Author.

Handsfield, L. J., & Crumpler, T. P. (2013). "Dude, it's not a appropriate word": Negotiating word meanings, language ideologies, and identities in a literature discussion group. *Linguistics \ and Education, 24*(2), 112–130.

Handsfield, L. J., Crumpler, T. P., & Dean, T. R. (2010). Tactical negotiations and creative adaptations: the discursive production of literacy curriculum and teacher identities across space-times. *Reading Research Quarterly, 45*(4), 405–431.

Handsfield, L. J., & Valente, P. (2016). "Momentos De Cambio": Cultivating Bilingual Students' Epistemic Privilege through Memoir and "Testimonio". *International Journal of Multicultural Education, 18*(3), 138–158.

Hunt, C. S., Crumpler, T. P., & Handsfield, L. J. (2016). "Do you want an idea of what they're doing?" Transgressive data generation and analysis within a bilingual writers workshop. *International Journal of Qualitative Studies in Education, 29*(3), 399–425.

Hunt, C. S., & Handsfield, L. J. (2013). The emotional landscapes of literacy coaching: Issues of identity, power, and positioning. *Journal of Literacy Research*, 45(1), 47–86.

Jacobs, G. (2007). Locating the local: Developing methodology for problematizing the construction of context. In M. V. Blackburn & C. T. Clark (Eds.), *Literacy research for political action and social change* (pp. 53–75). New York, NY: Peter Lang.

Jenset, I. S., Klette, K., & Hammerness, K. (2018). Grounding teacher education in practice around the world: An examination of teacher education coursework in teacher education programs in Finland, Norway, and the United States. *Journal of Teacher Education*, 69(2), 184–197. https://doi.org/10.1177/0022487117728248

Johnson, G. (2002). Moving toward critical literacies in the teaching of English. *Australian Journal of Language and Literacy*, 1(25), 49–57.

Juzwik, M., & Ives, D. (2010). Small stories as resources for performing teacher identity: Identity-in-interaction in an urban language arts classroom. *Narrative Inquiry*, 20(1), 37–61.

Kennedy, M. (2016). Parsing the practice of teaching. Journal of Teacher Education, 67(1), 6–17.

King, J. E. (1991). Dysconscious racism: ideology, identity, and the miseducation of teachers. *The Journal of Negro Education*, 60, 133e146.

Kemmis, S., & McTaggart, R. (2000). Participatory action research. In N. K. Denzin & Y. S. Lincoln (Eds.), *Handbook of qualitative research* (2nd ed., pp. 567–605). Thousand Oaks, CA: Sage.

Kinloch, V. (2010). *Harlem on our minds: Place, race, and the literacies of urban youth*. New York, NY: Teachers College Press.

Kress, G. (2011). 'Partnerships in research': multimodality and ethnography. *Qualitative Research*, 11(3), 239–260. https://doi.org/10.1177/1468794111399836

Kress, G. R., & Van Leeuwen, T. (1996). *Reading images: The grammar of visual design*. London: Routledge.

Ladson-Billings, G. (2001). The power of pedagogy: Does teaching matter. Race and education: The roles of history and society in educating African American students, 73–88.

Lankshear, C., & Knobel, M. (2003). *New literacies: Changing knowledge and classroom learning*. Open University Press.

Leander, K. M. (2002). Locating Latanya: "The Situated Production of Identity Artifacts in Classroom Interaction". *Research in the Teaching of English*, 198–250.

Lewis, C., Enciso, P., & Moje, E. B. (Eds.). (2007). *Reframing sociocultural research on literacy*. Mahwah, NJ: Lawrence Erlbaum.

Macías, R. F. (2016). Language ideologies and rhetorical structures in bilingual education policy and research: Richard Ruiz's 1984 discursive turn. *Bilingual Research Journal*, 39(3–4), 173–199. doi: 10.1080/15235882.2016.1230566

MacPhee, D. A. (2013). Professional development as the study of self: Using selfknowledge to mediate the act of teaching. *62nd yearbook of the Literacy Research Association*, 311–323.

McNeill, D. (2008). *Gesture and thought*. Chicago, IL: University of Chicago Press.

Miles, M. B., Huberman, A. M., & Saldaña, J. (2014). *Qualitative data analysis: A methods sourcebook* (3rd ed.). Thousand Oaks, CA: Sage.

Mills, K. A. (2010). A review of the "digital turn" in the new literacy studies. *Review of educational research, 80*(2), 246–271.

Moje, E. B., & Luke, A. (2009). Literacy and identity: Examining the metaphors in history and contemporary research. *Reading Research Quarterly, 44*(4), 415–437.

Morrell, E. (2008). *Critical literacies and urban youth: Pedagogies of access, dissent and liberation.* New York, NY: Routledge.

Noffke, S. E. (1997). Chapter 6: Professional, personal, and political dimensions of action research. *Review of research in education, 22*(1), 305–343.

Pella, S. (2015). Pedagogical reasoning and action: Affordances of practice-based teacher professional development. *Teacher Education Quarterly, 42*(3), 81–101. Retrieved from http://www.jstor.org/stable/teaceducquar.42.3.81

Pennycook, A. (2001). *Critical applied linguistics: A critical introduction.* London, England: Routledge.

Phillips, G., McNaughton, S., & MacDonald, S. (2004). Managing the mismatch: Enhancing early literacy progress for children with diverse language and cultural identities in mainstream urban schools in New Zealand. *Journal of Educational Psychology, 96*(2), 309.

Radinsky, J., Ping R., Hospelhorn, E., & Goldman, S. (2012). Making the absent present: Emergent representational fields in students' negotiations of meaning with spatial data. Paper presented at the American Educational Research Association, Vancouver, BC.

Richardson, V., & Placier, P. (2001). Teacher change. In V. Richardson (Ed.), *Handbook of research on teaching* (4th ed., pp. 905–947). Washington, DC: American Educational Research Association.

Rex, L., Bunn, M., Davila, B. A., Dickinson, H. D., Ford, A. C., Gerben, C., ... Thomson, H. (2010). A review of discourse analysis in literacy research: Equitable access. *Reading Research Quarterly, 45*(1), 94–115. doi:10.1598/RRQ.45.1.5.

Rex, L., Green, J., Dixson, C., & Santa Barbara Classroom Discourse Group. (1998). Critical issues: What counts when context counts?: The uncommon "common" language of literacy research. *Journal of Literacy Research, 30*(3), 405–433.

Riley, K. (2015). Enacting critical literacy in English classrooms: How a teacher learning community supported critical inquiry. *Journal of Adolescent & Adult Literacy, 58*(5), 417–425. doi:10.1002/jaal.371

Roskos, K., & Bain, R. (1998). Professional development as intellectual activity: Features of the learning environment and evidence of teachers' intellectual engagement. *The Teacher Educator, 34*(2), 89–115.

Strauss, A., & Corbin, J. (1990). *Basics of qualitative research.* Newbury, CA: Sage.

Street, B. (1995). *Social literacies: Critical perspectives on literacy in development, ethnography and education.* London, England: Longman.

Street, B. (2013). Literacy in theory and practice: Challenges and debates over 50 years, *Theory into Practice, 52*(Suppl.1), 52–62. doi:10.1080/00405841.2013.795442

Vangrieken, K., Meredith, C., Packer, T., & Kyndt, E. (2017). Teacher communities as a context for professional development: A systematic review. *Teaching and teacher education, 61,* 47–59.

Whang, P. A., & Waters, G. A. (2001). Transformational spaces in teacher education: MAP(ing) a pedagogy linked to a practice of freedom. *Journal of teacher education*, 52(3), 197–210.

Zeichner, K. M. (2010). Rethinking the connections between campus courses and field experiences in college- and university-based teacher education. *Journal of Teacher Education*, 61(1–2), 89–99. doi:10.1177/0022487109347671

FIRST INTERLUDE—DYLAN

As a child I read many books and wrote many stories, but the activity I feel stands out directly in my mind is playing computer games in elementary school. Both of the games Oregon Trail and Cross-Country USA exhibited journeys across the country trying to reach a specific goal. These games helped with responsibility and also managing money and food. This helped me learn how to balance regular day-to-day activities. There was also another game which I excelled at, and that was Math Blaster. In this game I was able to solve math problems and try to reach the ultimate goal and winning the round. I believe these games have influenced the interests that I have today. I am very interested in computer games as well as console video games, and I think that these games that I played in school helped to expand my interest in video gaming. These games not only helped me spend my leisure time, but they also helped me learn.

    I know now that I am certainly a different learner than the average student. I feel that I am a visual learner and enjoy hands on activity to help me learn. There are many people who excel as visual learners, but it is not the standard way of learning. I think that the games that I played in the computer lab while I was younger helped me learn certain things better. I excelled in math until I got to high school, and I feel that playing Math Blaster was the reason for my success. I was able to get all the hands-on experience and practice in math under a fun setting. Not only did all *the games I used to play use the "visual" language art, but it also let me express my "reading," "listening," and "visual representation." I felt that I was able to use these resources to help with school, when I didn't even realize that it was helping. I was just having fun. I had difficulty learning to ride a bike as a child and while my class would go to bike safety class, I would stay in the computer lab and play these games. Also, I took multiple summer school classes which would involve sitting in the computer lab and playing these "learning" type games all summer long. This would keep me learning while school was not in session, while at the same time I was not mentally thinking of it as school.*

—Dylan, Preservice teacher

Dylan articulates elements of two video games—Oregon Trail and Cross-Country USA—in terms of goal-driven activity; a mission of exploration! Enticements into play and adventure. And yet, he couches his recollections of these games in both academic and distant terms: The games "exhibited" journeys, and "helped with responsibility" and balancing the mundane day-to-day requirements of adulthood. Dylan's words are decidedly unemotional.

Of course, this itself surely reflects his purpose for writing, as the literacy memoir was an assignment for his class. As such, his words may also illuminate how popular culture texts were treated by Lara, Dylan's professor in his literacy methods course. Lara's and other course instructors' explicit framing of popular culture texts was as valid texts in and of themselves rather than as purely motivating texts to "trick" students into engaging in literacy practices. However, tacit messages regarding popular culture literacies may have filtered into course materials and discussions, resituating them as only marginally valid in comparison to traditional academic texts. And even if these dominant discourses were challenged in both explicit and tacit ways in the literacy methods course, their dominance perpetuates, seeping into discourse and practices in incipient ways. For instance, Dylan's memoir is saturated with professional vocabulary (e.g., hands-on, learning styles, visual representation) that he may have included to demonstrate to his professor his command of these terms, and he talks about visual literacies as running counter to standard assumptions about learning. However, while he mentions problem-solving, his arguments also function to situate video games as vehicles for learning math facts and algorithms (the focus of Math Buster). Further, nowhere in his memoir does he address teachers and teaching. Rather, teaching itself becomes programable into a video game.

In short, Dylan's memoir illustrates his own negotiation of power relations (e.g., professor-student) and multiple ideologies regarding literacy and teaching, and also offers evidence for how multiple discourses may bump up against one another simultaneously. These same tensions appear in the next three chapters as we explore how three other participants, who all joined Dylan in a study group work team focused on integrating popular culture texts, attempted to integrate students' interests and technologies into their literacy instruction.

· 3 ·
IDENTITY AS BECOMING IN PROFESSIONAL DEVELOPMENT

Isabel's Multiple Positioning

As we noted in Chapter 1, language and literacy ideologies are coconstructed alongside identities and relations of power. In this chapter, we explore the discursive coconstruction of "chronotopes of practice" (Artiles, 2011, p. 441) and identities, focusing specifically on Isabel and her bilingual fourth graders' negotiation of word meanings and language ideologies within a literature discussion. Significant portions of this chapter are reproduced from Handsfield and Crumpler (2013), in which we explored how ideologies of language and literacy and participant identities were constructed and contested during a literature discussion group in Isabel's classroom. In that article, we highlighted the students' discursive positioning and intersections between academic and social identities. Here, however, we shift our discussion to Isabel's participation in the event and implications for her professional identity construction.

As we explained in Chapter 2, we used microethnographic discourse analysis (Bloome et al., 2005) and analyses of body movements to theorize one classroom event. In this event, a group of Isabel's students—all boys—worked to identify an unknown and "inappropriate" word—"booger"—in their short novel, *Get Ready for Gabí!: A Crazy Mixed-up Spanglish Day* (Montes, 2003). In addition to grounding interpretations in Bakhtin's (1981) understandings regarding discourse and identity, we also integrate de Certeau's (1984) understandings of power, marginality, and cultural production in order to theorize Isabel's identity construction.

Isabel

Isabel, a White, middle class second and third year teacher during our research, participated in all three phases of our study. A native English speaker, she was also fluent in Spanish, and taught a fourth-grade bilingual class at Southend Elementary School. Isabel's class of fourth graders was unique in that it consisted entirely of eight native Spanish-speaking boys, who were all assessed at different levels of oral English proficiency as measured by the ACCESS test, and came from different countries of origin (Mexico, Guatemala, El Salvador, and the United States). Although her students had differing English knowledge and fluency, Isabel used English the vast majority of the time, particularly during whole group instruction. She did speak mostly in Spanish with one student (Esteban) who was categorized as a newcomer, having moved from Mexico several months previously. Her choice to speak predominantly in English with her class was informed by her school's bilingual program's emphasis on English and by her knowledge that her students would all be placed in monolingual English classrooms in fifth grade. However, Isabel invited both Spanish and code mixing between English and Spanish. Unless she was specifically engaged in a lesson designed to teach English vocabulary or aspects of the English language, Isabel rarely required students to speak or respond to her in English. She also taught students to use their knowledge of Spanish to help them read in English (e.g., identifying cognates, discussing concepts in Spanish to clarify understandings).

Isabel's instructional approach was difficult to characterize. She described her instruction as "outside the box," and based on our classroom observations, we would agree: She frequently used alternative assessments (e.g., multimodal projects, group activities), and her students were often engaged in group work and moved freely around the classroom, working at clusters of desks, and at other locations throughout the room. Throughout our two-year study, Isabel articulated concerns that the basal reading series and its ancillary materials were not responsive to the linguistic and cultural strengths and needs of her students. Although not part of the district's official curriculum at the time of our study, Isabel implemented a writing workshop approach, including opportunities for students to engage in co-authorship and online collaborative writing (Handsfield, Dean, & Cielocha, 2009). She also supplemented the basal reading series with literature discussion groups and a commercial curriculum designed to teach reading comprehension strategies, which she purchased with professional discretionary funds.

Isabel's principal, Greg, was complimentary of her teaching, and although Isabel was a novice teacher, he allowed her to diverge from and supplement the reading series (a privilege not afforded to many teachers at the school) as long as she used state standards as a guide. To be clear, on some occasions we also noted more teacher-fronted instruction, and the use of traditional assessment measures and classroom work (e.g., spelling tests, worksheets, etc.), as described elsewhere (Handsfield, 2012). On the whole, however, Isabel was critical of standardized and decontextualized approaches to literacy instruction, and her instructional practices reflected this view for the most part.

Five of Isabel's students (Jesús, José, Avery, Esteban, and Alejandro) participated in the focal event, and they were later joined by a sixth student (David). Two of these students, Avery and Alejandro, feature prominently in our analyses in their roles as co-directors of the literature discussion group. Alejandro was considered to be a leader socially among the group and was also the most fluent in English. Avery, on the other hand, was considered by teachers and other students to be socially awkward and to have limited facility with either spoken English or Spanish. Although we know few details regarding Avery's (or Alejandro's) home life, according to Isabel, she and other teachers were skeptical about how much oral interaction Avery had at home. While in general Isabel's assessments of Alejandro and Avery didn't seem too far off the mark to us based on our observations, our findings reveal a more complex picture with respect to the two boys' linguistic and literate repertoires.

Southend Elementary School

As we described in Chapter 2, Southend was one of four schools in which our participating teachers worked. In what follows, we articulate four chronotopes—material-discursive space-times—that were particularly salient in Isabel's professional context, and Southend in particular, that structured and were influenced by the daily language and literacy practices in Isabel's classroom. These chronotopes include: Transitional Bilingual Education (TBE), standardization, literature discussion, and strategic reading.

TBE

Southend was located in the city of Broadacre, and housed the district's Spanish-English TBE program. The program emphasized discrete language proficiencies and English, with the goal of moving students into all-English classrooms within three years. Although Southend had bilingual classrooms in Kindergarten through fourth grade, at the time of this study no such class existed for fifth graders. Instead, emergent bilingual fifth graders who were deemed in need of English language support received 30 minutes a day of pull-out English as a Second Language (ESL) instruction. This meant that all of Isabel's students would be moved into all-English instruction for fifth grade the following year. In fact, Isabel's occasional use of more traditional and teacher-fronted instructional approaches and her choice to mostly communicate in English in whole class contexts were meant to prepare her students for an all-English environment. As she explained, "when they go to 5th grade that is what they are going to do, so I let them get used to that." Indeed, the focal event analyzed in this paper occurred in May, only three weeks before the end of the school year, putting this issue into high relief.

The bilingual program was still in its infancy when this research was conducted, and it was embraced by many teachers at Southend. Several Southend teachers and the principal took EB certification courses at a local university to learn about teaching emergent bilingual (EB) students. However, according to some of the teachers in our study, once the program was off the ground, district support for the program waned. Moreover, Isabel's and some other teachers' stances toward bilingual education differed from the official transitional goal of the program. Several teachers, the district bilingual coordinator, and the principal hoped to implement a dual immersion program. Despite increased interest from a bilingual parent group and some advocacy on the part of some members of the local business community, this has not occurred. This is due in part to budget concerns, but largely stems from resistance from the more politically conservative community in which Southend is situated. In short, the tensions and sentiments regarding bilingual education and language policy in the district are reflective of the broader politics and history of bilingual education in the U.S. (Au, Brown, & Calderón, 2016).

Arguments for bilingual education have often been grounded in social justice concerns, and Isabel shared this interest. However, both research and policy conversations regarding bilingual education have been dominated by instrumentalist and technical-rationalist frames rather than equity (Grinberg

& Saavedra; 2000), which have been used to justify anti-immigrant and anti-Latino/a policies and practices (Au, Brown, & Calderón, 2016). These frames are manifested in mechanistic models of language acquisition and assessment (Baker, 2006) with an emphasis on outcomes of proficiency and efficiency of English language learning as measured by standardized assessments, rather than contextualized language use and classroom pedagogy (Leung, 2005). This is particularly the case in schools operating under legislation like No Child Left Behind (NCLB) (2002), which requires that EB students be assessed for decontextualized language skills (Baker, 2006, p. 193). The same sort of decontextualization characterizes dominant views of linguistic competence and communicative competence. Communicative competence is typically understood as an autonomous set of skills a speaker has and that can be measured in discrete ways. As Blommaert, Collins, and Slembrouck (2005) note, "[t]he issue of competencies is far too rarely dealt with as something which is connected to situated occurrences in an environment which has its own spatio-temporal characteristics" (p. 199).

Standardization

Much attention has been devoted to the effects of legislation such as NCLB in the US (2002), particularly how standardized language and literacy instruction, coupled with high stakes assessment, impact instruction. Such approaches emphasize decontextualized skills, and in literacy instruction specifically, this typically takes the form of isolated and direct code (phonemic awareness, phonics and spelling, and grammar) instruction. Such approaches contrast with embedded or holistic code instruction, in which graphophonic, syntactic, morphologic, and semantic features of print are taught within the context of authentic textual engagements (Goodman & Goodman, 2013). Dominant ideologies within a chronotope of standardization include a code/meaning dualism, in which the dominant assumption is that reading is a linear process where learning the linguistic code (e.g., standardized grammar, letter-sound relationships) will lead to meaning making, and universalist assumptions regarding teaching and learning—the notion that all "normal" individuals learn to read and interpret texts in uniform ways (Handsfield & Jiménez, 2009).

Bilingual teachers at Southend felt a great deal of pressure for their students to perform well on the state standardized test. At the time of our study, the school's EB student population was identified as the only demographic "subgroup" to not make Adequate Yearly Progress (AYP) as required by NCLB (2002). The chronotope of standardization became concretized in practices such as the district's adoption of a basal reading series with a strict scope and sequence, an emphasis on standardized test preparation, and no articulated writing curriculum beyond grammar instruction. Godley, Carpenter, and Werner (2007) point out that ". . . language ideologies that dissociate meaning from language form can hinder students' awareness of subtle changes in the meaning of texts" (p. 115) and argue that standardized approaches may hamper efforts to teach students how to distinguish between literal and figurative meanings in texts. This exact conundrum surfaces in the classroom event we spotlight in this chapter, as Isabel's students seek to identify an unknown word used figuratively in their novel. Importantly, however, Isabel carved out curricular space for meaning-based instruction, including literature discussion groups and comprehension strategies instruction.

Literature Discussion

An established body of research in literacy instruction supports the value of young readers responding to literature in small groups (e.g., Daniels, 2002; Gritter, 2012; Short & Pierce, 1990). Such approaches emphasize the active role of readers in constructing meaning and complex relationships between reader and text (Iser, 1978; Rosenblatt, 1978; Sipe, 2008). Sumara (1996, 2002) argues that meanings "emerge from the evolving relations among readers, texts, and contexts" (1996, p. 145). Other research bolsters Sumara's arguments, suggesting that students' participation in literature discussion groups involves complex social positioning with respect to peer group status and who is assigned or achieves interpretive authority (Allen, Möller & Stroup, 2003; Leander, 2002; Lewis, 2001).

As a curricular approach, literature discussion is designed to facilitate active conversations about authentic literature. In contrast to standardizing approaches, including isolated code instruction, literature discussion embraces ideologies of egalitarianism and collaboration in classroom interactions, peer-led discourse, and discussion of literary themes. That is, it emphasizes meaning before code. However, how to negotiate power relationships within such discussions is not always clear to teachers, particularly when considering how the teacher's discursive role may impact peer-led discussions (Maloch, 2002;

Zhang & Stahl, 2011). This became evident in the focal event. Isabel engaged her students in literature discussion groups as a supplement to the basal series, and she did so in conjunction with comprehension strategy instruction.

Strategic Reading

Since Dolores Durkin's (1978–1979) seminal research demonstrating that what often passed as comprehension instruction was in fact assessment (e.g., asking students to read from a textbook and answer "comprehension" questions), teachers have devoted increased attention to teaching comprehension strategies, such as generating questions, drawing inferences, clarifying, making connections, predicting, visualizing, identifying cognates, etc. (Pressley, 2002). While in theory strategic reading emphasizes active and flexible problem solving, research over the last ten years has called into question its effectiveness (McKeown et al., 2009) and cautioned that in practice such approaches are often reduced to skills-display, removed from purposeful reading (Handsfield & Jiménez, 2009; Palincsar, 2007). Still others (Aukerman, 2008) explicitly privilege strategic processes over accurate reading or comprehension. In short, several different ideologies shape the chronotope of strategic reading and exist in tension with one another.

The basal series Isabel was expected to use included a routinized approach to strategy instruction in which teachers were to teach specific strategies one at a time in a strict scope and sequence. However, Isabel supplemented the basal with a commercial curriculum emphasizing meaningful and flexible strategy use. The curriculum included lessons for explicitly teaching strategies and sets of children's literature in order to enhance engagement and readability for readers who struggle with grade-level texts. Of these texts, Isabel's students selected *Get Ready for Gabí* (Montes, 2003) for their literature discussion group. Isabel's expectation was that her students would engage in strategic reading as they read both individually and as a group and as they came together to discuss the story.

"I Don't Get This Word"

The focal event consists of a ten-minute video-recorded literature discussion in which Alejandro, Avery, Jesús, Esteban, José (and later David) came upon and worked to identify an unknown word, which was used figuratively in *Get ready for Gabí: A crazy mixed-up Spanglish Day.* The short novel tells the story of a spirited elementary-aged girl and her relationship with Johnny, her "worst enemy." Gabí, who is bilingual, begins mixing Spanish and English as her emotions get the best of her in her interactions with Johnny, who is monolingual. The portion of text under discussion in the focal event is the first page of chapter eight, titled "My secret identity." Gabí's father is talking with her regarding what she can do to control her temper, particularly with Johnny:

> "But, Papi," I said, "Johnny makes me see red."
> "I thought you liked Red."
> "I like red, not *Johnny*!" I said his name with my upper lip curled up—the way I say booger. (Montes, 2003, p. 51)

Gabí's use of "booger" is figurative—a metaphor for how she feels about Johnny, indicated both by the use of italics for the word and his name, and contextually. The word is also evoked with respect to its ending (-er) and the curling of the upper lip in disgust. As such language ideologies are infused in this excerpt, with the -er and a slight curling of the upper lip also representing the formation of the mouth when uttering the English -r sound, which differs from the rolled -r in Spanish.

The event centers around the students' attempts to identify the word "booger," beginning with José's appeal to Isabel: "I don't get this word, this-b-o-o-g-e-r." Rather than telling them the word's meaning, she leaves the task to the students to use different strategies to understand the text. Despite multiple efforts over the course of several minutes, they never arrive at either its literal or figurative meaning. During this time, they engaged in substantial interaction, in both English and Spanish, and movement as they sought assistance from Isabel, crisscrossed the room, accessed dictionaries, and generated questions, directives, and possible definitions of the word.

As the students moved about the room, some were intermittently off-screen. We tried to document students' speech when off camera, although this was not always possible. Ancillary conversations occurring concurrently sometimes merged with those of the literature discussion group, complicating our efforts to transcribe the event.

This event drew our attention for several reasons. First, we were curious about the sheer amount of time the students devoted to identifying one word. From a "time on task" perspective, some may question whether the event was productive at all, particularly since they never clearly accessed the meaning of the word. However, Isabel felt that the time the students spent was valuable, as they were attempting to use strategies that would benefit them in future reading engagements. In other words, she felt that the process (collaborative strategic reading) was valuable even if the product (their understanding) was sketchy. Finally, based on our understanding of identities and literacy practices as discursively coconstructed in classroom language and literacy events (Bloome et al., 2005; Duff, 2002; Handsfield et al., 2010; Hunt, Crumpler & Handsfield, 2015; Lewis et al., 2007), we speculated that more than word meanings were being produced in this event. We wanted to know what a close analysis might tell us about participants' identity construction.

The event began in an area of the room with a sofa and coffee table. José, Esteban, and Jesús were seated on the sofa, while Avery sat on a chair opposite José. Alejandro began standing opposite Jesús and the coffee table, and soon sat down in a chair to Avery's right. Isabel sat on a chair next to José, on the sofa. Isabel previously assigned Avery and Alejandro the roles of discussion directors, although it is unclear if any of the other boys were assigned roles. Some of the boys occasionally refer to small white slips of paper that they removed from an accordion folder provided by Isabel on a previous day. These papers had discussion prompts (e.g., ask a question) designed to help them manage their discussion. The description that ensues provides a chronological summary of the event, with references to IUs and line numbers.

Interaction Unit (IU) 1 begins with Isabel clarifying where the boys are in the book and asking Alejandro and Avery if the others have understood the book so far. She then prompts Avery and Alejandro to take over, stating, "well, get started" (line 27). Near the beginning of IU2 José says that he doesn't understand the word "booger," and looks to Isabel for assistance. Isabel gestures its meaning to José (line 34), although the other boys don't seem to notice. In IU3, Isabel initiates a discussion regarding the word, and directs José to re-read that portion of the text (lines 57–58). The rereading prompts Isabel to initiate a discussion of the figurative phrase "seeing red." Isabel then tells the group to "continue" on their own, and she steps away from the area to talk with Lara (lines 110–113), who was videotaping the event, and with an aide who was working with another student. The boys return to the word "booger" in IU4, and Alejandro states, "it's a booger that you pick your nose with" (line 136). Together Alejandro and José suggest that the group consult the dictionary. Despite Avery's assertion that it won't be in the dictionary because "it's not a appropriate word" (line 162), Alejandro and José jump up to move across the room to find dictionaries. Jesús follows, and Esteban and Avery then follow suit. In IU5a the group spends the next five minutes looking for the word in a variety of dictionaries, dispersing around the classroom. Ultimately, Isabel intervenes, calling Alejandro over to her and initiating IU5b. Avery follows, and Isabel prompts them to recall strategies they can use. She then poses a new problem to Alejandro: "Right now you are taking a lot of time to find one word" (lines 216–217), and she prompts him to reconvene the group. Following Alejandro's lead, they return to the sofa, ending IU5. In IU6, they quickly abandon their attempt to identify the word. Table 3.1 offers a summary of these IUs and the still images we discuss in the remainder of this chapter.

Stepping In and Stepping Out

We break up the following discussion into three sections: Framing of the event, theorizing word meanings, and "Let's wrap it up" (event conclusion). These sections follow the event somewhat chronologically, although not entirely. In each section we illustrate how participants' discursive moves (utterances and body movements) reinscribe, challenge, and play with different student and teacher identities and multiple language and literacy ideologies.

In our previous writing about this event (Handsfield & Crumpler, 2013), we focused on Avery and Alejandro. Here we also focus on Isabel, in particular how students' social and academic identity performances are coconstructed along with teacher identity performances.

Framing of the Event

The event is framed in ways that index particular normative expectations for social identities for the participants, most notably Isabel, Avery, and Alejandro, and this framing is produced alongside the indexing of different chronotopes as described above. We begin with Isabel's dual positioning as both authoritative teacher and as peer group member. We then show how Avery and Alejandro are positioned with respect to the chronotopes we identified earlier.

Isabel engaged in both physical and discursive moves that propelled the discussion of the word booger forward. As students first inquire about the word, Isabel gestures to José with her finger to her nose (see Table 3.2, line 35, and Figure 3.1), shifting her body slightly away from the camera, a move presumably meant to exclude Lara or perhaps to mark the topic as taboo.

Table 3.1: Data Summary.

Time	Lines	Main interaction units	Parallel interaction units	Figures
0:00–1:02	1–27	1. Getting started: establishing roles, orienting to task		
1:02–1:20	28–38	2. Identifying a problem: Unknown word		Fig. 1. Timestamp: 1:12. Isabel discretely gestures the meaning of the word to José.
1:21–4:01	39–109	3. Teacher intervention: re-reading; figurative language		
4:02–4:13	110–113	↓ (Off camera)	3a. Side conversation: Isabel conferring with Lara	
4:14–4:32	114–126	↓		
4:33–5:29	127–151	4. Theorizing word meanings		Fig. 2. Timestamps 5:25, 5:27. José and Alejandro jump up to retrieve dictionaries; Alejandro shouts in Avery's ear.
5:32–5:50	152–158	5. Consulting dictionaries	5a. World of words	Fig. 3. Timestamps 5:44, 5:49, 5:50. Avery argues that a dictionary should be called "The world of words" as he leans into the group.
5:51–8:47	159–196	↓		
8:48–9:40	197–228	↓ (Jesús, Esteban)	5b. Teacher intervention (Isabel, Alejandro, Avery, José)	Fig. 4. Timestamps: 9:15, 9:17. Isabel takes Avery by the shoulders and moves him to the side before addressing Alejandro.
9:41–9:57	229–236	↓ (David joins the group)		
9:58–10:58	237–264	6. Moving on		

At the same time, she makes playful utterances ("Where is a booger at?" "Was someone flinging boogers?," lines 39–41, and 48–50). These examples simultaneously signal the word's potential inappropriateness while validating body function humor and peer group discourse as a legitimate topic and mode of discussion. These kinds of participation serve to both encourage the discussion regarding the word and to position herself as co-learner or peer group member, rather than a traditionally authoritative teacher. This is particularly evident in line 41, in which she ends her question with preposition "at," a less formal or "schooled" syntax. Isabel's positioning here is consistent with the ideological commitments of literature discussion, in which the students are expected to assume more authoritative roles and teachers may attempt to minimize their own authoritative voices within such interactions.

At the same time, however, Isabel is the primary conversational pivot in IU1 and IU2. In lines 55–56 (see Table 3.3), she shifts to a more serious tone, taking control over the direction of the conversation and directing José to re-read the portion of text under question (lines 57–58). In this way she positions herself in a traditional teacher role, posing a series of known-answer questions about the phrase "seeing red" (see Table 3.4).

In short, in the earliest moments of the event, she positions herself in multiple ways as she moves between being a playful co-learner and traditional

Table 3.2: "I don't get this word"

Line	Speaker → Listener	Message Unit	Additional Contextualization and Movement
030	Avery → José	Ask your quest- uh ask your, uh	Spoken loudly, to get the floor
031	José → Isabel	I don't get this word, this- b-o-o-g-e-r	Spells out booger. José turns to Isabel, smiling.
032	Avery → José, Isabel	What does that mean↑	Alejandro sits back down, backing slightly away from Avery.
033		⌊Boo++ger	
034	José → Isabel	⌊Bohgar, booger↑	Isabel directs gaze away from camera and discretely motions with her finger to her nose. Only José sees it.
035	José	A++H, U+GH	José turns away in feigned disgust, waving hands in air; still smiling
036	Avery → Isabel	No, no, it must've been uh, uh, <u>Gabí</u>	
037		Cause she doesn't know-	
038		She doesn't really-	
		End interaction unit 2: Identifying a problem	
		Begin interaction unit 3: Teacher intervention	
039	Isabel → Group	Wait what- what's this talk about a *<u>booger</u>*	Emphasis on "booger" and ending with a preposition indicates approval of body function humor
040		You are talking about a <u>booger</u>↑	
041		Where is a <u>booger</u> at	
042	José → Isabel	There	Tone is skeptical
043		It says right there	
044		in the book	
045	Isabel → José	It says right <u>there</u> in the <u>book</u>↓	Directing José to show Isabel the text in the book?
046	Avery → José	Look	
047		Put it right there	
048	Isabel → Group	No, but I mean in the book were there boogers↑	Isabel chuckles as *students look in their books*.
049		Was somebody flinging boogers↑ or putting them	
050		under their desk or something↑	

Figure 3.1: Isabel.

teacher. This type of role switching is a practice that many teachers use to facilitate literature discussion. However, Isabel's discursive shifts achieve multiple simultaneous frames for the discussion context and expectations for student participation.

Simultaneously, Isabel has positioned Avery and Alejandro in multiple ways at the onset of the event. In preparation for the event, Isabel assigns both boys the discussion director role, which suggests that both were expected to act as group leaders. In an interview, Isabel explained that Avery was more socially awkward than the other students and that by partnering him with another student, she was hoping to provide him with peer support for a leadership role. However, Isabel's responses to his attempts at participation and word identification positioned him not as a leader but rather as a less competent participant. This happens first at the end of IU2, when Avery begins to theorize the word's meaning. He speaks in stops and starts, unable to fully articulate what he's thinking (No, no, it must've been uh, uh, Gabí/Cause she doesn't know- /She doesn't really-, lines 36–38), and he gets no uptake. In lines 85–87 (see Table 3.4), Avery states that he thought seeing red referred to the ability to "see in the dark," and later, he states that he thought Gabí had

Table 3.3: "You have the question."

Line	Speaker → Listener	Message Unit	Additional Contextualization and Movement
054	Alejandro → Group	I have David's question	*Flapping the question strip to get attention.* David is working with itinerant teacher during group meeting
055	Isabel → José	Okay, can- can I have you-	
056		You say *what does the word booger mean*	
057	Isabel → José	So, he should probably read that page	
058		So as a group you guys can decide *what does she mean*	
059	Alejandro → Group	What page is it	
060	José → Alejandro	51, paragraph	
061		Just read it	
062	Avery → José	51↑	
063	Isabel → José	Well <u>you</u> read it José	
064		<u>You</u> have the <u>question</u>	

"eye vision" (line 103). In doing so, he offers a possible meaning based on the strategy of using the surrounding context within the text. The chapter the students and Isabel are discussing is titled "My Secret Identity," and immediately following the portion of the novel in which "booger" and "seeing red" appear, Gabí is described as a superhero or secret agent, "fighting evil." We believe that Avery's interpretation of "seeing red" as "eye vision" relates to his knowledge of night vision and infrared goggles (which may be used to fight evil).

In both of the instances, Isabel responds to Avery by revoicing his statements slowly and with a flat (rather than rising or falling) pitch at the end. Similarly, her restatement of Avery's words is punctuated by her roll of her head and shift in gaze toward José and away from Avery, conveying either her lack of understanding of his comments or her dismissal of them as odd, an interpretation reinforced by Alejandro's response to Avery: "Huh↑" (line 88). In

Table 3.4: Seeing red.

Line	Speaker → Listener	Message Unit	Additional Contextualization and Movement
071	Isabel → Group	Okay, so <u>first</u> of all	
072		What does↑-	
073		She says, "<u>Johnny</u> is <u>making</u> me <u>see red</u>"	
074	Jesús → Isabel	She doesn't like Johnny-	
075	Isabel → Group	-Is she like <u>painting</u> something red↑	*Gestures with hand, as if painting*
076	Alej. → Isabel	[No	
077	Unknown → Isabel	[No	
078	Isabel → Group	What does that mean↑	
079	Jesús → Isabel	[She makes him mad	
080	Alej. → Isabel	[<Making her mad>	
081	Isabel → Group	<u>Why</u> do you think that↓	
082	Jesús → Isabel	[Because he does | bad stuff to her↑	
083	Alej. → Isabel	[<Because your face turns red when you're angry>↑	
084	José → Isabel	[She- she- she doesn't like Johnny	
085			
086	Avery → Isabel	[I thought- I thought- I think- I thought red, like you see in the <u>dark</u>	*Smiling sheepishly.*
087	Isabel → Avery	Like you see in the dark	*Revoicing, even tone*
088	Alej. → Avery	Huh↑	
089	Isabel → Group	Well, generally when you say *that makes me see <u>red</u>*	
090		And red is↑	
091		What do we think about red↑	
092	Alej. → Isabel	<Fire>	
093		Fire↑	
094	Isabel → Group	Or what <u>emotion</u> would you think red	*Gestures with arm in circular motion and tilts head, indicating that she's looking for a different response*
095	Avery → Isabel	I was-	

Continued

Table 3.4: *Continued*

Line	Speaker → Listener	Message Unit	Additional Contextualization and Movement
096	Jesús → Isabel	-Angry	
097	Isabel → Group	A+ngry	
098		It makes me see <u>red</u>	
099	Avery → Unknown	I-	
100	Isabel → Group	Her dad's like, "you <u>like</u> red"	
101	Avery → Isabel	I was thinking-	
102	Alej. → Unknown	XXX	
103	Avery → Isabel	[I, uh, I thought that it was- like he- she had <u>eye vision</u>	Lots of overlapping quiet talk
			Looking up at Isabel
104	José → Isabel	[OR MAYBE JOHNNY WAS WEARING RED	
105	Isabel → Avery	You thought she had <u>eye</u> vision	Isabel lifts head slightly, gaze directed a bit up, then rolls gaze to her left toward José

addition, the discursive (utterances and paralinguistic cues) features of Isabel's responses—her gaze, her slow and flat repetition of his statements—seem less characteristic of an authoritative teacher seeking to correct or instruct Avery, and more characteristic of a participant role in the literature discussion.

Isabel's responses marginalize Avery's participation and his role as discussion director despite the fact that he is, indeed, reading strategically. This is particularly interesting because Isabel framed the event in part as a time for them to apply strategic reading. This is evident in the literature discussion folder they used, which included ideas for questions to ask, and in her suggestion that they re-read the portion of the text that included the unknown word. She also explicitly prompts their strategy use later in the event (IU5, lines 200–202, Table 6). We speculate that Isabel's responses to Avery in IU3 are related at least in part to Avery's stops and starts (e.g., line 85) and his more limited familiarity with English terms such as "night vision" or "infrared goggles." The fact that she doesn't pick up on or make note of Avery's strategic reading is a missed opportunity that seems to relate to her positioning of herself as a participant rather than as authoritative teacher. That is, she steps into the role of a participant attempting to make sense of the passage rather than as a discursive authority who might recast Avery's contributions as attempts at strategic reading in order to scaffold meaning.

Isabel also explicitly framed the event as a peer-led literature discussion group, in which participants were to work collaboratively. However, in IU3 she temporarily re-inserts herself into an authoritative teacher position. Isabel's explicit instructions to read around the word "booger" quickly morphs into the Initiation-Response-Evaluation (I-R-E) exchange regarding the meaning of the figurative phrase "seeing red." In lines 96–98, Jesús is verbally rewarded for his correct arrival at the target word (angry). Thus, we see an instructional interaction regarding figurative language and strategic reading performed via I-R-E. This includes her determination of when the correct meaning of the word is accessed, with no discussion of what figurative language is or how students may use different semiotic (e.g., color) resources to access complex word meanings.

The examples above illustrate how the event was framed in ambiguous, or indeterminate ways (Bloome et al., 2005). This framing was permeable to multiple simultaneous positionings for Isabel as teacher and for her students. This indeterminacy is also evident in later portions of the event, in which Isabel steps out and students begin to theorize word meanings and consult dictionaries.

Theorizing Word Meanings

In IU4 (lines 127–151) and IU5 (beginning on line 152) (see Table 3.5), Avery and Alejandro position themselves in very different ways, articulating different ideologies of language and literacy learning: strategic reading versus discrete word identification. While Avery begins to theorize the meaning of booger in IU3, it is in IU4, after Isabel leaves the group, that the students' theorizing takes off. Alejandro positions himself in a traditional teacher role as he makes a declarative statement offering a definition (a booger is something you "pick your nose with," line 136). The event unfolds with Avery and Alejandro vying for control of the group and leadership with respect to what strategies or approaches they should use to identify the word. Avery argues for using a variety of strategies to solve the problem. This includes his assertion that booger must refer to a person based on the -er suffix indicates his recognition of an important aspect of English morphology. He also applies pragmatic

Table 3.5: World of words.

Line	Speaker → Listener	Message Unit	Additional Contextualization and Movement
127	Jesús → Group	Answer my question↑	
128	Alejandro → Jesús	Jesús, it's your turn	Avery leans forward, as if to listen to Jesús
129	Jesús → Group	My question-	
130	José → Group	-Wait, you haven't answered mine	Interrupting Jesús
131	Avery → José	Yeah we did	
132	José → Avery	What↑	
133	Avery → José	Boo+ger | is-	
134	José → Avery	-It's a di+fferent o+ne	*José smiles, covers his face with his open book.*
135	Avery → José	What↑	Confused expression
136	Alejandro → Avery	It's a booger that you pick your nose with	*Jesús and Esteban lean together, consulting book.* [the next chapter has the word hamburger in the title.] *José looks to Jesús and Esteban. Avery softly hits José's knee with accordion folder. Alejandro rolls his eyes, then leans toward Jesús and Esteban to speak.*
137	Jesús → Group	Maybe- maybe a hamboo+ger	
138	Avery → Group	No, like booger | like booger | like booger	
139	Unknown, multiple	XXX hambooger	
140	Alejandro → Jesús, Esteban	Dude, hamburger is spelled h-a-m-b-u-r-g-e-r	
141		The booger that he's talking about is spelled b-o-o-g-e-r	
142 143	Avery → Jesús, Esteban	The booger | that you're talking about must be like someone is a booger	
144	Jesús → Avery	U+h <I don't know>	Spoken dismissively
145	Avery → Group	Like, like booger means to a person	
146		which that means it's a yuh	*Stomps foot gently* when he says "yuh," likely referring to—er suffix
147	Alej. → Avery	I know what we could check	
148	José, Alej., Jesús	The dictionary	*Alejandro and José rise, José enthusiastically, to find dictionary across room.*

Table 3.5: *Continued*

Line	Speaker → Listener	Message Unit	Additional Contextualization and Movement
149	Avery → Others	The dictionary doesn't have b<u>oo</u>ger	
150	Alejandro → Avery	It has <u>words</u>	*Alejandro stops, leans over Avery from behind as if to whisper in his ear,* but speaks line 150 loudly. *Jesús smiles, gets up to follow Alejandro.* Line 151 spoken while looking over shoulder.
151		Why do you think they call it a <u>dictionary</u>	
152	Avery → Group, A1	Why- why can't we call it um uh *the world of words*	*Glancing around and at video camera; showing one hand as if to emphasize "world of words" Esteban, Alejandro, and José are standing around dictionary.*
153		It's much better	
154	Alejandro → Avery	The best dictionary	*Alejandro looks to Avery. José flips through the dictionary. Jesús has a different dictionary two desks away.*
155		For <u>students</u>	
156	Avery → Other group members	Why did they it um- why did they call it a <u>dictionary</u>	
157	Avery → Camera/A1	I think we should call it *The <u>World</u> of Words*	No uptake of Avery's comments. *He joins group, placing his fingertips on desk*
158	Alejandro → José	B-o-o- End parallel interaction unit 5a: World of words	*Looking at camera, Avery extends his arms outward, emphasizing "world," then leans in toward the group.* Alejandro spells out booger while others looking for word in dictionary
		Continue interaction unit 5: Consulting dictionaries	
159	Avery → Others	[No↑ No está↑	Alejandro closes dictionary without having found the word.
160	José → Alejandro	[We'll go get one over there	
161	Avery → Alejandro	[<u>Told</u> you	*José points toward Isabel's desk*
162		booger is not a- | a appropriate word	*Alejandro quickly goes over to shelf by Isabel's desk. Others follow.*

Continued

Table 3.5: *Continued*

Line	Speaker → Listener	Message Unit	Additional Contextualization and Movement
163	Alejandro à Avery	[It's not a word↑	
164	Avery à Alej.	Well it is	Walking away. Avery follows.
165	Unknown à Self	b-o-o-g-e-r	Uttered softly, even tone

understandings, which is evident in line 149 and in IU5, when he argues that booger won't be in the dictionary because it is "a inappropriate word" (line 162). Importantly, however, throughout IU3 and IU4, neither Isabel nor Avery's peers acknowledge his strategic reading. In many respects, Isabel has taken on an observer role.

We attribute the lack of uptake in part to Avery's lower social status. However, this social positioning may be reinscribed in combination with different ideologies recruited by Avery and Alejandro during the event. This is emphasized when Alejandro and José suggest using the dictionary, a source of decontextualized word meanings. As José and Alejandro get up to move across the room, Avery counters that the word will not be in the dictionary (line 149). As he moves away from the group, Alejandro stops behind Avery's chair, leans over, and shouts directly in his ear, "It has WORDS" (see Figure 3.2). While walking away, and looking over his shoulder, he adds, "Why do you think they call it a dictionary" (line 151).

Alejandro's physical stance, combined with shouting directly in Avery's ear, positions Avery as less powerful, both socially and academically. Also notable is Alejandro's reasoning that booger will be in the dictionary because a dictionary has words, and that's why it is called a dictionary. Alejandro's utterance displays a high level of English fluency (without the stops and starts and awkward word choices often made by Avery), but less contextual and semantic competency (e.g., the root of the word dictionary, which references pronunciation rather than words, per se). In fact, at the beginning of IU5 (lines 152–153), Avery demonstrates his own understanding in this regard: "Why- why can't we call it um uh *the world of words*/It's much better." Avery is quite persistent in his assertion that booger won't be in the dictionary, and Alejandro is equally persistent in his belief that it will. But in the end, it is Alejandro, rather than Avery, who receives uptake from the

Figure 3.2: Literature Discussion Group.

other boys, which reinforces Alejandro's social position, his academic position, and the ideological commitments supported by Alejandro's discursive and physical moves. Further, as we describe later, it is Alejandro's communicative competence rather than Avery's strategic reading, that also garners Isabel's uptake, and it is in these interactions that both student and teacher identities are discursively coconstructed.

"Let's Wrap It Up!"

Eventually, once the students have exhausted their resources, Isabel re-enters the literature discussion. Table 3.6 includes all of IU5b (lines 197–228), in which Isabel steps back into the interaction and prompts Alejandro to use strategies. Several things stand out in this portion of the event. First, Isabel's I-R-E and modified I-R-E discourse pattern once again positions her as an authoritative teacher, moving Alejandro into a position of being evaluated with respect to his leadership as discussion director. While this discourse pattern could index standardized approaches to instruction, Isabel uses it to spur

Table 3.6: "Let's wrap it up."

Line	Speaker → Listener	Message Unit	Additional Contextualization and Movement
197	Isabel → Alejandro	XXX	José is looking on.
198	Alejandro → Isabel	No↑ Yes no	Avery and Esteban move over
199		I don't know	toward desks. Avery joins Isabel
200	Isabel → Alejandro	What can you do if you can't find it in the dictionary	and Alejandro, while Esteban joins José off to the side. Esteban looks off to the side. Isabel is
201		or you don't know what it is	prompting strategy use, and students are offering ideas, but they don't satisfy Isabel.
202		What did we talk about	Quietly
203	Esteban → José	No sé en español (I don't know in Spanish)	
204	Avery → Isabel	the XXX	
205	José → Isabel	Computer	
206	Isabel → Group	No	
207	Avery → Isabel	Reference-	"re" pronounced with long-e.
208	Alejandro → Isabel	-Context clues	
209	Isabel → Alejandro, Avery	You can infer	Quietly
210	Avery → Isabel	We can't infer	
211	Alejandro → Isabel	We don't know the words	
212	Avery → Isabel	We don't have the picture	Avery clarifies as to why
213		We don't have the words	they can't infer. He nudges
214		We don't have the clues	Alejandro onto a nearby desk,
215	Isabel → Avery	Watch what you're doing Avery	apparently by accident. Isabel sees this and rolls her head
216	Isabel → Alejandro	Because right now you are taking a lot of time	slightly. Laughing, placing hands on Avery's shoulders
217		to find just one word	and turning him to the right, so he's facing Alejandro, but off to the side. Esteban joins Jesús at Isabel's desk. Isabel's gaze directed toward Alejandro, not Avery, who is now off to the side.
218	Alejandro → Isabel	That's really hard	Quietly; gazing ahead, into space, rather than at Isabel
219	Avery → Isabel	I did find Boston	
220	Isabel → Alejandro	So what can you do	

Table 3.6: *Continued*

Line	Speaker → Listener	Message Unit	Additional Contextualization and Movement
221		to bring your group back together at some point	
222		'cause they're just probably gonna keep doing that unti:l	*Isabel gestures with arm to indicate students dispersed around the classroom. Avery's gaze is toward boys at Isabel's desk. He gestures "come on over" with arm to return to sofa area, presumably to continue their discussion.*
223	Avery → Group	[Keep going	
224	Alejandro → Group	[Alright guys let's go	
225	Isabel → Avery	[Keep going↑	*Isabel has an expression of confusion*
226	Alejandro → Group	[Let's *wrap it up*	
227	Isabel → Alejandro	Way to go Director	
228	Alejandro → Jesús, Esteban	Sorry XXX	*9:37–9:43: Alejandro moves toward Jesús and Esteban at Isabel's desk, who are looking at dictionaries. Avery follows Alejandro.*

students' strategic reading (lines 200–202, 209). At the same time, she also directs her prompts toward Alejandro rather than toward both Alejandro and Avery, who are co-discussion directors. It could be that Isabel has not noticed or understood Avery's strategic reading attempts, as she was engaged with another set of students and an itinerant teacher as IU5 was unfolding. However, the utterances and physical movements in lines 209–227 suggest another likely explanation.

In line 199, Avery joins Alejandro and Isabel unsolicited, and in line 212 he explains why they could not infer the word's meaning, building on Alejandro's assertion that "we don't know the words" (line 213) to emphasize his thorough use of strategies. This is evident in the repeated phrase "we don't have the . . ." in lines 212–214. Isabel has taught them how to make explicit inferences as a comprehension strategy, and Avery's argument that they don't have the requisite information in the text or enough context to successfully infer indicates both his understanding of the strategy itself and his confident meta-level awareness of the limitations of these strategies in this instance. This moment could be interpreted as a rare and fleeting alliance between Avery and Alejandro: Avery joins Alejandro and provides additional arguments regarding their inability to infer the meaning of the word. This interpretation would make sense given their joint confusion regarding the word booger.

At the same time, Alejandro's utterance in line 211 still favors discrete word knowledge ("we don't know the words"), while Avery's contributions center on resources for effective strategy use. Furthermore, Avery's physical movements indicate continued and persistent competition for recognition as discussion director. As Avery speaks in lines 212–214, he bumps into Alejandro, almost knocking him over. It is unclear from the video whether or not Avery intended to knock Alejandro over; however, he clearly intended to gain access to the representational field of interaction and possibly to remove Alejandro's access. These attempts, however, are not taken up favorably by Isabel, who responds by stating, "watch what you're doing, Avery" (line 215), and by moving Avery back to the side, outside the representational field (see Figure 3.3). In the process, any alliance that was formed between Avery and Alejandro, and their tactical request for further instructional support, are compromised.

Figure 3.3: Isabel and Alejandro.

Rather than responding to Avery's statements regarding his strategy use, or their joint plea, Isabel shifts to procedural concerns, turning to Alejandro and asking him what he can do to get his group back together. Through these directing and access moves (Radinsky et al., 2012) and her utterances, Isabel repositions Alejandro as the group leader, marginalizing Avery. Thus, despite Isabel's explicit prompting to engage in strategic reading, Avery's application of this approach garners no uptake, calling into question the ideologies that are "heard" in the event.

Moments later, Alejandro appears to receive validation from Isabel based on his facility with English. After Isabel prompts Alejandro to reconvene the group, Avery gestures with his arm toward the reading area behind him and calls out, "KEEP GOING" (line 223). We believe Avery meant for the group to continue reading and discussing the novel. However, Isabel interprets his meaning as a directive to continue searching for the word ("Keep going↑," line 225), perhaps not seeing his arm gesture. When Alejandro shouts "Let's *WRAP IT UP*" (line 226), Isabel validates his performance as discussion director (line 227). Indeed, throughout the event there is a tacit misrecognition (Bourdieu & Passeron, 1977) of what counts as a discussion director, a role characterized by social and academic leadership. Alejandro demonstrates a strong social-communicative repertoire in English, which effectively scales up the interaction in a way that is recognized by Isabel as authoritative, but Avery demonstrates a sophisticated knowledge of language and a strategic approach to word identification—a strategic reading repertoire. Nevertheless, the social-communicative repertoire trumps the strategic reading repertoire and becomes the primary criterion for being a successful discussion director.

In the end, the word is not in the dictionary. In IU6 (see Table 3.7), the group is reconvened on the sofa, but with Avery positioned in a more authoritative discussion director role. This is indicated by his directives to the others ("Okay guys. A llegar (come on)," line 240; "Cállate (Be quiet)" lines 241 and 245; and "Dáme eso (Give me that)," line 249), and his comment to José (but perhaps indirectly also to Alejandro), "Too bad so sad/you cannot find the answer" (line 254).

This last example shows Avery engaging in a kind of peer group discourse in English, much like Alejandro used in IU5 ("Let's *WRAP IT UP*" [line 226]). Avery's utterances indicate that he has successfully (even if temporarily) disrupted Alejandro's leadership within the peer group: in lines 260–261, it is Avery who garners uptake from his peers while Alejandro's question goes unrecognized.

Table 3.7: "Too bad, so sad."

Line	Speaker → Listener	Message Unit	Additional Contextualization and Movement
237	Jesús → Unknown	XXX-ese otra vez (that one again)	Boys sitting in their original places on sofa and chairs around coffee table.
238	Alejandro → Avery	What's wrong with you eating man↑	
239		It's like you wanna make everyone hungry	Critical tone; spoken as Alejandro takes his seat.
240	Avery → Group	Okay guys	A llegar. (come on)	Avery glances at camera and smiles, as does Jesús.
241		Cállate	cállate (Be quiet | be quiet)	Avery turns head away from Alejandro. Esteban, Jesús, and David are on sofa; José comes to group, but stays standing perhaps referring to growling stomach
242	Alejandro → no one	Ayayay	
243		Se due+le (It hurts)	
244		sí se duele (It sure hurts)	
245	Avery → rest of Group	Cá+lla+te+ (BE QUI+E+T)	
246	Jesús → Alejandro	I have a que+stio+n	
247	Alejandro → Jesús	Yes↑	Looking at Alejandro, leaning forward.
248		No we haven't answered his question	Indicating José; Jesús leans back in sofa again. José tries to take slip of paper out of accordion folder Avery grabs folder back.
249	Avery → José	Dáme eso (Give me that)	
250	Jesús → Alejandro	Hey maybe it's Booker T↑	Cross-talk about booger.
251	Alejandro → Jesús	Booker T↑	Leaning forward, smiling
252		Oh I forgot that's a wrestler	Jesús and Alejandro laughing; Booker T is the adopted name of a professional American wrestler.
253	Alejandro → Group	Okay	
254	Avery → José	Too bad so sad	Peer group discourse
255		you cannot find the answer	
256	José → Avery	Hey	José has an exaggerated frown, indicating feigned dejection

Table 3.7: *Continued*

Line	Speaker → Listener	Message Unit	Additional Contextualization and Movement
257		Oh well	
258		Just skip it	
259	Avery → Isabel	Miss Schmidt can we skip an answer↑	
260	Alejandro → Group	What does *sha-rock-a* mean	
261	Avery → Group	Any questions↑	Ignoring Alejandro's question

Indeterminacy, Tactics, and Reshaping Identities

Throughout the event we see Alejandro and Avery jockeying for status, forwarding different approaches to word identification, and garnering qualitatively different uptake from Isabel, all within an apparently cohesive group. However, through Isabel's ongoing informal assessments of the boys' different kinds of participation, she confers more weight to Alejandro's communicative repertoire than to Avery's strategic reading repertoire. This enables Alejandro (for the majority of the event) to assume the leadership position in the group. Gestures, body movements, and utterances by Isabel tacitly favored Alejandro's communicative repertoire (and by association his emphasis on discrete word proficiencies), despite Isabel's explicit prompting for students to try to infer the word's meaning. Thus, while Avery is the one who does the academic work of bringing his own pragmatic and morphological understandings to bear in the event, Alejandro gets the interactional validation as discussion director.

What is particularly interesting in this event is Isabel's decision making regarding when to move off script; that is, when to remove herself from the discourse, and when to move back on script to reinsert herself as the teacher into the interaction. In addition, her active participation includes both traditional teacher scripts or discourse, such as when she scolds Avery or praises Alejandro, and nontraditional scripts, as when she feigns placing her finger up her nose early in the event. This multiple positioning—moving on and off script in different ways and at different times—is both tactical in a de Certeauian sense and generative of new possibilities for both student and teacher identities.

Possibilities for Alternative Identity Trajectories

We see a tactical recasting of dominant structures to generate new possibilities for participant identities in these interactions. Avery waits for cracks to form in Alejandro's discrete word knowledge frame, and in the end Avery's tactical maneuvers threaten the coherence of Alejandro's leadership. In the process, multiple simultaneous identity performances are made possible by and for Avery (strategic reader, competent English speaker, and productive literature group member (if not discussion director)). Isabel was central in setting the stage in this regard by framing the event in indeterminate ways. First, she assigned Avery to a leadership role (discussion director) while simultaneously positioning him as in need of support for fulfilling that role by making him a co-discussion director with Alejandro. Second, while she intervened in the event in key ways (e.g., leading them into a discussion of "seeing red" and prompting Alejandro rather than Avery to reconvene the group), she also separated herself physically and verbally for large portions of the event.

We also wish to emphasize the importance of attending to both utterances and larger body movements for understanding identity construction and disruption in classroom language and literacy events such as this. Movements such as Alejandro leaning in to shout in Avery's ear, or Isabel putting her hands onto Avery's shoulders to move him out of the way, suggest particular ideologies about language and literacy that simultaneously criss-cross multiple chronotopes of language and literacy learning.

Like Gabí, Avery tactically recasts himself as a particular type of protagonist as he, the other students, and Isabel move through the space/times of the event. Extending Sterponi's work (2007), in which she describes a student "animating a text gesturally" (p. 19) as a type of double voicing in interactive reading, Avery uses utterances, gesture, and larger body movements in ways that Bakhtin (1981) would identify as "comic, ironic, or parodic" (p. 324). Rather than animate the text in this case, these moves "refract" his positionality and open possibilities for him to re-narrate his role in the discussion group.

It is also worth pointing out that neither a decontextualized approach to word identification, nor strategic reading with or without Isabel immediately present, nor literature discussion groups independent of the teacher were sufficient for accessing the figurative meaning of the word. In other words, the problem at hand could not be solved by bringing together the chronotope of strategic reading, with its commitment to metacognition, and standardization, with its dissociation of meaning from language form. And certainly, student-directed literature discussion by itself would not have sufficed. Even when Isabel steps into the literature discussion and a more authoritative teacher role by prompting students to engage in strategic reading, the focus does not appear to be on accessing the word's figurative meaning, but rather on doing strategies.

In short, procedure is valued over interpretation, and ironically, strategy use itself becomes decontextualized. This is problematic given expectations for student achievement that include interpretation of figurative and symbolic uses of language in literature and other texts. It is also significant that Isabel does not prompt Avery, Alejandro, or the other students to consider how their knowledge of Spanish may be recruited to interpret the text. Might they have been able to access examples of figurative language in Spanish to help them begin to decipher complex uses of language in their English text?

Teacher Identity Performances in the Context of Classroom Research

Central to these questions of pedagogical possibilities is teacher positioning—in this case, what kinds of professional identities was Isabel taking up and for what purposes? Particularly given the purpose of the third phase of our research project—to explore challenges and successes in how participants such as Isabel were able to implement strategies discussed in our study groups—it is likely that Isabel was intentionally trying to situate herself as less authoritative in order to generate space for student-directed interactions and literature discussion. This may have made her less inclined to clarify word meanings for the students or to take on a more teacher fronted role in the discussions. In other words, this may have prompted her to move "off script."

Moreover, the skills-focused curriculum and English-focused ideologies, characteristic of a chronotope of standardization, also likely served to structure—to scale up—Isabel's decisions with respect to her positioning and participation. This may have played a role, even tacitly, in her privileging of Alejandro's English communicative competence over the strategic reading and meaning making goals of the literature discussion group. Even if Isabel's identity performances were not for the sake of the research team, dominant ideologies function as flows (Ahmed, 2017; Lysaker & Handsfield, 2019) within everyday life that are difficult to swim against, even when no one else is watching.

Scholars have illustrated the value of permeable curricula (Dyson, 2003) and textual discussion (Gritter, 2012) for enabling students to use their cultural and linguistic resources in the interest of academic engagement and achievement. Permeability invites indeterminacy, or the destabilization of chronotopes. However, a teacher, team of teachers, or district making the decision to use approaches such as literature discussion or reading and writing workshop does not necessarily lead to alternative identity trajectories. Rather, our analyses paint a more complex picture, in which such permeability also opens the door to the reinscription of standardized and autonomous ideologies of language and literacy learning. This does not constitute an argument against permeable learning engagements, such as literature discussion. In fact, we believe that working such engagements into her instruction within a fairly restrictive curricular environment and within a political climate focused on high stakes assessment is one of Isabel's strengths as a teacher. However, as noted above, this is not enough. Teachers must be able to recognize students' tactical maneuvers, and then mediate, or scaffold, such moments with an eye toward students' social positioning and identity (re)visions.

Elsewhere we have analyzed Isabel's tactical negotiations of restrictive literacy mandates to support her students' literacy learning (Handsfield, 2012; Handsfield, Crumpler, & Dean, 2010; Hunt, Crumpler, & Handsfield, 2015). We speculate that Isabel's inclinations to seek out cracks in the structures that function to manage teachers' and students' work might dispose her to noticing her students' tactical negotiations and complex positioning. However, we believe that teachers might benefit from professional development efforts in which they engage in micro-level analyses of their own instruction, particularly moments of contingency in which dominant ideologies may seep in to structure teaching flows within the framework of standardizing chronotopes. Based on our analyses, it would be important that within such reflective work, teachers are supported in noticing students' tactical negotiations and the different chronotopes that form the warp and woof of everyday instructional engagements. Such efforts might prompt teachers to reconsider their own roles in such instructional activities as they seek to scaffold textual meanings with an eye toward the different ideological commitments at play in their classrooms.

In the next chapter, we continue to explore these dynamic kinds of negotiations, turning our attention to Isabel's colleague, Paula. Specifically, we explore Paula's integration of digital technologies into her instruction, and tensions between authoritative discourses of teaching and learning and the mobilities that digital literacies invite into classroom spaces.

References

Ahmed, S. (2017). *Living a feminist life*. Durham, NC: Duke University Press.

Allen, J., Moller, K., & Stroup, D. (2003). "Is this some kind of soap opera?": A tale of two readers across four literature discussion contexts. *Reading and Writing Quarterly, 19*, 225–251.

Artiles, A. (2011). Toward an interdisciplinary understanding of educational equity and difference: The case of the racialization of ability. *Educational Researcher, 40*(9), 431–445.

Au, W., Brown, A. L., & Calderón, D. (2016). *Reclaiming the multicultural roots of U.S. Curriculum: Communities of color and official knowledge in education*. New York, NY: Teachers College Press.

Aukerman, M. (2008). In praise of wiggle room: Locating comprehension in unlikely places. *Language Arts, 86*(1), 52–60.

Baker, C. (2006). *Foundations of bilingual education and bilingualism*. Clevedon, UK: Multilingual Matters.

Bakhtin, M. M. (1981). *The dialogic imagination: Four essays*. Austin, TX: University of Texas Press.

Blommaert, J. (2005). *Discourse: Key topics in sociolinguistics*. New York, NY: Cambridge University Press.

Blommaert, J., Collins, J., & Slembrouck, S. (2005). Spaces of multilingualism. *Language & Communication, 25*, 197–216.

Bloome, D., Carter, S. P., Christian, B. M., Otto, S., & Shuart-Faris, N. (2005). *Discourse analysis and the study of classroom language and literacy events: A microethnographic perspective*. Mahwah, NJ: Lawrence Erlbaum.

Bourdieu, P., & Passeron, J. C. (1977). *Reproduction in education, society, and culture*. London, England: Sage.

Cazden, C. (2001). *Classroom discourse: The language of teaching and learning*. Portsmouth, NH: Heinemann.

Daniels, H. (2002). *Literature circles: Voice and choice in book clubs and reading groups*. Portland, ME: Stenhouse.

de Certeau, M. (1984). *The practice of everyday life*. Berkeley, CA: University of California Press.

Duff, P. A. (2002). The discursive construction of knowledge, identity, and difference: An ethnography of communication in the high school mainstream. *Applied Linguistics, 2*(3), 289–322.

Dyson, A. H. (2003). *The brothers and sisters learn to write: Popular literacies in childhood and school cultures*. New York, NY: Teachers College Press.

Godley, A., Carpenter, B., & Werner, C. (2007). I'll speak in proper slang: Language ideologies in a daily editing activity. *Reading Research Quarterly, 42*(1), 100–113.

Goodman, Y. M., & Goodman, K. S. (2013). To err is human: Learning about language processes by analyzing miscues. In D. E. Alvermann, N. J. Unrau, & R. B. Ruddell (Eds.), *Theoretical models and processes of reading* (6th ed., pp. 525–543). Newark, DE: International Reading Association.

Grinberg, J., & Saavedra, E. R. (2000). The constitution of bilingual/EB education as a disciplinary practice: Genealogical explorations. *Review of Educational Research, 70*(4), 419–441.

Gritter, K. (2012). Permeable textual discussion in tracked language arts classrooms. *Research in the Teaching of English, 46*(3), 232–259.

Handsfield, L. J. (2012). Mediating learning and negotiating curricular ideologies in a fourth-grade bilingual classroom. In B. Yoon & H. K. Kim (Eds.), *Teachers' roles in second language learning: Classroom applications of sociocultural theory* (pp. 41–61). Information Age Publishing.

Handsfield, L. J. (2007). From discontinuity to simultaneity: Mapping the what ifs in a classroom literacy event using rhizoanalysis. In D. W. Rowe & R. T. Jiménez (Eds.), *56th yearbook of the National Reading Conference* (pp. 216–234). Oak Creek, WI: National Reading Conference.

Handsfield, L. J., & Crumpler, T. P. (2013). "Dude, it's not a appropriate word": Negotiating word meanings, language ideologies, and identities in a literature discussion group. *Linguistics and Education, 24*(2), 112–130.

Handsfield, L. J., Crumpler, T., & Dean, T. R. (2010). Tactical negotiations and creative adaptations: The discursive production of literacy curriculum and teacher identities across space-times. *Reading Research Quarterly, 45*(4), 405–431.

Handsfield, L. J., Dean, T. R., & Cielocha, K. M. (2009). Becoming critical consumers and producers of text: Teaching literacy with Web 1.0 and Web 2.0. *The Reading Teacher, 63*(1), 40–50.

Handsfield, L. J., & Jiménez, R. T. (2009). Cognition and misrecognition: A Bourdieuian analysis of cognitive strategy instruction in a culturally and linguistically diverse classroom. *Journal of Literacy Research, 41*(2), 151–194.

Hunt, C. S., Crumpler, T. P., & Handsfield, L. J. (2015). "Do you want an idea of what they're doing?" Transgressive data generation and analysis within a bilingual writers' workshop. International Journal of Qualitative Studies in Education, 29(3), 399–425.

Iser, W. (1978). *The act of reading: A theory of aesthetic response.* Baltimore, MA: Johns Hopkins University Press.

Leander, K. M. (2002). Locating Latanya: The situated production of identity artifacts in classroom interaction. *Research in the Teaching of English, 37,* 198–250.

Leung, C. (2005). Language and content in bilingual education. *Linguistics and Education, 16*(2), 238–252.

Lewis, C. (2001). *Literary practices as social acts: Power, status, and cultural norms in the classroom.* Mahwah, NJ: Lawrence Erlbaum.

Lewis, C., Enciso, P., & Moje, E. (Eds.). (2007). *Reframing sociocultural research on literacy.* Mahwah, NJ: Lawrence Erlbaum.

Lysaker, J., & Handsfield, L. H. (2019). Integrative research syntheses as sites of disruption and dialogue. *Journal of Literacy Research.* (Impact Factor-JCR: 1.710).

Maloch, B. (2002). Scaffolding student talk: One teacher's role in literature discussion groups. *Reading Research Quarterly, 37*(1), 94–112.

McKeown, M. G., Beck, I. L., & Blake, R. G. K. (2009). Rethinking reading comprehension instruction: A comparison of instruction for strategies and content approaches. *Reading Research Quarterly, 44*(3), 218–251.

Montes, M. (2003). *Get ready for Gabí: A crazy mixed-up Spanglish day.* New York, NY: Scholastic.

No Child Left Behind (NCLB) Act of 2001. (2002). Pub. L. No. 107–110, § 115, Stat. 1425.

Palincsar, A. S. (2007). Reciprocal teaching 1982 to 2006: The role of research, theory, and representation in the transformation of instructional research. In D. Rowe, R. Jimenez, & D. Compton, et al. (Eds.), *56th yearbook of the National Reading Conference* (pp. 41–52). Oak Creek, WI: National Reading Conference.

Pressley, M. (2002). Comprehension strategies instruction: A turn-of-the-century status report. In C. Block, & M. Pressley (Eds.), *Comprehension instruction: Research-based best practices* (pp. 11–27). New York, NY: Guilford.

Radinsky, J., Ping R., Hospelhorn, E., & Goldman, S. (2012). Making the absent present: Emergent representational fields in students' negotiations of meaning with spatial data. Paper presented at the American Educational Research Association annual meeting, Vancouver, BC.

Razfar, A. (2005). Language ideologies in practice: Repair and classroom discourse. *Linguistics and Education, 16*(4), 404–424.

Rosenblatt, L. (1978). *The reader, the text, the poem.* Carbondale, IL: Southern Illinois University Press.

Short, K., & Pierce, K. (1990). *Talking about books: Creating literate communities.* Portsmouth, NH: Heinemann.

Sipe, L. (2008). *Storytime: Young children's literary understanding in the classroom.* New York, NY: Teacher's College Press.

Sterponi, L. (2007). Clandestine interactional reading: Intertextuality and double-voicing under the desk. *Linguistics and Education, 18*(1), 1–23.

Sumara, D. (1996). *Private readings in public: Schooling the literary imagination.* New York, NY: Peter Lang.

Sumara, D. (2002). *Why reading literature in school still matters: Imagination, interpretation and insight.* Mahwah, NJ: Lawrence Erlbaum.

Zhang, J., & Dougherty Stahl, K. A. (2011). Collaborative reasoning: Language-rich discussions for English learners. *Read Teach, 65,* 257–260. doi:10.1002/TRTR.01040

· 4 ·
MOBILE LITERACIES, SCALING PRACTICES, AND MOBILE IDENTITIES

In this chapter, we turn our focus to mobile literacies and sociolinguistic scaling practices as a way to understand the negotiation of power relationships within teaching and teacher development, including the relative regulation of bodies and writing practices. We highlight Paula, a colleague of Isabel's and a teacher in a third-grade bilingual classroom at Southend, and how she began shifting her writing instruction toward digital and multimodal composing and including students' popular culture interests within writing workshop. In particular, we highlight shifting mobilities in Paula's writing instruction, including how she and her students negotiated curricular affordances and constraints.

Mobile Language and Literacy Practices

What do we mean when we talk about mobile literacies or mobilities? We think about mobility as partially literal (bodies moving across the classroom, communication across networked spaces) and partially figurative (texts and languages moving and being recruited across ideological and cultural borders). Either way, as Stornaiuolo, Smith, and Philips (2017) suggest, "movement must always be understood in relation to what does not (or cannot) move" (p. 69). This requires identifying both fluidity and agency, but at the same time attending to the material and discursive restriction and marginalization of some language and literacy practices and identities (Stornaiuolo & LeBlanc, 2016). In an analysis of literacy practices among immigrant youth across languages and geographical locations, Leonard (2013) articulates a paradox of mobility: "As global activities become more fluid, national boundaries tighten. . . . As capital circulates more freely, laborers experience more restriction" (p. 14). The idea is that mobility across geographical, national, linguistic, cultural, economic, and/or linguistic boundaries corresponds to concomitant efforts to solidify extant power relationships and social boundaries. Importantly, these restrictions are both ideological and structural, and therefore material. Leonard's analysis is sobering, as she emphasizes the paradox of students' writing practices as simultaneously mobile and immobilized (Leonard, 2013).

Like Leonard (2013), Paula also worked with students with personal and/or family histories of immigration, and her students' writing also traversed languages and cultural boundaries. This included practices such as writing in Spanish, integrating elements of Spanish letter-sound and grammatical relationships into their English writing, and writing themselves into fan-fiction narratives based on the soap opera, *Rebelde*. These students' writing was also networked, as they used the internet to research information for nonfiction writing. One student (Wilfredo), for example, researched and wrote in English about the Brazilian *fútbol* (soccer) star, Ronaldinho, who played for an Italian club (Handsfield & Seglem, 2012). As Paula helped him interpret information on websites about Ronaldinho, Wilfredo used knowledge of his first language to decipher English vocabulary. But while Paula and her students utilized the mobilities of the internet, as we illustrate in this chapter, physical mobility within the classroom writing space was limited in the instruction we observed during our two-year study. Paula expected students to stay seated at their desks as they worked on creating PowerPoint presentations to report on their research projects. While we can't say for sure that their restricted movement was connected to their relative freedom to explore digital writing with their laptops, the literacy events we documented seem to reflect this paradox of mobility.

Mobilities and Identities

So, what does mobility, and the paradox of mobility more specifically, have to do with identity? As we have argued throughout this book, identities are co-constructed in practice alongside ideologies and power relationships. As such, identities shift as practices shift, and the mobilities of digital resources and the movements of bodies, capital, and material resources across geographical spaces and temporalities are tied up in such shifts. For example, imagine a bilingual fourth grader is using a word processing application on a laptop computer to recast an English text he has written on paper into a digital format. In doing so, he moves back and forth between paper and pencil technologies to digital tools and page space, trying to leverage his computer skills along with his knowledge of language, genres, and social contexts. He notices that the student next to him is more adept and fluid with the keyboard, and he wants his help. Despite the expectation that students will work quietly and independently, he begins joking with him in Spanish and gently teasing him about how well he is doing. Using humor and moving across languages, he shifts his identity toward being a collaborator, softening his request for help. And in the process, he shifts the discourse of the activity into somewhat subversive territory while simultaneously seeking to succeed within the normative academic task.

This imagined event is actually similar to the kinds of practices in which we see Paula and her students engaging. As we illustrate in this chapter, it is through Paula's and her students' mobile practices that their identities—as teacher and as students, among others—wobble and flow (García & O'Donnell-Allen, 2015). Just as learning often emerges out of moments of disequilibrium, it is within unsettled spaces—paradoxical spaces—that identity becomings may also occur. These identity becomings may follow well-worn trajectories as people try to reconcile and relieve tensions and discord. However, they may also shift trajectories in important ways. And these mobilities occur at multiple scales of space and time.

Sociolinguistic Scales

The theoretical constructs of sociolinguistic scales and scaling practices come out of the fields of sociolinguists, social geography, and world-systems theory, as a frame for understanding and interpreting complex social processes (Canagarajah & De Costa, 2016; Collins, 2012). This framework rests on the understanding that circulations of both people and material resources within and across social contexts are asymmetrical with respect to power (Collins, Slembrouck, & Baynham, 2009). In what follows, we briefly articulate how the notions of scale and scaling practices connect to the constructs of discourse, positioning, and chronotopes, which we have elucidated in previous chapters.

While the concept of scale has been used to understand how social processes unfold over an array of timescales, from short periods of time (e.g., seconds or minutes) to longer (even geologic) timescales (Lemke, 2002), we focus here on sociolinguistic scales. We understand sociolinguistic scales as horizontally distributed and vertically ordered semiotic resources for constructing meaning and power relationships. Such semiotic resources may include discursive norms, materials and artifacts, and ideologies that function to govern the norms of interaction, social practices, and identification within a given context (Blommaert, Collins, & Slembrouck, 2005; Collins, 2012). The inclusion of materiality here is intentional, as scales can be understood as semiotized in practice as people engage in everyday practices (Blommaert, 2007).

The notion of sociolinguistic scales resembles Bakhtin's (1981) concept of chronotopes in important ways (Blommaert, 2015; Stornaiuolo & LeBlanc, 2016). Blommaert (2015) describes chronotopes as "invokable chunks of history that organize the indexical order of discourse" (p. 105). As such, they are dynamic but durable ideological constructions—persisting over time, and difficult to disrupt or change—that guide social practices, thus producing material effects that in turn constrain or afford further social practices. The key difference between chronotope and scale, however, involves how these constructs address semiotic resources. According to Stornaiuolo and LeBlanc (2016), chronotopes conceptualize the *availability* of discourses, while "scales account for the *accessibility* of such contextual discourses in interaction" (p. 267, emphasis added). Scale, then, more keenly addresses unequal power relationships, which influence not just what meaning making resources exist or are available, but the extent to which they are accessible to different people in different contexts and practices.

A scalar analysis can help researchers discern how chronotopes are not only distributed with respect to space and time, but also vertically ordered with respect to power. "Lower" scales are temporally fleeting or momentary with respect to time, and as local or highly contextualized with respect to space. In other words, the semiotic resources of lower-scaled chronotopes may be accessible in local and temporary contexts of practice. "Higher" scales, however, are considered timeless—as global or translocal with respect to space and time (Blommaert, 2007). Canagarajah and De Costa (2016), however, caution against viewing scales according to deterministic relationships between more powerful global scales and less powerful local ones. Instead, they recommend scaled configurations that may be "nonlinear, unpredictable, layered, and multidirectional" (p. 3) rather than static and hierarchical. Additionally, we argue that scales should be construed as dynamic or mobile.

Mobility, Power, and Scaling Practices

The notion of mobility is central to a scalar analysis, as it places emphasis on processes of *doing* instead of on state states of *being*. Similar to the recent emphasis in applied linguistics on the doing of language, or languaging (Pennycook, 2012) rather than on language as a thing, a scalar analysis focuses on the *doing* of scales, or how "scales are practiced in social life" (Canagarajah & De Costa, 2016, p. 3).

As a verb, scaling resembles the construct of discursive positioning (Harré & Langenhove, 1999), which we describe in Chapter 3. However, scaling differs from discursive positioning in that its focus on semiotic resources expands processes of social interaction and identification to include a wider array of ideological and semiotic resources beyond language. These include narratives, utterances, material objects, gestures, and body movements (Wortham & Rhodes, 2012) that are recruited in power-laden and mobile networks of activity (Stornaiuolo, Smith, & Phillips, 2017). Returning to Bakhtin, it is through such scaling practices that a chronotope "takes on flesh" and "becomes artistically visible" (1981, p. 84). A scalar analysis, then, seeks to understand how people engage in scaling practices to open up or constrict access to such available resources. We are particularly interested in how those in less powerful positions may shift scales or scale jump in everyday practices and interactions and how scale jumping informs our understandings of teacher identity construction. Students may use tactics to negotiate power in a classroom to negotiate their own learning space within a teacher-driven literacy instruction.

Sterponi (2007) offers an example of how children engage in such tactical negotiations during a relatively normative and restricted classroom literacy event: independent silent reading. Sterponi examined how students injected interactional episodes into this literacy event, illustrating students' "clandestine interactional reading" (p. 2). In addition to analyzing students' linguistic utterances as they furtively shared texts, Sterponi attended to their nonverbal moves, including gaze, body movements, and the positioning of objects such as books. A key finding from Sterponi's analysis is the recognition that even those in positions that are relatively powerless within restricted spaces will agentically engage with one another in ways that disrupt proprietary powers. We can imagine the students remaining relatively immobile in terms of moving across the classroom space and relatively silent as per classroom norms, but becoming mobile at a micro-level through their gaze and expressions, and by whispering, pointing, and subtly placing a text (or screen) so that others may view it simultaneously.

What Sterponi's analysis does not highlight, however, are the scaling practices through which students accessed different semiotic resources to disrupt the higher-scaled chronotope of independent silent reading. In this chapter, we present our scalar analysis of similar clandestine moves by Paula's third grade students as Paula begins having her students use laptops to engage in multimodal writing using PowerPoint.

Paula

Unlike Isabel, during our two-year study, Paula was not yet fully certified as a bilingual teacher. During Isabel's first year teaching, which was also the year prior to our study, Paula served as the bilingual liaison for the district. During that time, she received a provisional certificate, which allowed her to teach in a bilingual classroom prior to completing required bilingual education coursework and endorsement. The first year of our study was Paula's first year teaching bilingual third grade. She and Isabel collaborated closely with respect to instructional support and planning, and Paula viewed Isabel as a mentor, despite the fact that Isabel was also a novice teacher, only in her second year at the onset of our study.

Paula was critical of the lack of a writing curriculum. The district expected that writing would be covered using a basal series, which focused primarily on grammar and included prompts that Paula and Isabel felt were dry and disconnected from their bilingual students' experiences and interests. In the first study group (on literacy instruction for linguistically diverse learners), Paula joined with Isabel, a special education teacher from Southend, and the school social worker to form a work team centered on writing instruction, for which they read and discussed *When English Language Learners Write: Connecting Research to Practice, K-8* (Samway, 2006).

In the second study group, which focused on multilingualism, popular culture literacies, and new digital technologies, Paula and Isabel also joined the same work team, this time joined by a fifth-grade teacher from Southend, and four preservice teachers. Their work team explored the use of popular culture texts during literacy instruction and read *Trading Cards to Comic Strips: Popular Culture Texts and Literacy Learning in Grades K-8* (Xu, 2005). The pedagogical goal Paula articulated prior to phase three of the study was to incorporate digital technologies into her writing instruction, which was a challenge for her given that she felt she did not have much expertise with digital technology.

Throughout the study however, Paula emphasized structure—both in terms of structuring her teaching of writing and helping students structure their writing. Indeed, finding "help structuring writers' workshop" was her primary learning focus for the first study group. She created uniform graphic organizers for her students to use while writing, and she frequently prompted her students to stick to their writing plans as they wrote.

Motivated in part by the second study group, Paula and her students used the school's mobile laptop lab during writing so that students could compose digitally rather than by hand. However, her emphasis on structure seemed to work against her goal of having students digitally compose: Her insistence that students not diverge from their graphic organizers often resulted in students copying written sentences or chunks of text from their graphic organizers onto the screen. Paula also restricted student talk while writing, reserving student-student discussion time about their writing for planning or pre-writing stages. Her expectation was that once students sat down to write at the computer with their graphic organizers in hand, they would no longer need to discuss their writing or modify their plans. This resulted in a fairly static structure both of students' writing and of their bodily positioning during writing, despite the potential for mobility with wireless laptops. Students were mostly seated individually at their desks, rarely moving about the room or conversing, and the student discussions and movement that we observed centered almost entirely around technology assistance rather than composing. Paula was the one person who was consistently on the move during writing instruction, circulating about the room to provide writing guidance and technology help.

Nevertheless, we also noted patterns with respect to how both Paula and her students negotiated mobilities during writing time. In what follows, we offer examples of how both Paula and her students strategically and tactically scaled and rescaled interactions and activity to curb or foster mobilities. We focus first on translingual mobilities and visual textual mobilities, and then shift to spatial embodied mobilities across the classroom space.

Cultivating Mobilities

During the first two of our observations, Paula's students were working on PowerPoint presentations in which they reported on research projects on topics of their choice related to U.S. government. Topics included Ellis Island, bald eagles, the Jefferson Memorial, and the pledge of allegiance, the Pentagon, etc. Students were expected to build their presentations from graphic organizers, completed with paper and pencil, copying text from one to the other. The space was fairly quiet, with the primary noises being the clicking of keyboards, rustling of papers, and the voices of Paula and students as they conferred. However, there was mobility in terms of translanguaging, or moving across languages, as students quietly, and sometimes furtively, conferred with one another.

Translingual Mobilities

Along with Isabel, Paula taught within a transitional bilingual education (TBE) program, which meant that students were being prepared to move into monolingual English classrooms. Thus, English was the upscaled language. However, Paula did not restrict their language use and often prompted some students to work in Spanish. Students tended to use Spanish and to code mix between English and Spanish when talking with one another, although this was more prevalent in Paula's absence. The following video transcript portrays a typical student-student conversation during writing workshop. Moises seeks assistance from Bobby to insert a picture file into his presentation (Bobby and Moises's desks are positioned side-by-side.) (Table 4.1):

Their body positioning, with bottoms in their chairs, and their quiet voices fulfill bodily expectations, perhaps enabling more mobile language practices quietly between each other. However, the tenuousness of their linguistic freedoms is not to be taken for granted. As Bobby becomes frustrated with something in his presentation, Moises helps him troubleshoot (Table 4.2):

Moises's glance to see if Paula is watching or notices them illustrates the surveilled nature of the broader event and the Moises's understanding that some aspect of his interactions with Bobby are out of bounds.

MOBILE LITERACIES, SCALING PRACTICES, AND MOBILE IDENTITIES   97

Table 4.1: Bobby and Moises.

Time	Speaker • Hearer	Message units	Video stills & additional contextualization
001	Bobby •	There	Smiling slightly, still looking at his screen
002	Moises		
003	Moises •	| | X	Turns to Bobby, smiling broadly;
004	Bobby		
005	Bobby •	Look X	Bobby looks at Moises
006	Moises		
007	Bobby •	He was X <u>around</u>	
008	Moises		
009	Moises •	X	
010	Bobby		
011	Bobby •	Cómo se usa el X↑	Moises doesn't respond; gaze on
012	Moises	Dos Ls	own screen; "Ls" as in English name for the letter L.
013			Bobby tries some keys;
014			

Table 4.2: Bobby Stands.

Time	Speaker • Hearer	Message units	Video stills & additional contextualization
001	Bobby • Moises	Au+++gh	
002		otra así-	
003	Moises • Bobby	Ugh	Bobby stands up out of his chair
004		así no <u>E++S</u> Bobby+	Louder than previous talk
005		Es <u>aba+jo+</u>	Moises turns around to see if Paula is watching
006			

Stability and Mobility in Troubleshooting Encounters

The expectation of relative physical immobility of students' bodies was accompanied by an overall focus on technological procedures (e.g., how to save a file, how to change a font style), as well as an emphasis on discrete skills and language conventions. The vast majority of Paula's questions and feedback to students had to do with mechanics:

- "This looks like a really good paragraph. Don't forget to indent."
- "You know what? You did a really good job moving your mouse"
- "Do you ↑ have 10 sentences >"
- "So let's work on two slides today. My goal for you is two slides: your title and your first slide."

These bits of talk function to upscale and stabilize the interaction into controlled activity as Paula circulated around the room and the students maintained their positions at their seats. In doing so, Paula positioned herself as the sole troubleshooter.

Mobilities and "Breathe, Moises, breathe!"

Interestingly, however, students seemed to also recruit these procedural and troubleshooting interactions in order to create space for physical mobilities and collaborative engagements around their multimodal writing. In other words, troubleshooting the technology became the ticket to bodily mobility across the classroom space. This was evident, for example, during the second observation. Paula was just beginning a mini-lesson using the LCD projector connected to Andrés's laptop when Moises announced that his computer did not show the icon that she had prompted them to locate on their screens (Table 4.3):

Although not captured on screen, it is the moment when Moises announces his technical difficulties with his laptop that opens up space for mobilities in this destabilizing moment, and prompts Andrés to get up to investigate. Andrés recasts the moment as a moment of potential danger (Wait. WAIT.), parodying the common fear and even panic among those with less facility and confidence with digital technologies that one wrong click may damage a file or the hardware (DON'T BREAK IT. Breathe Moises breathe).

Table 4.3: Paula, Andrés, and Moises.

Line	Speaker • Hearer	Message units	Video stills & additional contextualization
001	Paula • Ss	Okay-->	Moves over to a student's desk
002		Here is what we are going to	takes student's paper with graphic organizer on it
003		do-->	
004		We have been worki+ng > | |	
005		o++n >	
006		getting our paper completed |	
007		Do you remember	
008		the things we needed to have	
009		in each bo+x-->	
010	S1 • Paula	Yeah	
011	Paula • Ss	This was our introduction >	
012		Then we had three facts	
013		three pieces of information >	
014		And our last one wa+s->	
015	US • Paula	X	
016	S2 • Paula	[Symbol]-->	
017	Paula • S2	Yes-->	Paula turns to Student 2
018		This is a symbol of	
019	Paula • Ss	And so	Paula turns back to class
020		What we're going to do toda+y	
021		is we're going to turn this into	
022		the presentation	
023		that I was talking to you about-->	
024	Paula •	So	Paula moves over to Andrés and asks to sit in his desk. Andrés stands two feet away next to whiteboard.
025	students	What you need to do i+s >	
026			
027			Paula looks up at screen
028		to- at your computer	
029		do you see a screen like this-->	
030	2–3 Ss	Ye+s*	tone is a bit tired
031	Paula • Ss	You need to find	
032		this little orange | | |	Paula looks up at screen.

Continued

Table 4.3: *Continued*

Line	Speaker • Hearer	Message units	Video stills & additional contextualization
033		see the little picture--> ||	Moves mouse to highlight the icon
034		it says Microsoft PowerPoint-->	
035		Click two times-->	Moises raises his hand
036		fast *click click*	*uttered in rapid fire*
037		What do you need Moises >	
038	Moises • P	Nothing's showing in X	Off camera; Inferred: Andrés quickly moves to Moises's desk
039			
040	Andrés • P	Oh yeah	Off camera
041		It doesn't have nothing	
042	Moises • P	It only has this	Camera pans back to Andrés and Moises
043		but it's X	
044	Andrés •	Wait	Looking at computer with hands on hips[1] and quickly turns to Moises, puts his hands out as if to calm him on "WAIT."[2] Paula lifts up her head[3], noticing their activity, and begins walking toward them, with Andrés looking over his shoulder on "breathe Moises."[4] Brian at far left, looks toward Paula. Paula gently moves Andrés to the side[5], and bends over and reaches to take control of Moises's laptop.[6]
045	Moises	WAIT	
046		DON'T BREAK IT	
047			
048		Breathe Moises	
049		breathe	
050			
051			
052			
053			
054			
055			
056	Moises • P	I turned it on	Additional student voices/ conversation in background Andrés is now back at his own desk and laptop.[7] Other students now focused on their own screens.
057		and it just goed like that	
058	P • Moises	What happen+ed >	
059			
060			

Table 4.3: *Continued*

Line	Speaker • Hearer	Message units	Video stills & additional contextualization
Clip		**Video Still**	**Utterances**
1			Andrés • Moises: Wait
2			Andrés • Moises: WAIT DON'T BREAK IT
3			Andrés • Moises: Breathe Moises Breathe
4			
5			

Continued

102   PRESERVICE AND INSERVICE TEACHER IDENTITIES

Table 4.3: *Continued*

Line	Speaker • Hearer	Message units	Video stills & additional contextualization
6			Moises • Paula: I turned it on and it just goed like that
7			Paula • Moises: What <u>hap- pen+ed</u> >

An important backdrop to this dramatic parody is Paula's discomfort and minimal expertise with computers. It is Andrés who assumes the authoritative voice, using directives with Moises. Andrés's parodic shift temporarily rescaled the interaction to one in which he is the one to the rescue—the first responder—calming the scene prior to Paula's arrival. This is evident not only in his movement toward Moises and his utterances, but also his body movements and positioning. In clip 1, Andres's hands are on his hips—a gesture of authority that takes up space, signaling importance. In clip 2, he turns toward Moises, placing his hands out, palms down, in a gesture intended to settle things down, which also functions to position himself as the one in charge.

In addition to mobilizing a new potential identity for Andrés as the primary first responder (Paula's typical role), this moment also generates mobilities with respect to other students, whose gazes shift from their own computers to Andrés and Moises, and then to Paula. In addition, when Andrés arrives on the scene, other students begin more freely communicating with one another. Paula's gaze toward Andrés and Moises (clip 3) and her movements to get up and move toward them ultimately rescale the interaction back toward traditional power relationships, with stable student bodies fixed on their own individual laptops. Part of Paula's upscaling involves authoritatively taking Andrés by the shoulders, from behind, and moving him out of the way and back toward his desk.

While it could be that Paula was simply refocusing Andrés back toward his own writing, we argue there is more going on here. In particular, Paula's regulation of student bodies in the midst of mobile literacies illustrates how the paradox of mobility constitutes upscaling. We can see similar scaling practices—both discursive and embodied—about 10 minutes later during the same lesson, when Paula introduces different design options to students within PowerPoint.

Mobilities and Stable Designs

After Moises's technical difficulties are resolved, Paula announces to her students, "now you have a lot of choices. You get to experiment and see what you want to do." She briefly shows them how to create different slide format options (Table 4.4). This begins with changing styles and colors, inserting images from a file or the internet, and ends with how to insert text animations into slides.

In this excerpt, Paula is the one controlling, or attempting to control, both digital and bodily mobilities—both in terms of utterances and body movements. The "experimentation" is more hers than the students' in that she has chosen what to show them or what they can experiment with, and as soon as students begin to murmur, Paula upscales by reinforcing control over students' bodily attention—both their utterances and their gaze (lines 003–005). Paula also upscales after moments in which students' verbal interactions increase by shifting to authoritative IRF discursive scripts (e.g., lines 033–035). Interestingly, the paradox of mobility also describes Paula's teacher identity constructions. In particular, we see a tension between Paula being comfortable in role of "traditional" teacher, while simultaneously desiring to shift her practice as a result of the study group. (We also see this paradox in the next chapter, as Camille negotiates multiple tensions in her literacy instruction.)

Mobilities and Eclipse Motion

The moment analyzed above continues through Paula's instructions on how to add in animations (Table 4.5). There continues to be a need for troubleshooting, and thus for technology consultants. However, it is not just Paula who takes on that role, particularly as the buzz of activity intensifies at around line 21.

Table 4.4: Paula, Raúl, and Andrés.

Line	Speaker • Hearer	Message units	Video stills & additional contextualization
001	Paula • Ss	Okay→	
002		I want you to |	
003		put your hands in your lap	
004		for a second >	
005		and just look up here→ | |	
006		I want to show you a few↑ things >	
007		and then I'm just going to give you	Only one or two students
008		time to work	do this; Paula looks around
009		Now	and then continues with
010		Do you remember	instructions.
011		how to make new slides	
012	USs • Paula	Yes	
013	Paula • Ss	All you have to do	
014		is click here > |	P demonstrates from desktop
015		and you can pick	
016		how you want it to look	
017		Now he+re >	
018		it says design→ | | |	P demonstrates from desktop
019		We can click there |	
020		There are all different ways-	
021		-different designs	
022		that you can make your slides have	
023		If Andrés would pick this one	
024	Andrés • Paula	I X like X	No uptake
025			Paula changes Andrés's slide
026			to orange
027			
028			
029	Several Ss	WOA+++H	moves hand to mouse
030	Paula • Ss	Now	Quizzical look on her face;
031		this looks like it has a runner	looks up at students
032		standing here	
033		is his presentation about running	
034	Several Ss	No++	
035		Ma+ybe that's not the best design to	Paula selecting additional designs as she talks
036		pick	

Table 4.4: *Continued*

Line	Speaker • Hearer	Message units	Video stills & additional contextualization
037		if you're doing something |	*Higher pitch, excited tone; no pause between this utterance and previous one*
038		about something else …	
039		*OH LOOK*	
040		it looks like a curtain	
041		doesn't it	
042		Like a stage	
043	Raúl • Paula	How do you <u>get</u> there	
044	Paula • Raúl	| Remember Raúl >	Andrés gets up to help Raúl
045		I went right here	
046		<u>design</u>	
047	Andrés • Raúl	Here	While walking over
048	Paula • Ss	There are some <u>simple</u> ones <u>too</u>	Andrés and Raúl can be heard talking quietly in background while Paula continues.
059		that just ha+ve |	
050		different <u>colo+rs</u> >	
051		or different little <u>designs</u>	Andrés returns, but buzz of students' voices continues
052		You can go through	
053		and pick <u>any</u> of those you <u>want</u>	
054		Now-	Paula looks up; continued buzz
055		-<u>Hold</u> on	Paula leans back a bit, takes hands off keyboard
056		Hands in your lap	on here, P lightly claps hands together
057		for a second	
058		hands in your lap	
059		pay attention up <u>here</u>	
060		so you can <u>see</u>	

Continued

Table 4.4: *Continued*

Line	Speaker • Hearer	Message units	Video stills & additional contextualization
061		what you want to <u>do+</u>> |	
062		when you <u>get</u> there	
063		Now↓	
064		If you remember	
065		did <u>my</u> | PowerPoint	
066		have the <u>same</u>-	
067		were all the slides the <u>same</u>	Still a few students murmuring in background
068	Ss • Paula	Unh uh	
069	Paula • Ss	I made each of mine <u>different</u>-	
070		Let me show you <u>how</u>	

Paula continues on with a few reminders, including other formatting features they've used before, such as changing the color or the font. She then ends by telling them that she'll give them a little time to write, and that they'll work on "two slides today."

One of the most notable shifts in this excerpt is how Paula's introduction of textual mobilities in the form of inserting animations—mobilities on the screen—appear to open up space for other kinds of mobilities. As soon as the first animation is shown, student-student overlapping talk ensues, as well as student-student and student-teacher talk across languages. This includes the use of Spanish not just between students (e.g., 41–43), but between students and Paula (e.g., line 27), as well as code mixing (e.g., lines 26 and 28–29).

Ironically, however, during this time they are all (including Paula) sitting in their seats, fairly static or immobile, while looking up at the screen, even as they are getting excited about different animations or mobilities. In other words, mobilities seem to be limited to screen (not online) and voice while any significant bodily mobilities are muffled, or in Moises's words as he talks to himself, "eclipse motion."

At line 44, Paula rescales the event and the interactions back toward stable ground, by shifting back toward an IRE script. This appears to occur as a response to Moises and Bobby's quiet but persistent troubleshooting simultaneous to her instruction. In terms of content, her IRE script focuses on completing their print text first before designing with colors, styles, and animations. In other words, Paula upscales the pedagogical space toward

MOBILE LITERACIES, SCALING PRACTICES, AND MOBILE IDENTITIES

Table 4.5: Paula Addresses the Discussion Group.

Line	Speaker • Hearer	Message units	Video stills & additional contextualization
001	Paula • Ss	So these are things	*Enunciating clearly*
002		that you can work on <u>too</u> > |	
003		do you <u>see</u> over <u>here</u>	
004		it says *<u>slide design</u>*	
005	2–3 Ss • P	Yeah	
006	Paula •	If you remember	
007		I clicked right here	
008		and then all this information came up↑	
009		This is also where |	
010	Moises • P	Oh <u>yeah</u>	
011	Paula • Ss	We picked > |	
012	Moises • P	yeah [for the-	
013	Paula • Ss	-different] ways	Paula makes text in slide spin
014		for the <u>letters</u> to come in→	
015		there's <u>all</u> different <u>kinds</u>-	
016	Moises • P	-SPI+N	
017	Paula • Ss	Maybe-	Paula moving mouse; students
018		let's do one of these <u>exciting</u> ones	looking up at screen
019		| |	
020	Andrés •?	I don't X	Quietly, possibly to self
021	Several Ss	OH	
022		XXX	
023		I like <u>tha+t</u>	
024	US • Paula	<u>how'd</u> you do that	
025	Several Ss	OO+H	
026		Estaba <u>cool</u> (that was cool)	
027	Marco • Paula	Dónde vas a ir	Glancing briefly at Paula, but watching screen. No uptake
028	Moises • Self	Es la de e- eclipse mo- motion	
029		Eclipse Motion	

Continued

Table 4.5: Continued

Line	Speaker • Hearer	Message units	Video stills & additional contextualization
030	Marco • Moises	Cuándo XX (When XX)	Briefly glances at Moises's screen, then quickly back to his own, grabbing his mouse
031			
032			
033	Andrés • P	[I don't see nothing]	Looking at screen
034	Paula • Andrés	[Do you see	Looking at screen
035		how the little letters	Lines xxx-xxx simultaneous
036		are coming up]	
037	Moises • Self	[Eclipse motion	
038		Eclipse motion	
039		Eclipse motion]	
040	Marco • Paula	Can you do some more	
041	Moises • Bobby	Que estoy- (What am I-)	Andrés starts to get up
042		mira [la X (look the X)	
043		aquí está+] (it's here)	
044	Paula • Ss	[So remember >]	Andrés sits back down as
045		I clicked o+n > -	Paula continues; Paula shifts
046		all this information	gaze toward students, then
047		is here where I clicked [on desi+gn >	toward screen
048	Andrés	[Design]	Looking at screen
049	Moises • Bobby	[X eclipse motion]	Lines xxx-xxx simultaneous
050		XX	
051		Eclipse motion]	
052	Paula • Ss	[and then that's where	Notices Bobby and Moises
053		I got to pick]	continuing to murmur
054		how I wanted all my slides to look >		Selecting a new animation
055		I got to pick		

Table 4.5: *Continued*

Line	Speaker • Hearer	Message units	Video stills & additional contextualization
056		different colo+rs	
057		and I can also pick	
058		how I want my words to [appear]	
059	USs	Oo+h	Quietly
060	Andrés • P	I like that	Smiling
061	Paula • Ss	NOW→	Turning to look at Ss
062	Andrés • P	Do we just need one?	No uptake
063		or two	
064	Paula • Ss	What you need to do+ >	
065	Paula • Luís	Hang on Luís	Luís is off camera; on first
066		HA+NG on >	"hang on," Ss look back up at
067		HA+NG on >	Paula and screen.
068	Paula • Ss	is	wiggling mouse to make
069		before you go too crazy	cursor move, glances at computer, then at
070		looking at all this cool stuff	Ss
071		what do you need to do++ |	
072		over he+re | |	
073			
074	US • Paula	Type	
075	Paula • US, Ss	Yeah	Nodding yes
076		You need to put your information on	
077		Right.	

standardized practices and autonomous literacies. Such upscaling is part and parcel of paradox of mobility.

Mobilities and Technology Consultants

Interestingly, it's when Paula recruits or appoints helpers that movement happens around the room and that design elements beyond language conventions come into play. And it's when "major" issues of formatting, such as the font getting extremely big, or the margins getting extremely narrow, that buzz occurs, and bodies move across the classroom space. At first, this is just Paula's body, and she sits down to troubleshoot, but later, two-thirds of way through, several bodies move to look at the screen (Table 4.6).

Table 4.6: Paula, Luís, Bobby, and Moises.

Line	Speaker • Hearer	Message units	Video stills & additional contextualization
001	Bobby •	Dónde está X↑ (Where is X)	Looks briefly at Moises; Paula
002	Moises	Yo voy a poner boy (I'm going to put boy)	standing behind them, looking at Moises's screen
003	Moises • Paula	How do you get the picture↓	Moises notices Paula behind
004			them, then looks up at her Paula taps Bobby's shoulder
005	Paula • Bobby	Show him how to find the picture	Bobby gets up and starts to reach for Moises's mouse; Paula
006		No <u>tell</u> him	remains standing behind them
007		so <u>he</u> knows how to do it	
008			Paula taps on Bobby's shoulder
009			as she speaks
010	Bobby • Moises	Insert	spoken quietly
011	Paula • Bobby and Moises	Inse++rt >	enunciated each sound
012	Bobby • Moises	pictu+re>	Bobby points to Moises's screen
013	Luís • Paula	<u>we</u> want to get a pictu+re >	Luís (at desktop computer) looks
014			at group, smiles as he finishes
015			speaking; Bobby smiles, sits back
016			down at his desk
017			
018			
019	Paula • Luís	Are you <u>ready</u> ↑	Paula moves slowly toward Luís.

Bobby's and Moises's interaction has a very performance-like quality to it, with Bobby only speaking in one to two word phrases. This is partially indicated by both Bobby's and Luís's smiles in lines 13–18 (although it is difficult to detect Luís's smile given our need to blur the video still). This affective moment, in which Bobby completes his performance, and Luís initiates his interaction, constitutes another form of mobility in this pedagogical space. Stornaiuolo, Smith, and Phillips (2017) state that "remaining open to multiple ways of knowing and experiencing expands how researchers might attend to the ways the paradox of mobility emerges in interaction, especially the embodied, material, and affective dimensions and consequences of everyday practices" (p. 75). This affective moment is similar to Sterponi's (2007) clandestine interactions in an otherwise teacher-controlled space.

Paula's proximity to students also seems to have an inverse effect on the extent of student talk. As Paula moves away and toward Luís, for instance, Bobby and Moises engage in extended talk about their text designs and consulting with one another about how to perform certain tasks. This discussion ends in line 1 of the interaction included in Table 4.7, which occurred about

Table 4.7: Paula, Bobby, and Luís.

Line	Speaker • Hearer	Message units	Video stills & additional contextualization
001	Bobby • Moises	You have to put it like <u>that</u>	
002	Paula • Bobby	Bobby↑	Paula is fixing a barrette in her
003		Luís needs a <u>picture</u> >	hair. Bobby gets up and quickly
004			heads over to the desktop
005			computer where Luís is seated.
006			Paula moves to help other student.
007	Bobby • Luís	Insert | |	Bobby pointing at Luis's screen
008			
009	Luís • Bobby	XXX↑	Exasperated tone
010	Bobby • Luís	Insert XX picture↓ | |	Extended talk, with flow of
011		Now you have to type XX	complete sentences
012		XXX	

a minute after Bobby's performance. Subsequently, Paula asks Bobby to help Luís insert a picture (lines 2–3). This time, however, she moves away to help another student.

Interestingly, Bobby's instructions for Luís include the same vocabulary (e.g., insert) that he used under Paula's direction with Bobby, but with more extended talk (lines 7–12). Not only does this appear to be a more authentic teaching moment for Bobby, but it also is a richer episode of talk, indicating a connection between bodily mobilities and opportunities for language development. Similar episodes of extended talk a few minutes later, when Paula invites a girl to help Bobby insert a title into his presentation using a technique that Paula was previously unaware of.

Importantly, however, Paula still maintains discursive and bodily control in the assignment of students as tech consultants (which can only be assigned by Paula). In essence, physical mobility becomes a reward for "mastering" technological skills. Luís is the first tech consultant, followed by Bobby, and then (finally) a girl. While Paula relinquishes minimal explicit control by assigning these students as her proxies, their official mobilities seem connected to other clandestine mobilities (linguistic, social, etc.). In essence, the mobilities produced through Paula's assignment of students to offer procedural assistance as technology consultants to other students become opportunities for student-produced tactical down-scaling.

Mobilities and Identities

The ways in which students recruit linguistic, bodily, and affective mobilities to tactically open up spaces of interaction serve as reminders of how social identities and academic identities, in particular digital composition, are intertwined (Wortham, 2006). Over the course of this one writing workshop, we see a shift from Paula as the sole technology consultant and the only one physically on the move, to Andrés's parody of a technology emergency, to students being allowed to move across the room to help others, to several students being formally named as technology consultants. This ultimate designation includes the privilege of movement across the classroom space, rescaling the space to one that is less authoritarian.

These mobilities and scaling practices are the stuff of teacher identity construction. As students take over Paula's roles as first responder and technology consultant, Paula becomes a different kind of teacher, moving from authoritarian positionalities with surveillance as a tool for maintaining power to a teacher who apprentices her students into new roles. We could think about Paula's mobility with respect to her teacher identities in these episodes as moving from someone who animates behaviorist theories of teaching to one who animates sociocultural-historical theory. Rogoff (1995), for example, might argue that Paula has very astutely supported her students in participatory appropriation, whereby her students *become* text designers and technology consultants as they are engaged in cultural activity. However, this doesn't explain the tactical negotiation of power relationships that occurs as Paula and her students scale and rescale the pedagogical space.

Unlike sociocultural-historical theory, a scalar analysis draws our attention to the constant and complex mobilities and positionalities that are produced simultaneously through these events. In short, Paula's and her students' becomings are multiple and simultaneous rather than unidirectional and fixed. This begs the question, what if Paula's writing workshop had been differently scaled, with more explicit invitations from the onset for students to explore and experiment with tools rather than direct instruction on how each tool can be used? And how might teacher educators engage preservice and practicing teachers explicitly with rescaling practices?

Process drama is one way to facilitate this type of engagement. Specifically, we see promise in Edmiston's notion of "dramatic positioning" (2014, p. 233). Edmiston built on Heathcote and Bolton's (1994) concept of "mantle of the expert" to argue that dramatic positioning has a "double-voiced" facet. As a facilitator moves in and out of role, they position and reposition participants in role as parents, teachers, or students to explore ideas that are important to the group; however, it is made clear that this is just imaginative play and they are not really those individuals.

In Chapters 6 and 7, we explain how dramatic positioning might work in contexts of teacher development and research. But first, in the next chapter, we shift our focus to Camille, a preservice teacher participant in our study. Camille participated along with Paula and Isabel in a work team focused on integrating popular culture into literacy instruction, and was also was experimenting with technology integration. However, her positionality as a student teacher and also as a nontraditional student—a mother pursuing her second profession—and the more restrictive literacy curriculum in her student teaching context, offers a novel view of teacher identity negotiation.

References

Bakhtin, M.M. (1981). *The dialogic imagination: Four essays.* Austin, TX: University of Texas Press.

Blommaert, J. (2007). Sociolinguistic scales. *Intercultural Pragmatics, 4*(1), 1–19.

Blommaert, J. (2015). Chronotopes, scales and complexity in the study of language and society. *Annual Review of Anthropology, 44,* 105–116.

Blommaert, J., Collins, J., & Slembrouck, S. (2005). Spaces of multilingualism. *Language & Communication, 25,* 197–216.

Canagarajah, S., & DeCosta, P. (2016). Scales analysis, and its uses and prospects in educational linguistics. *Linguistics & Education, 34,* 1–10.

Collins, J. (2012). Migration, sociolinguistic scale, and educational reproduction. *Anthropology & Education Quarterly, 43*(2), 192–213.

Collins, J., Slembrouck, J., & Baynham, M. (Eds.). (2009). Globalization and languages in contact: Scale, migration, and communicative practices. London, England: Continuum.

García, A., & O'Donnell-Allen, C. (2015). *Pose, wobble, flow: A culturally proactive approach to literacy instruction.* New York, NY: Teachers College Press.

Handsfield, L. J. & Seglem, R. (2012). Global literacy instruction meets the Common Core: Integrating waves of change. *Florida English Journal, 48*(1), 26–38.

Harré, R., & Van Langenhove, L. (Eds.). (1999). Positioning theory: Moral contexts of intentional action. Malden, MA: Blackwell.

Heathcote, D., & Bolton, G. (1994). *Drama for learning: Dorothy Heathcote's Mantle of the Expert approach to education.* Portsmouth, NH: Heinemann.

Lemke, J. L. (2002). Language development and identity: Multiple timescales in the social ecology of learning. In *Language acquisition and language socialization,* 68–87.

Lorimer Leonard, R. (2013). Traveling literacies: Multilingual writing on the move. *Research in the Teaching of English, 48,* 13–39.

Pennycook, A. (2012). *Language and mobility: Unexpected places.* Bristol, UK: Multilingual Matters.

Rogoff, B. (1995). Observing sociocultural activity on three planes: Participatory appropriation, guded participation, and apprenticeship. In J. V. Wertsch, P. del Rio, & A. Alvarez (Eds.), *Sociocultural studies of mind* (pp. 139–164). New York, NY: Cambridge University Press.

Samway, K. D. (2006). *When English language learners write: Connecting research to practice, K–8.* Portsmouth, NH: Heinemann.

Sterponi, L. (2007). Clandestine interactional reading: Intertextuality and double-voicing under the desk. *Linguistics and Education, 18*(1), 1–23.

Stornaiuolo, A., & LeBlanc, R. J. (2016). Scaling as a literacy activity: Mobility and educational inequality in an age of global connectivity. *Research in the Teaching of English, 50,* 263–287.

Stornaiuolo, A., Smith, A., & Phillips, N. (2017). Developing a transliteracies framework for a connected world. *Journal of Literacy Research, 49*(1).

Wortham, S. (2006). *Learning identity: The joint emergence of social identification and academic learning.* Cambridge, UK: Cambridge University Press.

Wortham, S., & Rhodes, C. (2012). The production of relevant scales: Social identification of migrants during rapid demographic change in one American town. *Applied Linguistics Review* 3(1), 75–99.

Xu, S. H. (with Perkins, R.S., & Zunich, L.O.). (2005). *Trading cards to comic strips: Popular culture texts and literacy learning in grades K–8.* Newark, DE: International Reading Association.

· 5 ·
PERFORMING MULTIPLE IDENTITIES IN STUDENT TEACHING

Introduction

"And so, strictly from being a mom . . ."—Camille interview with Lara

Camille was not a typical preservice teacher: She was significantly older than her peers, was pursuing teaching as a second career, and was a married mother of two children. The short phrase above is excerpt from an interview Lara conducted with Camille about bringing video game manuals into her classroom during student teaching for a grammar lesson. Camille was initially tentative about using this type of popular culture in her classroom, but working in the study group that was part of the larger project persuaded her of its value. With this short phrase, she positions herself as a mother within a larger discussion about this student teaching lesson. Motherhood is one of the identities Camille performs; it was not the only one, but it was key because it mediated how she positioned herself in the contexts of student teaching and of the research project. The phrase "And so, strictly from being a mom," suggests that Camille separated her identity as a mother from her role as a student teacher and that she could navigate between those roles to analyze her student teaching experience, suggesting the fluidity of identities even in small moments of interaction (Lewis, Encisco, & Moje, 2007).

In this chapter, we return to an analysis of interview and observational data from Camille's student teaching to explore how she takes up an identity as a mother in her development as a preservice teacher. We used microethnographic discourse analysis as we described in Chapter 2 to focus on how identities are fashioned moment by moment. Our analyses indicated that Camille's identities were multiple and tactical (de Certeau, 1984; Jackson, 2001), and being a mother is one of those identities (Biklen, 1995; Landeros, 2011). More specifically, Camille shifted among the identities of student teacher, experienced teacher, and mother during her student teaching and demonstrated that identities are constructed in short interactions and moments of discourse.

Substantive research exists investigating relationships among identities of motherhood and teachers (Biklen, 1995; Estola & Elbaz-Luwisch, 2003; Galman, 2012; Griffith & Smith, 1987; Landeros, 2011; May, 2008; Smythe, 2006). For example, Biklen (1995) examined relationships between teachers and mothers and argued that social construction of gender created an "interdependence" (p. 130) between the two. She theorized how the "mother's gaze" (p. 127) constructs tensions of cooperation and contention between mothers and teachers as they work together to educate students in classrooms and how those tensions shaped identity. May (2008) analyzed narratives of women to understand how identities of being "good mother" were presented in contexts of public norms. Landeros (2011) investigated how the construct of being a "good mother" shaped the views of women toward student achievement after they had put aside careers aside to raise families. Drawing on feminist poststructural theory Jackson (2001) tells the story of a preservice teacher supervised by two cooperating teachers who articulated divergent discourses about instruction and mentoring. The preservice teacher "constructed her subjectivities as a teacher" (p. 386) within the tensions and uncertainties of those conflicting discourses.

Together, these studies suggest that motherhood is constructed by powerful cultural discourses. In this next section, we review scholarship on nontraditional preservice teachers and motherhood to understand the confluence of these discourses.

Nontraditional Preservice Teachers and Motherhood

Second career preservice teachers bring more extensive life and professional experiences into their teacher development programs (Resta, Huling, & Rainwater, 2001; Tigchelaar, Brouwer, & Korthagen, 2008), but the research literature on how these differences may impact their teacher development is mixed. Gonzales, Brown, and Slate (2008) found that second career teacher candidates felt their primary needs were time and practical experiences, whereas first career candidates more likely identified the need to learn pedagogical skills. Second career teachers were also more likely to work beyond traditional pedagogies and to connect classroom work to the real world. However, other research shows that while second career first year teachers felt that textbook curricula should not be central to their teaching, by the end of their first year teaching, they taught in very textbook-centered ways (Powell, 1997). More recently, Nielsen (2016) drew on the Bourdieu's theoretical insights to argue that second career teachers' identities are dynamic and complex and that more research is needed to understand how they transition into classrooms.

Historically, U.S. teachers have been predominantly female, paid less than their male counterparts, and assumed to be natural nurturers (mothers) (Alsup, 2006; Rury, 1989). More recent research illustrates the persistence of this expectation with respect to teacher identities. In an ethnographic study of programs that prepare elementary teachers, for example, Galman (2012) found that programs socialize young women into what she calls the "Wise Virgin" (p. xiii) identity to take up traditional roles of marriage and motherhood. But mothering is also constructed as a protective practice, in which the protection of children is paramount. This issue is often brought into debates about parenting and children's uses of popular media, such as video games and the internet, and also permeates discussions of teachers' responses in the midst of school shootings (Steinkuehler, 2016; Willett, 2015).

Mothering as a discursive practice has also been investigated by sociologists, feminist educational researchers, scholars working in gender studies, and researchers in literacy (Estola & Elbaz-Luwisch, 2003; Griffith & Smith, 1987; Landeros, 2011; May, 2008; Smythe, 2006). Griffith and Smith (1987), for instance, argue that understandings and experiences of mothering "are linked to the social and institutional fabric, particularly school" (p. 87), and are culturally constructed in relationships among families and schools. Being a "good mother" is a cultural construction situated within competing discourses of gender roles (May, 2008), and this construct informs discourses that flow over into what it means to be a teacher. Additionally, both teaching and motherhood have also been construed as embodied activities. Estola and Elbaz-Luwisch (2003), for instance, use body positioning to look at how Finnish and Israeli teachers' bodies are "on stage and in the audience" when they are in their classrooms (p. 704). They theorize five body positions which "connect the physical, cultural, and personal of teaching bodies; presence, control, love and care, listening to oneself, and protection" (p. 697). They analyzed teachers' classroom narratives to identify and represent these five body positions. One of their findings was that "bodies echo many voices" (p. 702), which they also align with Bakhtin's (1990) notion that all identities are multi-voiced.

Camille's teacher identities were similarly multi-voiced in a Bakhtinian sense (1990). Bakhtin's conceptualization of chronotope (1981) informed our understanding of identity because he theorized historical events as spatiotemporal (Blommaert, 2015). The implications for teacher identities are important. Blommaert (2015) argued that "in their simplest form, chronotopes as historically configured tropes point us to the fact that specific complexes of 'how-it-was' can be invoked as relevant context in discourse and affect what can and does happen in discursive events" (p. 111. Therefore, identities that were formed in the past, such as being a mother in Camille's case, are brought into play into the discourses of student teaching as a way to scale power relationships (Blommaert, 2007; Collins, Slembrouck, & Baynham, 2009). Motherhood can also be viewed as another scale in language practices. As we described in Chapter 1, scale is rooted in geographical analysis, and recently sociolinguists have asked how notions of scale and scaling practices can be used in discourse analysis (Collins, Slembrouck, & Bayham, 2009). Again, we follow Blommaert's conception of scale (2007) as a "vertical metaphor" (p. 1) so that language practices are both hierarchical and layered. Camille's identity as a mother is layered onto her identity as a student teacher through specific language practices evident in the analyses presented in this chapter.

Multiple positioning and identity development are complex, and throughout this book, we argue that identities mediate one another and are performed moment by moment (Bloome, Carter, Christian, Otto, & Shuart-Farris, 2005; Caldas-Coulthard & Iedema, 2016). However, our analyses also show that motherhood was both an identity in its own right and was used by Camille and Lara to mediate identities of novice and experienced teacher, suggesting the fluidity and sedimented nature of identity in even in small moments of interaction (Caldas-Coulthard & Iedema, 2016). This next section of the chapter briefly reviews our research practices pertinent to this chapter, building on our more general introduction to our analytical approach in Chapter 2. Then we describe Camille's student teaching experiences and present findings from our microethnographic discourse analysis to illustrate this claim.

Research Practices

We selected interview and video excerpts to micro-analyze that were multiply coded, both with lower inference codes and across chronotopes, and also selected data from across year two of the study. We transcribed the audio and video recordings using transcript conventions from Green and Wallat (1981) and Bloome et al. (2005) (see Table 2.1). This involved identifying speaker turns, semantic features of utterances, volume, and other contextualization cues (e.g., falling or rising intonation, stress, double voicing [Bakhtin, 1984]). Contextualization cues, including descriptions and video stills of small-scale body movements (e.g., shifts in gaze, gesture) and larger-scale body movements (e.g., Camille moving across the room to the interactive whiteboard) appear in the far right-hand column of the transcripts. Our next step was to separate utterances into message units—what Green and Wallat (1981) describe as the smallest units of meaning in conversation—using line breaks. We then divided the transcripts into IU, or stretches of "conversationally tied message units" (Green & Wallat, 1981, p. 200). We did this by using contextualization cues, changes in speakers' goals, topical shifts, changes in participatory demands (e.g., a shift from a responsive/collaborative structure (Gutiérrez et al., 1995) to IRE, and body movements.

Participants in our study often moved across the classroom space in ways that extended beyond gestural spaces—the physical spaces immediately encompassing an interlocutor's torso (McNeill, 2008). We included video stills and descriptions in the microethnographic transcripts to capture these body movements. Goodwin (2007) proposed the notion of participation frameworks to conceptualize how individual people's bodily positioning contributes to emergent stances, or positioning, arguing that embodied actions and participation frameworks are co-constructed, rather than independent from one another. Roberts, Radinsky, Lyons, & Cafaro, (2012) build on Goodwin's understandings, conceptualizing representational fields as spaces of representation constructed through embodied actions. They differentiate between use moves, or uses of the representational field, and assembly moves, the making of the representational field. The category of assembly moves may include access moves and directing moves to gain, deny, invite, and request access to the field as students and teachers engage in classroom events. This framework offers tools for analyzing body movements alongside utterances to understand Camille's positioning. However, our approach differs in that we are interested not only in the representational meanings, but also indexical meanings (Blommaert, 2005)—how participants' body movements alongside utterances index different ideologies of literacy and teaching.

Camille's Multiple Identity Positioning

Organizations and institutions in our current globalized economy change and shift on "shorter timescales" (Lemke, 2013, p. 39). New enterprises start up and fizzle in a few years or less. Paralleling these phenomena, individuals also move across careers, organizations, and institutions in shorter timescales so that as Lemke argues, "the meaning of our lives is made across institutions rather than within them" (2013, p. 39). Analogously, teacher identities are made across identities rather than within them. In Camille's case, her teacher identity of motherhood served as an affordance, which she used to tactically mediate student and more experienced teacher identities. It is important to note as a mother, Camille brought cultural capital associated with white middle class women into a predominantly white classroom, and she was therefore able to use this capital to as a way to perform motherhood in particular ways. An African American or Latino mother/student teacher would likely have different experiences and would bring different cultural capital and language practices to this same classroom (Cho, 2018; Collins, 2016).

Scaling practices may be tactical as people import or laminate one spacetime onto another, recontextualizing discourses and ideologies into different timescales and spaces to construct new or alternative identities (Collins & Blot, 2003; Collins, Slembrouck, & Baynham, 2009; Handsfield & Crumpler, 2013). Analytically, this means closely examining everyday practices through which a preservice teacher may tactically loosen a role like motherhood and use it to position herself in discourses of instruction. In the next section, we contextualize instructional practices of Camille's student teaching experience.

Camille as a Student Teacher

As noted earlier, Camille's work team within the second study group in phase two of our study inquired more specifically into the use of popular culture texts. In fact, Camille participated in this work team along with Isabel and Paula. Camille viewed motivation as a primary reason to use popular culture texts (including graphic novels, comics, and videogames) in the classroom. However, in her coursework and in the study group, we promoted popular culture texts as valuable in their own right; not simply as motivational tools for traditional literacy practices.

Camille student taught in spring in a third-grade classroom at Central Harvest Elementary, a small rural school approximately an hour away from the university with a predominantly white and economically diverse student population. Camille's cooperating teacher, Jean, was traditional in her approach to instruction. The reading series used at Central Harvest and the district as a whole emphasized isolated grammar instruction with little differentiation. Students rarely had opportunities to engage meaningfully with texts or work in groups, and the teachers in her school focused heavily on test preparation and making AYP under NCLB (2001). As Camille explained in an interview, "they are very very- I mean they are constantly having curriculum meetings and making sure everybody follows the same page." We are not suggesting that Camille's cooperating teacher delivered poor instruction; rather, we are characterizing the predominant instructional discourse as focused on a standardized view of teaching and learning. Such a discourse provides certain spaces for teacher identities while closing off others (Wortham, 2003, 2006), creating tensions that may result in a teacher's identities shifting within a short sequence of instruction as she repositions herself vis-a-vis conflicting discourses. We view these tensions as productive and argue that Camille wielded the identity of motherhood during student teaching to mediate tensions between expert and novice teacher positions.

Observations of Camille's student teaching experience indicated that Jean and Camille were also positioned in a traditional cooperating teacher-to-student teacher relationship. Indeed, Jean monitored Camille's practice carefully, never leaving her by herself in the classroom. This context of close supervision informed the larger discourse of standardization. Camille's choice to bring video game manuals into the classroom and pedagogically connect them with the third-grade students' popular culture knowledge unfolded in this context. Discourses of teaching and learning, curricular expectations, and other features of a classroom converge to shape teacher identity development. To illustrate this point, we briefly return to Paula's third grade bilingual classroom that was highlighted in the previous chapter and contrast it to Jean's.

Prior to entering the classroom, Paula worked as the bilingual liaison for the district, and while in this role, she received a provisional certificate to teach in a bilingual classroom. She completed required bilingual education coursework for her bilingual certification during our study, and the first year of our study was Paula's first year teaching bilingual third grade. Like Jean's district, Paula's district used a basal series as the primary aspects of their curriculum. The district expected that teachers' writing instruction would be based on this basal series, which privileged grammar and included prompts that Paula criticized as disengaged from bilingual students' experiences and interests. Consequently, Paula used writer's workshop to provide more authentic writing experiences for her bilingual students that were missing from a basal-centered approach.

To be fair, Paula taught her students to write in highly structured ways. She developed graphic organizers for her students and insisted that students to stick to the writing plans they had developed rather than let writing processes guide composing (Graves, 1983). However, Paula was not a teacher who was afraid to question the district's preferred curriculum; also, she sought out ways to engage in writer's workshop while participating in our research project. Overall, Paula seemed to exercise more professional agency in how she blended the required curriculum with her own knowledge of her students.

While the discourses of learning in Paula's classroom were more organic and centered on students' strengths, Jean's classroom, in contrast, focused more exclusively on the basal. We believe this matters in terms of understanding how teacher identities are mediated and performed in student teaching experiences such as Camille's. Again, we are not claiming that Paula was a better teacher than Jean. Rather, we are arguing that, in terms of identity development, particular discourses of teaching and learning open spaces for student teachers to take up certain identities and not others. Camille performed identities of student teacher and more experienced teacher in Jean's classroom and used her identity as a mother to scale up from a student teacher chronotope to reposition herself as more experienced.

In the next section, we illustrate analyses that support this argument. We present three tables as evidence: The first two are transcript excerpts from an interview that Lara completed with Camille in which Camille articulates her view of literacies and talks about her experience as a mother. The third includes video images juxtaposed with dialogue from a lesson Camille taught using video game manuals as the basis for a grammar lesson on pronouns.

Mediating Identities as a Student Teacher

In a study that investigated identity development of a student teacher who worked with two cooperating teachers, Jackson (2001) argues: "In teacher education, the teacher/student, expert/novice binaries are laden with meaning, meaning constructed by those who are situated within the unstable relationships between power, knowledge, experience, and subjectivity (p. 387)."

Denotatively, the phrase "student teacher" positions an individual in a binary opposition to an inservice or experienced teacher that involves power and knowledge. Yet as Jackson claims, these types of identity binaries are "unstable," and boundaries between them are porous. A student teacher performs the role of expert teacher at times as well as other identities in the processes of becoming a practicing teacher. In the interviews below Camille positioned herself with respect to multiple chronotopes simultaneously and engaged in temporal scaling throughout the first interview, which occurred at the very onset of the study group on multimodal literacies. Within the interview, Camille and a graduate student researcher (Tami) focused much of their conversations on digital literacies and classroom uses of popular culture texts.

When asked what she understood about the term "multiliteracies," a focus of the larger study group, Camille initially emphasized a wide array of semiotic modes (Table 5.1, lines 04–06, 31–33, 44–48), consistent with the view of literacy advocated in her methods course and a chronotope of popular culture. Her utterances suggest that she was conscious of researcher expectations regarding valuing multiple forms of literacy. For example, in lines 30–38, Camille paused eight times, and extended the vowels of some words, a move that serves as a placeholder to collect one's thoughts. These frequent pauses, stops and starts, and self-corrections indicate her desire to align herself with the researchers within this chronotope. Similar discursive patterns appear in lines 44–48. Camille proceeded with caution, positioning herself as the kind of teacher she likely believed we wanted her to be. Her awareness of the power relationships in the interview context is punctuated when she asked, *Am I passing* (line 63) in a hushed tone, making clear her position as preservice teacher who felt she was being evaluated. Camille's acute awareness of her tentative positioning, the evaluative context of student teaching, and the potentially evaluative context of the interview spotlights how researcher positionality can significantly impact participants' responses during data generation. At the same time, Camille did not adhere neatly to the researchers' perspective that such texts hold academic value in themselves, or the idea that the affordances of popular culture texts go beyond interest and motivation. This is evident in line 09, when Camille explicitly emphasized the word interest.

In Table 5.2, Tami is talking with Camille about popular culture and its role in the classroom. When asked her perspective on this, Camille framed them as tools to engage students in traditional print texts rather than as legitimate academic texts in their own right ("obviously if you can use it as a learning tool then-"; Table 5.2, line 27). Notably, Tami provided immediate

Table 5.1: Interview 1, Excerpt 1 (R = Researcher, C = Camille).

Line	Message Units	Additional Contextualization
000	R: So what- is that- what does multiliteracies mean to you	
001		
002	C: Multiliteracies↑ u++h | I guess I would say being able to	
003	<u>function</u> um |	
004	within varyi+ng | environments	
005	whether it be reading writing |	
006	technologically+ uh you know <u>compute+rs</u> um |	
007	using different things in the classroom whether be | videos	
008	| like and computers	
009	just tapping into all these different avenues	
010	you can basically express the same idea to the kids |	
011	for <u>interest</u>	
012		
013	R: Yeah | There are lots of different <u>facets</u>	
014	C: Uh hum	
015		
016	R: A conglomer<u>ation</u> of things	
017		
018	C: Uh hum	
019		
020	R: So if a person then is <u>defined</u> as <u>literate</u> |	
021	in your eyes what is that- what can that person can do↓	
022		
023	C: That is the hardest question	
024		*Spoken while laughing
025	R: It's my <u>job</u> that's why the <u>hired</u> me*	
026		
027	C: So what do I consider- if someone's <u>literate</u> ...	
028		
029	R: Yeah if I was to say this person over here is <u>literate</u> |	
030	what can that person <u>do</u> then↓	
031		
032	C: It depends on what there're being | what there're | deemed literate at |	
033	you know if somebody is literate at | | car repair	
034	I would say they could fix my car |	
035	if some one's literate at | computers and technology	
036	they can- they're able to-	

Table 5.1: *Continued*

Line	Message Units	Additional Contextualization
037	I don't know define your parameters I suppose |	
038	but they're able to complete tasks related to that | | particular object or item or …	
039		
040		
041		Nervous laugh
042	R: So how would that look that in literacy | if they are literate	
043		Laughs
044	C: Ay | literacy if they're literate uh	
045		
045	R: Yeah literacy if they're literate	
047		
048	C: If they can communicate ah of those ah you know verbally+ | |	
049	uh | in written fo+rm |	
050	they're able to rea+d | uh whether be+ um |	
051	I guess you can express themselves through art as well drawings things of that nature |	
052	be able to convey their ideas through some form they com-	
053	can communicate to other people	
054		
055		
056		
057	R: Okay | okay so+ | since I am I am literate	
058	and I can communicate to you via either you know | I can rea+d	
059	and I can communicate via text or picture or a | variety of different ways	*Spoken quietly*; laughter
060	what does that mean for teaching↑ |	
061	if all these things make someone literate	
062	what does that mean then-	
063		
	C: Well then as a teacher you have to try to incorporate all those different facets in your class you are teaching and style as well *am I passing↑*	

Table 5.2: Interview 1, Excerpt 2 (R = Researcher, C = Camille).

Line	Interaction Unit 1, Broken up by Message Units	Additional Contextualization
001	C: Ah yeah we did talk about the avata+r um	
002	I don't know if graphic <u>novels</u> fall to that-	
003		
004	R: [Definitely	
005		
006	C: -or not]	
007	yeah we did address that	
008	and that's-	
009	my eleven year old is <u>very</u> into graphic novels	
010	and so um | <u>that's</u> something that I have	
011	experienced <u>personally</u>	
012	and I mean he just absolutely loves them	
013	uh so we just discussed sort of where that would <u>fa+ll</u> |	
014	uh hum off the top of my head-	
015		
016	R: -So with your experience	
017	then your son and graphic novels	
018	would you feel comfortable like using them in your classroom	
019	[how do you feel-]	
020		
021	C: [Oh <u>certainly</u>]	
022		
023	R: -about pop culture in your classroom	
024	Yeah↑	
025		
026	C: I <u>definitely</u> think it has a <u>place</u>	
027	I mean | you're surrounded by it	
028	so | obviously if you can use as a learning tool then-	
029		
030	R: -Why- you know they're <u>reading</u>	
031		
032	C: Yeah	
033		
034	R: That's what I always said	
035	<u>woohoo</u> you're <u>reading</u>	

Table 5.2: *Continued*

Line	Interaction Unit 1, Broken up by Message Units	Additional Contextualization
036		[4] sympathetic tone, slightly higher pitch
037	C: I kno+w[4] I know↓[4]	
038	that's X that whole Captain Underpants debate	
039		
040	R: O+h gosh	
041		
042	C: It just absolutely kills me	
043		
044	R: I kno+w	
045		
046	C: And I was like you know what ↓ |	
047	and I'm sure | you have these with other people too	
048	they're- they are reading a book↓ |	
049	it's they're excited about it	
050	and I read it for my Lit class	
051	and so I was reading it with my kids |	
052	we were drivi+ng | I think to Chicago |	
053	my husband was driving	
054	I wasn't reading and driving at the same time	
055		Laughing
056	R: oh that's good I feel better about that	
057		Laughing
058	C: but I was reading it out loud	
059	and they're just dying laughing	
060	and I thought you know↑	
061	it's so infrequent that you see kids | so into	
062	and so excited I think it's so fun to read so . . .	

uptake, and expressed a similar view (lines 29, 33–34). Their conversations here and in lines 47–48, when Camille states, "they're- they are reading a book / it's they're excited about it," suggest that while graphic novels are not ideal, they have motivational value for promoting reading. Camille's stress on "reading," "book," and "excited" indicate a confidence that is likely derived from the interviewer's uptake of her stance on graphic novels in the classroom.

No scaling is necessary, as Camille and the researcher are on the same page, or in step with one another, with respect to space and time.

The apparent synchrony between Camille and the researcher appears to be a result not just of similar views of reading and popular culture, but also Camille's tactical positioning with respect to her experiences as a mother, which indexes a different timescale, laminating it atop the immediate timescale of the interview. This enables Camille to capitalize on the discourses of motherhood. For instance, in line 07, Camille stated that she recalled discussing graphic novels in her coursework, indicating her student teacher status. But in she abruptly reframed her response with respect to her experience as a mother, emphasizing the word "personally" (lines 09–11), before shifting back to her coursework in line 12. Camille got uptake from Tami, and continued to frame the potential of popular culture texts in the classroom according to her experiences as a mother and reading graphic novels such as Captain Underpants (Pilkey, 1997) with her children. In lines 45 to 53, she said she read the text for her literature class, but then placed additional emphasis on "kids" (line 50), positioning herself as a parent. Camille tactically scaled from the chronotope of student teacher status, situated within a timescale of one to two years, to her nontraditional preservice teacher status, grounded in a timescale of several years, that offers life experiences of motherhood as capital on which to ground her assertions.

Camille is not simply reframing the conversation with regard to her positions or identities as preservice teacher and mother, but also with regard to the timescales. By shifting the discourse to a broader timescale, she is able to position herself as more expert and experienced to successfully negotiate the political tensions and power relationships at play during the interview, her teacher preparation coursework, and in the study group. We view these negotiations as central to Camille's identity development, and suggest that teacher identities are informed by multiple positionings and rehearsal as student teachers forge professional identities of an inservice teacher. These rehearsed identities are also re-performed in classroom settings such as student teaching. In the next section, we present a portion of transcript from one of two observations of Camille student teaching in Jean's classroom.

On two occasions, we video recorded Camille during student teaching, as she attempted to work toward her study group goal of integrating popular culture into her literacy instruction. Both video-recorded lessons involved teaching pronouns, a curricular topic determined by the scope and sequence of the district curriculum. In the second lesson (displayed in Table 5.3), Camille invited her students to bring video game manuals from home, and had them

PERFORMING MULTIPLE IDENTITIES IN STUDENT TEACHING

Table 5.3: Video Two, Excerpt 1.

Line	Speaker • Hearer	Message Units	Additional Contextualization
001	T • Students	Oka:ay | who hasn't been up today at all even during math time↑	Several hands stretch hands way up in the air, eager to be picked.
002			
003			
004	T • Krista	Krista | go on up there	
005		And we are now talking about	
006		Princess Peach	Side conversation between two girls
007		"Your character is Princess Peach"	
008	Several Boys		
009		**Ee++++w**	
010			
011			
012			
013	T • Students	Hey | That's *my* character	
014		*I* was just Princess Peach	Students laugh.
015			
016		Is that the one that can turn into a *ninja*↑	Girls raise hands, look eager
017	Students • U		
018			
019			Krista moves to Active Board
020			
021			
022			
023			
024		Let's see which one Krista chooses	
025	T • Student	"Your *character* is Princess Peach"	
026		Test them *out*	
027		"*Your* character is Princess Peach"	
028		Not you *are* character	Student circles the word your
029		Now | what should that- should	
030		that probably be *capitalized*↑	
031			
032		Yeah	
033	Krista • T	Yes it *should*	
034		I found an error	

Continued

Table 5.3: Continued

Line	Speaker • Hearer	Message Units	Additional Contextualization
035	T • Student	Okay who hasn't been up today at	T retrieves Jeremy from back
036		all to the active board	of room. He walks to Smart
037			Board and T. walks around
038		*Jeremy* hasn't been	him to the left of the board.
039			She talks in quieter voice
040	Student • T	Everyone *else* in here has had a turn	directly to him, pointing to
041		today↓	the words as she reads. She
042		Okay *Jeremy*	"They're racing in	points at the word "they're"
043	T • Student	the mushroom cup at 100 cc's"	as she says, "they are."
044			Jeremy circles "they're"
045	T • Jeremy	Okay	well let's take a look	
046		Look at this contraction	
047		They are racing in the mushroom cup at 100 cc's	
048		Does that make sense↑	
049		They are racing in the mushroom cup	
050		Okay, nice job	
051			
052		All right	Peter	
053	T • Peter	"Quickly slide your car to the right	
054		while attacking"	
055			
056	T • Student	So	do you guys know what game	
057		I was thinking of while I was	
058		writing these	
059		sentences↑	
060	Student • T		
061		**Mario Cart**	
062			Significant cross-talk
063	T • Student	Mario Cart	
064			
065		I *have* that game	
066	Student • T		
067		*Raise* your hand	
068			

Table 5.3: *Continued*

Line	Speaker • Hearer	Message Units	Additional Contextualization
069	T • Student	"Quickly slide your cart to the right while attacking"	
070			
071			
072	T • Student	You *wrote* these↑	Two girls now appear disengaged
073			
074		Yeah I *did*	
075	Student • T	All by myself	
076		*Amazing* isn't it↑	
	T • Students	I guess	
		Okay | so we're showing possession	
		Your cart	
	Students • T	That cart belongs to you	
		Possessive pronoun	
	T • Students		

work in partners to find sentences in the manuals that included pronouns and copy them onto a worksheet. Camille tried to establish a game-like quality to the lesson, but this was countered by her desire to comply with the standardized curriculum and the school's teacher-directed instructional culture. Notably, and as we mentioned previously, Jean, who adhered tightly to the standardized curriculum, remained in the room during Camille's student teaching. In addition, Lara was Camille's literacy methods course instructor the previous year and study group facilitator, and she was also present as the videographer. Given the multiple sets of eyes on her and different ideologies framing the context and the lesson, it is not surprising that Camille positioned herself in multiple ways.

Throughout the lesson, Camille's physical and linguistic positioning constructed an authoritative teacher space consistent with an expert teacher chronotope. Camille maintained a fairly controlled IRE script in her interactions with students, as we see in Table 5.3, when she calls student volunteers to the interactive whiteboard (directing moves) to circle the correct pronoun in different sentences (lines 22–44). By circulating around the desks and positioning herself alternately at the back and front of the room (assembly moves), Camille maintained authority over the other students, who remained seated, strictly controlling their access to the teacher fronted representational field (Roberts et al., 2012).

Reimagining Positionality in Student Teacher Identity

Our findings in this chapter indicate that Camille refashioned identities in response to changing expectations, accountability, and curriculum to meet the educational needs of the students she taught during her student teaching in Jean's classroom. At times, she positioned herself as a novice teacher, other times she performed as an experienced teacher, and her identity as a mother helped her navigate between them. Camille's positioning and repositioning also involve shifting the discourse to a broader timescale.

Positioning in social interactions (Harré & Van Langenhove, 1998) is well established. However, Edmiston's recent work argues for "dramatic positioning" (2013, p. 233) as a way to enrich our thinking about using positioning as a pedagogical tool to work with learners. He views dramatic positioning as tactical, and an aspect of its power is that when someone is positioning themselves or participants in roles in process drama, they are using their imaginations, and taking risks in role that they may not take as themselves. This imaginative play "is nested within whatever everyday social positions have been established" (Edmiston, 2013, p. 234). Extending this idea, student teachers as socially positioned in classrooms and position themselves as well. Dramatic positioning has the potential to help student teachers inquire into concepts of positioning to better understand identity development if it is incorporated into teacher education programs. We explain how this can work more specifically in Chapter 7.

To conclude, we build on these ideas and our own thinking about "ongoing active positioning" (Crumpler, Handsfield, & Dean, 2011, p. 79) to explore how we could work with student teachers like Camille and others to inquire into identity development and analyze and replay moments to explore issues of power as part of their teacher preparation programs. Ongoing active positioning with student teachers involves providing feedback during their student teaching by using a dramatic lens to reframe moments of instructional success, uncertainty, discomfort, or others and re-envision how issues of power may inform teaching possibilities. This reframing will be part of the support and debriefing for them as student teachers.

Research has suggested the importance of identity development for student teachers (Pillen, Den Brok, & Beijaard, 2013; Stenberg, 2010) and how discourse creates expectations, and even stereotypes of student teachers (Alsup, 2006). Using ongoing active positioning helps student teachers better understand the role of identity in teacher development. Ongoing active positioning is analogous to member checking, in which a researcher shares initial interpretations of data with participants in order to increase trustworthiness in a study (Bogdan & Biklen, 1997). However, using ongoing active positioning as a feature of a process drama approach to supporting student teacher development repositions student teachers more agentically in their own identity development. We imagine student teachers meeting in small groups to candidly reflect on their teaching practices, interactions with students, and other aspects of their experience. As with all process drama work, it is vital to develop trust among group members. Once this context is established, a facilitator can lead the group to examine to examine moments in student teaching, work in role to replay those moments and open spaces to ask how these moments could have unfolded differently to reposition student teachers. Ongoing active positioning moves beyond discussing other possibilities and imaginatively re-enacts them to create new data (Norris, 2009) about how teacher identities are created moment by moment in classroom interactions.

Of course, there are issues of power in any student teaching experience. Britzman's foundational work (1986, 2012) has demonstrated that power is enmeshed with biographical experiences and institutional structures as teacher candidates learn the practices of teaching. These include power of cooperating teachers such as Jean in Camille's case, power of university supervisors or faculty to influence instructional approaches and the power of schools and districts to privilege some discourses of teaching and learning learning over others. We recognize that our approach does not erase these dynamics. However, we believe process drama work informed by ongoing active positioning can help make these dynamics more visible and help student teachers begin to navigate them more effectively.

In the next chapter, we report some of our findings about teacher study groups as an approach to professional development. Specifically, we demonstrate how research interludes, tableau, working role, and other process drama can be used deepen understanding regarding teacher identity.

References

Alsup, J. (2006). *Teacher identity discourses: Negotiating personal and professional spaces.* New York, NY: Routledge.

Bakhtin, M. (1984). *Problems of Dostoevsky's Poetics* (Ed. and Trans. Caryl Emerson. *Theory and history of literature*, Vol. 8, p. 124). Minneapolis, MN: University of Minnesota Press.

Bakhtin, M. M., Holquist, M., & Liapunov, V. (1990). *Art and answerability: Early philosophical essays* (Vol. 9). Austin, TX: University of Texas Press.

Biklen, S. K. (1995). *School work: Gender and the cultural construction of teaching.* New York, NY: Teachers College Press.

Blommaert, J. (2005). *Discourse: A critical introduction.* Cambridge, UK: Cambridge University Press.

Blommaert, J. (2007). Sociolinguistic scales. *Intercultural Pragmatics, 4*(1), 1–19.

Blommaert, J. (2015). Chronotopes, scales, and complexity in the study of language in society. *Annual Review of Anthropology, 44,* 105–116.

Bloome, D., Carter, S. P., Christian, B. M., Otto, S., & Shuart-Faris, N. (2005). *Discourse analysis and the study of classroom language and literacy events: A microethnographic perspective.* New York, NY: Routledge.

Bogdan, R., & Biklen, S. K. (1997). *Qualitative research for education.* Boston, MA: Allyn & Bacon.

Britzman, D. (1986). Cultural myths in the making of a teacher: Biography and social structure in teacher education. *Harvard Educational Review, 56*(4), 442–457.

Britzman, D. (2012). *Practice makes practice: A critical study of learning to teach.* New York, NY: Suny Press.

Caldas-Coulthard, C., & Iedema, R. (Eds.). (2016). *Identity trouble: Critical discourse and contested identities.* New York, NY: Springer.

Cho, S. (2018). "A Personal Touch of Advocacy to My Profession": Counter-narratives of immigrant Latina teachers in English as a second language education. *Ethnic Studies Review, 39*(1), 19–35.

Collins, P. H. (2016). Shifting the center: Race, class, and feminist theorizing about motherhood. In *Mothering* (pp. 45–65). New York, NY: Routledge.

Collins, J., & Blot, R. (2003). *Literacy and literacies: Texts, power and identity.* New York, NY: Cambridge University Press.

Collins, J., Slembrouck, S., & Baynham, M. (Eds.). (2009). *Globalization and languages in contact: Scale, migration, and communicative practices.* London, England: Continuum

Crumpler, T. P., Handsfield, L. J., & Dean, T. R. (2011). Constructing difference differently in language and literacy professional development. *Research in the Teaching of English, 46*(1), 55–91.

de Certeau, M. (1984). *The practice of everyday life.* Berkeley, CA: University of California Press.

Edmiston, B. (2013). *Transforming teaching and learning with active and dramatic approaches: Engaging students across the curriculum.* New York, NY: Routledge

Estola, E., & Elbaz-Luwisch, F. (2003). Teaching bodies at work. *Journal of Curriculum Studies, 35*(6), 697–719.

Galman, S. (2012). *Wise and foolish virgins: White women at work in the feminized world of primary school teaching*. Lanham, MD: Lexington Books.

Goodwin, C. (2007). Participation, stance and affect in the organization of activities. *Discourse & Society, 18*(1), 53–73.

Graves, D. H. (1983). *Writing: Teachers and children at work*. Exeter, NH: Heinemann Educational Books.

Green, J. L., & Wallat, C. (1981). Mapping instructional conversations: A sociolinguistic ethnography. *Ethnography and Language in Educational Settings, 5*, 161–195.

Griffith, A. I., & Smith, D. E. (1987). Constructing cultural knowledge: Mothering as discourse. *Women and Education: A Canadian Perspective, 3*(1), 87–103.

Gutiérrez, K., Rymes, B., & Larson, J. (1995). Script, counterscript, and underlife in the classroom: James Brown versus Brown v. Board of Education. Harvard Educational Review, 65(3), 445–472.

Handsfield, L. J., & Crumpler, T. P. (2013). "Dude, it's not a appropriate word": Negotiating word meanings, language ideologies, and identities in a literature discussion group. *Linguistics and Education, 24*(2), 112–130.

Harré, R., & Van Langenhove, L. (Eds.). (1998). *Positioning theory: Moral contexts of international action*. London, England: Wiley-Blackwell.

Jackson, A. Y. (2001). Multiple Annies: Feminist poststructural theory and the making of a teacher. *Journal of Teacher Education, 52*(5), 386–397.

Landeros, M. (2011). Defining the 'good mother' and the 'professional teacher': Parent–teacher relationships in an affluent school district. *Gender and Education, 23*(3), 247–262.

Lemke, J. L. (2013). Thinking about feeling: Affect across literacies and lives. In O. Erstad & J. Sefton-Green (Eds.), Identity, community, and learning lives in the digital age (pp. 57–69). Cambridge, UK: Cambridge University Press.

Lewis, C., Enciso, P., & Moje, E. B. (Eds.). (2007). *Reframing sociocultural research on literacy: Identity, agency, and power* (pp. 1–11). Mahwah, NJ: Lawrence Erlbaum.

May, V. (2008). On being a good mother: The moral presentation of self in written life stories. *Sociology, 42*(3), 470–486.

McNeill, D. (2008). *Gesture and thought*. Chicago, IL: University of Chicago Press.

Nielsen, A. (2016). Second career teachers and (mis) recognitions of professional identities. *School Leadership & Management, 36*(2), 221–245.

No Child Left Behind Act of 2001, Pub. L. No. 107–110.

Norris, J. (2009). *Playbuilding as qualitative research: A participatory arts-based approach*. New York, NY: Routledge.

Pilkey, D. (1997). *Adventures of Captain Underpants*. New York, NY: Scholastic.

Pillen, M. T., Den Brok, P. J., & Beijaard, D. (2013). Profiles and change in beginning teachers' professional identity tensions. *Teaching and Teacher Education, 34*, 86–97.

Powell, R. R. (1997). Teaching alike: A cross-case analysis of first-career and second-career beginning teachers' instructional convergence. *Teaching and Teacher Education, 13*(3), 341–356.

Resta, V., Huling, L., & Rainwater, N. (2001). Preparing second-career teachers. *Educational Leadership, 58*(8), 60–63.

Roberts, J., Radinsky, J., Lyons, L., & Cafaro, F. (2012). Co-census: Designing an interactive museum space to prompt negotiated narratives of ethnicity, community, and identity. Symposium conducted at the meeting of the American Educational Research Association, Vancouver, BC.

Rury, J. L. (1989). Who became teachers? The social characteristics of teachers in American history. In *American teachers: Histories of a profession at work* (pp. 9–48). New York, NY: Macmillan.

Smythe, S. (2006). The good mother: A critical discourse analysis of literacy advice to mothers in the 20th century (Doctoral dissertation). University of British Columbia.

Steinkuehler, C. (2016). Parenting and video games. *Journal of Adolescent & Adult Literacy, 59*(4), 357–361.

Stenberg, K. (2010). Identity work as a tool for promoting the professional development of student teachers. *Reflective Practice, 11*(3), 331–346.

Tigchelaar, A., Brouwer, N., & Korthagen, F. (2008). Crossing horizons: Continuity and change during second-career teachers' entry into teaching. *Teaching and Teacher Education, 24*(6), 1530–1550.

Weedon, C. (1997[1987]) *Feminist practice and poststructuralist theory*. Oxford, UK: Blackwell

Willett, R. J. (2015). The discursive construction of 'good parenting' and digital media–the case of children's virtual world games. *Media, Culture & Society, 37*(7), 1060–1075.

Wortham, S. (2003). Accomplishing identity in participant-denoting discourse. *Journal of Linguistic Anthropology, 13*(2), 189–210.

Wortham, S. (2006). *Learning identity: The joint emergence of social identification and academic learning*. Cambridge, UK: Cambridge University Press.

SECOND INTERLUDE—CAMILLE

Camille used video game manuals in her effort to integrate her students' popular culture interests to teach elements of grammar (specifically pronouns) in a lesson during her student teaching. At one point in the instructional sequence (Table 3, lines 13–29), the students showed excitement about the notion of character that Camille had introduced, but she quickly redirected the conversation to the goal of grammar instruction. However, we wondered, what if Camille and her students explored a different opportunity and used structures of process drama? This interlude describes that possibility.

Imagining Video Game Characters

Following the lead of her students, Camille shifts the instruction away from parts of speech to a conversation about character. She invites the students to brainstorm who are some other video game characters they know, and as the students shout them out, she lists them on the interactive white board. She listens carefully, and asks questions about the characters' powers to engage them more deeply in discussion. The goal is to generate as many names of video characters as possible so that the students will have choices to make in the next phase of the lesson.

Now that Camille has scaffolded the discussion with the large group, she selects one character from the students' list and asks the whole group to brainstorm new powers for that video game character. She lists them on the interactive white board so that the students have a shared understanding of these powers. Then, Camille invites the students to stand at their tables, and as she says a power out loud, she asks the students to physically perform that power in slow motion when she counts to three. For example, we imagine that one new power could be the ability to leap over buildings. Camille and her students slowly raise their bodies up to mimic leaping over a building. Slow motion helps the students manage their bodies in the classroom space. This move enacts meaning and helps prepare the students for more focused small group discussions about character. After they have moved in slow motion, Camille invites the students to sit back down and talk with her about what they were thinking about as they readied themselves to leap in slow motion. This debriefing can help students become aware of their decision making and learning processes.

Next, she puts them in groups of four and request that they choose one of the other video characters from the list and discuss what new powers and personality traits they would add to the character. Camille designates one student in each group to make a list of powers for the group. Students have about ten minutes complete this list. Then each group shares what they have created with the larger class. To provide closure to this lesson, Camille ask each group to create a tableau in which they arrange themselves in a silent, frozen moment to represent one of the powers they have identified. The rest of the class interprets each tableau with Camille.

From here, Camille could choose multiple instructional options to finish the lesson. For example, the students could draft a short narrative in role as the video game character. Then, they share their drafts with a partner at the table. Camille could use the texts the students have composed to teach pronouns (or other aspects of grammar) the next day.

This interlude asked, what if Camille noticed the students' interest in character and shifted instruction to engage the students in more imaginative work? In this short sequence imagined here, Camille and her students begin to create a drama world, a new field of meaning that opens possibilities to access multiple meaning systems. These meaning systems include popular culture, personal experience, and collaborative dramatic interactions which converge as the students think about character. In Chapters 6 and 7, we focus on how teachers can use some of these same process drama structures in professional development and research on identity.

· 6 ·
EXPLORING TEACHER IDENTITY DEVELOPMENT THROUGH STUDY GROUPS

Introduction

"I feel like we have so many children that we're, that are coming from Chicago from disadvantaged families with tough situations with lack of experiences and a lot of it is completely different for the ELs." (Kathy, study group transcript)

The comments above were voiced by a teacher in our first study group. This section of transcript is from a larger discussion about EB students (which she refers to as ELs—English learners) coming into a classroom and how best to teach them. She is commenting on EB children coming into her smaller school district and classroom as "disadvantaged." Kathy's comments reflect a deficit view of language, learning, and types of families, but teacher identities are also being constructed within this moment of discourse. From a professional development standpoint, what are possible responses to her comment? If we as facilitators do nothing, is this deficit perspective reaffirmed or validated? From a researcher perspective, is this an ethical dilemma in which we recognize problems and intervene? How does that inform data generation?

All of these questions are important, and we believe that process drama, while not providing clear answers, can be a tool for exploring such questions more deeply and generating dialogic relationships within teacher study groups. Bakhtin (1984) theorized dialogic relationships by contending that, "They must clothe themselves in discourse, become utterances, become the positions of various subjects expressed in the discourse, in order that the dialogic relationships might arise among them" (p. 183). In other words, dialogic relationships are already situated within teacher study groups as a facet of the discourses produced by the participants. Bringing process drama to these kinds of dialogic relationships helps us unpack them to better understand how identities are "clothed" in discourses of teachers' and researchers' professional conversations.

In this chapter we share our findings about the role that process drama can play within study groups to examine the nuances of teacher identity work. In doing so, we introduce the concept of *research interludes* a research practice that uses role play and other process drama tools as a tactic for pausing, replaying, and examining interactional moments with study group participants. Further, we demonstrate how research interludes can be used in professional development to help teachers delve more deeply into how identities are constructed.

We define teacher study groups as a group of teachers systematically focusing on a specific topic and thinking collaboratively for improving pedagogical practices (Butler & Schnellert, 2012; Stanley, 2011). In our project, we designed two teacher study groups. The first brought practicing teachers together for professional conversations based on reading and studying professional texts about teaching multilingual students. The second brought together preservice and practicing teachers to explore digital and multimodal literacies in multilingual classrooms. Bringing teachers together into communities to improve teaching, address student learning, study problems of practice, and develop other aspects of professional growth has a long history in teacher education (Kennedy, 2016; Vangrieken, Meredith, Packer, & Kyndt, 2017). Goals for teachers include learning about new instructional practices, curricular planning, reviewing student data to make instructional decisions, or studying a professional text.

However, whether these groups are called professional learning communities (PLCs), study groups, or another similar term is of little consequence if teachers are not positioned as independent decision makers. Too often, teachers are situated as passive technicians who are directed to focus on primarily improving test scores, implementing prepackaged curricula, or other outcomes-based agendas (Britzman, 2012; Mockler, 2012). This type of professional development, although well intentioned, diminishes the complexity of teachers' work and the potential for more dialogic learning by fostering technocratic or instrumentalist thinking. Instrumentalist thinking assumes that the right instrument or tool is key to successful learning rather than viewing learning as relational and contextual (Acton & Glasgow, 2015; Chan & Elliott, 2004). Instrumentally driven professional development becomes one more meeting teachers have to attend that takes them out of their classrooms. Our research findings indicate that teacher study groups that introduce research interludes into their interactions can potentially enact a more relational and meaningful type of professional development for teachers.

We grounded the two study groups in our project on a funds of knowledge perspective (Moll, Amanti, Neff, & Gonzalez, 1992). We introduced this concept to participants as it relates to working with multilingual students and drawing on students' and families historically and culturally-situated sets of understandings and ways of viewing the world, building on it in subsequent large group and work team meetings. We also extended this notion to consider peer group and popular culture funds of knowledgs. In addition, we emphasized the cultural and linguistic knowledge that both preservice and inservice teachers bring to their work, and more specifically, the understandings and experiences they brought to the study group and their work teams.

We sought to position ourselves as co-learners within the groups and actively construct understandings of how to more effectively teach diverse students, share understandings about the professional texts, and explore the limits of a deficit view of children and families, particularly EB students. Based on research with these groups, we developed a dialogic, dramatic approach to explore teacher identities and replay moments in which teacher identities are being constructed. A central feature of this approach, which we call *research interludes* (Crumpler, Handsfield, & Dean, 2011), involves creating opportunities to replay moments of understanding, discomfort, new awareness, and affirmation. Replaying these moments provides insights into how teacher identities are constructed in interactions and activity among teachers.

In the next section, we revisit scholarship that informed our thinking about teacher study groups as an approach to teacher professional development. Then, we theorize research interludes based on scholarship in process drama and share a re-analysis of study group data to demonstrate the potential of this approach to examining teacher identity.

Professional Development and Teacher Identity

In the past, the nature of the teaching profession has been characterized as individualistic (Lortie, 2002) as well as autonomous (Little, 1993), in which teachers worked in their classrooms with minimum scrutiny and support. However, in the past 15 years the culture of teaching has shifted to one of accountability (Avalos, 2011; Hollins, 2015) with evaluation of teacher performance increasingly tied to student test scores and meeting learning standards. We argue that to respond to this shift, professional development should engage teachers in thinking deeply and critically about these changes, consider what are the best curricular approaches for promoting deep learning, and how identities of teachers are constructed and reconstructed as a feature of professional development. However, too often, such activities are absent from professional development.

In a comprehensive review of research on professional development, Kennedy (2016) argued that many professional development programs, while well intentioned, do not view teachers as individuals with their "own motivations and interests" (p. 30) and fail to provide intellectually engaging opportunities for learning. Similarly, Mockler (2013) studied professional development in Australia and found that discourses of professional development emphasized skill "acquisition and competency development" (p. 35), positioning teachers as technicians rather than professionals engaged in identity work. Other researchers in the United States (Endacott et al., 2015) and United Kingdom (Hall & McGinity, 2015) have made similar arguments and identified parallel concerns.

Together, these studies have raised questions about the purposes of professional development and how an approach to professional development that privileges technical aspects of teaching ignore teachers' identity development. We agree with Mockler (2012) that teacher professional development *is* identity work (p. 42), and our research with teacher study groups shows that when identity work is positioned as a key aspect of professional development, the experiences can become more meaningful. In what follows, we describe how the study groups we facilitated were conceptualized in our project, the expectations for participation, and the dialogic relationships needed to create a different kind of professional development experience.

Teacher Study Groups

Our purposes in designing and facilitating the study groups were to conduct research on professional development focusing on literacy instruction with linguistically diverse students and multimodal literacies, support teachers in identifying and shifting away from deficit views of teaching EB students, and to create opportunities for rich pedagogical conversations. A facet of the study groups was to participate in four small group work team meetings over the course of a semester. Each work team, consisting of four to eight participants, selected a professional text from variety of titles we had chosen to stimulate thinking about working with EBs and with digital and popular culture texts. These meetings were held at schools where teachers who participated in the study worked. Six guidelines were developed for the work team meetings.

Guidelines for Study Group Work Team Meetings

1. Form teams around a common interest and text.
2. Establish a structure and schedule for meetings that meets the group's needs.
3. Ask one member of group to document in the form of notes key ideas, strategies, questions, and whatever else is discussed when the team meets. These will be useful when we meet as large group. Also, include the date and a starting and ending time for each meeting. We suggest rotating this task.
4. We ask the teams to meet for a total of 6 hours over the course of the semester to be in alignment with the 12 hours that the district requires for professional development experiences.
5. The meetings should be opportunities to learn from one another, discuss your reactions to the readings, share strategies you have tried or will try in your own classrooms, and other ideas you have to build on your teaching practices.
6. We ask that the last 5 minutes of the team meeting, each of you write a short response in a journal that reflects on what happened in the team meeting that day.

These guidelines were designed to foster choice and create a professionally engaging space where teachers could honestly express their opinions, discuss strategies, and ask questions about teaching EBs.

The meetings lasted about two hours and were comprised of a large group discussion that we facilitated and a block of time for the groups to meet and discuss the professional text they were reading in relation to the larger group. We report on initial development of the concept of research interludes elsewhere (Crumpler, Handsfield, & Dean, 2011). In the next section, we expand this concept to show its potential for research on teacher identities, focusing our examples on the first study group, focused on literacy for linguistically diverse students.

Research Interludes

An interlude is a pause, or break in what goes on before or after. It is a breathing space for reflection. The term is also associated with theater and signifies a break in acts or action of a performance. We developed the term *research interludes* as moments when as participants in a study group conversation, we would pause their interactions for the purpose of replaying and reimagining a moment where teacher identity is being constructed (Crumpler, Handsfield, & Dean, 2011). Bakhtin's concept of double-voiced discourse is key to our conception of research interludes. Bakhtin argued (1984) "Someone else's words introduced into our own speech inevitably assume a new (our own) interpretation and become subject to our evaluation of them; that is, they become double-voiced" (p. 195). Implementing research interludes into teacher study groups uses process drama tools as a way to explore the double-voicedness of constructing teacher identity as a feature of social interaction.

Additionally, we see a potential for research interludes to elucidate and interrupt scaling practices and power relationships. For example, imagine a teacher study group that was composed of more experienced and new teachers discussing instruction for EB students. One of the more experienced teachers comments that he has been teaching those students for years, he is not bilingual, and the best practice is for them to be pulled out of the general classroom and work with a bilingual teacher. One of the newer teachers responds that she believes it is important to keep emergent bilinguals in her classroom and view their second languages as a affordance for learning. Further, imagine that the more experienced teacher rolls his eyes and states that the district policy suggests that is not what she should do. Using research interludes, we pause the conversation, and replay that moment in which the experienced teacher has positioned himself in a position of power and scaled up the discourse by introducing district policy.

Research interludes are also instances for data generation and analysis of those moments, and position participants in agentive roles in the inquiry process. The term is informed by the notion of role playing as it has been taken up in process drama (Bolton & Heathcote, 1999). Role playing is stepping into role as someone other than ourselves for the purposes of gaining multiple perspectives on a problem, situation, issue, or our own motivations. As the researcher-facilitators, we use this concept to step out of the roles of teacher and researcher and into other roles that allow us to explore how identities are being constructed within the context of the study group interactins. Roles are developed based on recorded study group conversations, as we show later. Then, we step back again and reflect on how identities we examined in role shape the teachers we are and those we aspire to become. All of these interactions involve purposeful language and actions by the researcher facilitating the study group.

Two theorists have shaped our further development of research interludes, O'Toole's (1992) study of drama and meaning and Berry's work in drama and cultural studies (2002). O'Toole's (1992) study of how dramatic meaning is negotiated among participants, contexts, and texts helps clarify how language and actions inform research interludes. He theorized the relationship this way:

> In all drama, language and physical action are polyfunctional, multi-dimensional, with all of their constituents dependent on each other; furthermore, in process drama, those constituents are constantly being renegotiated. (1992, p. 199)

The processes of renegotiation are central to research interludes as a research practice for exploring teacher identity. Through the uses of specific language functions and actions, teachers in professional study groups can renegotiate their own identities while exploring the content upon which the group has chosen to focus. They can become reflective practitioners (Edmiston & Wilhelm, 1996) researching their own identity work.

Another aspect of research interludes is Berry's (2002) idea of "re-authoring the text through drama" (p. 86). Berry draws on cultural studies and argues that re-authoring a text can mean taking a position from a different cultural perspective-one that is marginalized for example. In teacher study groups, conversations, which involve both utterances and paralinguistic communication (e.g., gaze, gesture, facial expression, bodily positioning), provide rich opportunities for a facilitator/researcher to stop a conversation, work in role with the participants, replay a moment where identities are being constructed, invite teachers to re-author that moment, and reposition themselves to see other perspectives.

Research interludes also uses gesture and body movements as analytic tools. In this regard, we draw not only on traditions in theater (Kershaw, 1992; Rodenburg, 1993), but also on work by Denzin (2003) in performance ethnography. Shifting the space between participants, moving in an out of a circle, asking individuals to turn away from a group and all the while remaining silent allows us to shift a scene, and create a different interpretation of what is happening. For example, if in a group of five, everyone is standing shoulder to shoulder and facing inward, group cohesion is suggested. If we ask two members to step back, turn, and face outward with their hands on their hips, the relationships among members change. This type of tableau work is a potentially powerful way to invite teachers to take on different perspectives and compose embodied texts that inform the discourse of the study group (Branscombe & Schneider, 2013). Together, O'Toole and Berry's scholarship helps us ground research interludes in the multimodalities of literacy and argue for teacher identities as constructed, fluid, and potentially reimagined.

To illustrate how this works, we provide examples taken from transcripts of two large group meetings during the first study group. We identified two moments from these two discussions in which deficit discourses were being produced. We want to be clear that the purpose of developing research interludes as an inquiry tool is not to denigrate teachers or evaluate instructional practices. And too be clear, these were not the only such moments, and we had our own complicity in their production. In the application and understanding of research interludes, it is imperative to recognize our own role in the creation of these moments/discourses. Although we attempted to position ourselves as co-learners, we participated in the creation of the discourse as well. In process drama, the facilitator/researcher is not separate from the research interlude but rather is a participant in it. This leads to possibilities for critically reflecting on researcher–participant relationships and the role of the researcher as part of the research process.

This next section includes a section from a discussion during one of the work team meetings at an elementary school and a different work team meeting at a middle school. These transcripts are part of broader discussions the study group participants were having around new EB students being placed in their classrooms, new families entering the school and communities, and how they were accommodating the new students. Rather than using the microethnographic discursive approach described in earlier chapters, our analysis of these data involved drawing on elements of critical discourse analysis, especially as it is informed by sociolinguistics (de finna, Schiffrin, & Bamberg, 2006). This approach allowed us to focus on how identities were being constructed within participant interactions and conversational turns.

We first conducted a close thematic reading of the transcripts and identified "moments" in which the discourse suggested a deficit perspective. After these moments were identified, we re-analyzed the discourse within each moment and looked for discursive constructions of identities—turns in the conversation in which particular positions toward EB students or approaches toward literacy teaching and learning were being articulated. As demonstrated below, teachers were positioning themselves within these interactions in particular ways (Greer, 2006) that shape their identities. Research interludes offer opportunities to examine those positions and then reimagine them. As a research strategy it can help researchers understand how teacher identities are constructed (and de- and re-constructed) moment by moment in social interactions.

Working With Teacher Study Groups

Moment One

In this first conversation, there were five K-8 teachers who comprised the work team. The discussion was about instructing EB learners who were arriving at the school where the teachers taught and challenges the teachers perceived as part of that work. Tami, a graduate assistant who worked on the research project with us, was facilitating and recording the conversation.
The discussion began with the teachers discussing linguistic resources (who spoke Spanish and who did not) and the fact that the district had decided that the EB students would be sent to a particular elementary school. As a teaching staff, they wanted to accept this and do their best to teach the new students. Prior to the moment analyzed here, the conversation had focused on the programmatic resources available in the building for EB students, after which Tami inquired about the affordances in the teachers' own professional backgrounds that could help them be successful with EB learners. Kathy begins by positioning herself as a new teacher, mentions "learning disabilities," and then states "we took the ELLs too," effectively linking EB students

and learning disabilities. Before she finishes her statement, Becky enters the conversation and introduces the ideas of disadvantaged families lacking experiences and how different their school and classrooms are from Chicago. Tami asks the teacher to tell her more, and Becky produces language that suggested a deficit view of EB students and families. Within this exchange, she negotiates her identity as a teacher who focuses on what EB students do not have (communication skills, vocabulary, certain experiences) and thus as someone who tries to give them these things—a discourse of white saviorism (Sondel, Kretchmar, & Hadley Dunn, 2019).

KATHY: We got ... I was kind of a teacher brand new and first year and so (unintelligible) learning disabilities, you know (laughing slightly) and so we took the ELLs too and it's, um ....

BECKY: I feel like we have so many children that we're, that are coming from Chicago from disadvantaged families with tough situations with lack of experiences and a lot of it is completely different for the ELLs.

TAMI: Tell me more

BECKY: The vocabulary that they come with. The support they come with from families. The communication that we have is lacking in those children and so they have that experience that requires that we build up their vocabulary. We are trying to give them books. We are trying to give them experiences and so everything is at a much slower pace and its where we are and helping these kids has so much to do with helping the families with so much that I don't think it's a lot different than what we are supporting.

We want to be clear here that all the teachers in this study group were committed professionals who wanted their students to succeed. Although we do want to shift deficit perspectives on learning, using research interludes as a tool to examine teacher identity work is not designed to perform a "gotcha" discourse or to denigrate teachers. Instead, this approach offers opportunities to re-perform and reimagine discourses, ideologies, and power relationships, as well as the identities that are coconstructed along with them, by inserting ourselves as researcher/participants into the conversation, and using role play and tableau to re-author other stances and possible identities with participants. What follows is moment one reimagined. Notice that we do not change the original words of the study group participants; however, we do speculate about what other participants might say in response within the research interlude work. This practice is important for re-dramatizing the study group scene so that we better understand how identities are *clothed in discourse* as Bakhtin (1984) argued. We also include stage directions to indicate physical movement and repositioning of individuals as part of the reimaging of this moment (Crumpler, Handsfield, & Dean, 2011).

Moment One Reimagined

> As researcher/facilitators, we physically step into the study group conversation. This shifts our position to being in the middle of the exchange and signals that we are participants in the moment as well. Our language is invitational, and we use phrases such as "what if ..." or "I wonder how" to suggest possibilities for renegotiation of perspectives.
>
> KATHY: We got ... I was kind of a teacher brand new and first year and so (unintelligible) learning disabilities, you know (laughing slightly) and so we took the ELLs too and it's, um ....
> BECKY: I feel like we have so many children that we're, that are coming from Chicago from disadvantaged families with tough situations with lack of experiences and a lot of it is completely different for the ELLs.

In this exchange, we note frustration of a newer teacher as well as the discursive linking of ELL students and students with learning disabilities. The teacher's slight laughter suggests nervousness, at which point the second speaker comes in and shifts the discourse to "disadvantaged families" with a "lack of experiences."

> TOM: It is difficult sometimes to understand families in the abstract, and we can be frustrated by our own lack of interactions with diverse families. I would like us to step back and think about what if we could talk to a family who has just arrived in our community? I wonder if two of the group members would come sit beside me and we create a tableau. Let's imagine the two of them are parents who have just recently moved to this community from a large urban city. What experiences might they have had that could be resources to help them transition into this community? What are their worries or concerns now that they are here?
> We work with silence and ask that no one speak aloud for 30 to 60 seconds. This allows the group to reflect upon the figures who represent the family that is sitting beside them.
> Using a technique called "tapping" in, Lara stands behind one of the three figures and asks the group to verbalize whatever is in their mind in regard to this family. By listening to whatever is spoken at this point, we begin to disturb the silence and possibly deconstruct the deficit discourse that was articulated in the study group. Shifting roles, Tom moves the conversation within the research interlude directly to the family represented.
> TOM: What if I were the child of these two parents? A student who will be entering school next week. [Tom moves closer to the other two participants.] If

you could ask a question to one of the parents or the student, I wonder what questions you would ask us. Think for a minute, and when you are ready, state your question to one of the family members.

Important to note here is that Tom has stepped into role as a family member and used the pronoun "us." The abstract family that was characterized as "disadvantaged" and lacking experiences is now more concrete. Further, by inviting the participants to speak to the family, a dialogic relationship is initiated through "double-voiced discourse" (Bakhtin, 1984 p. 199). The tableau of the family is embodied discourse (Branscombe, & Schneider, 2013) because creating a tableau requires participants to draw on multiple meaning systems (personal, linguistic, communal) and arrange themselves in a way that silently signifies meaning to an audience who then interprets that meaning. By asking questions to the figures in the tableau, the other study group participants are revoicing interpreted meaning in the embodied discourse of the tableau into their own words and asking, "what if?" (Edmiston, 2003). Research interludes tap into embodied discourse and recasts this meaning into the double-voiced questions, thus opening space for re-authoring identities.

Predicting exactly what would be said is difficult. However, if discourse that is problematic were to continue, additional opportunities to renegotiate perspectives and examine teacher identities arise.

TAMI: Tell me more.
BECKY: The vocabulary that they come with. The support they come with from families. The communication that we have is lacking in those children and so they have that experience that requires that we build up their vocabulary. We are trying to give them books. We are trying to give them experiences and so everything is at a much slower pace and its where we are and helping these kids has so much to do with helping the families with so much that I don't think it's a lot different than what we are supporting.
LARA: *As teachers, we certainly want EB students to be successful. If I were one of the students who is enrolled in this school, I wonder what experiences I have had that I would want my teacher to know about that would help her or him see my strengths as a learner. Also, if bilingual teacher were to come into the conversation, I wonder what he or she would add.*

Remain silent for thirty to sixty seconds for the participants to think about their words and what they might say as a student.
Kathy (in role): My aunt likes graphic novels. She brings them to me in English, and helps me read them.
Becky (in role): My sister is a year younger than me, and she likes video games. I teach her how to play some of my games and she is almost as good as me now.

Lara (in role as bilingual teacher): I have met several of the families and children, and I have been impressed by their eagerness to become members of our community. What an opportunity for all of us students to engage in rich language learning experiences.

Others may continue the conversation, and after a period of time, when it appeared that all of study group members who desired to speak had done so, we would step out of role and become ourselves again to debrief the interactions of the research interlude.

Debriefing entails reflecting on how individuals who voiced the inner thoughts of others and stepped into role decided to do so. This metacognitive part of the process encourages participants to notice the multiple meaning systems and modalities (Leu, Lankshear, Knobel, & Coiro, 2014) they may draw on during the research interlude. These may include personal knowledge and experience, popular culture, other texts (linguistic, visual, and gestural), and ideas generated by the dramatic interactions. The debriefing is part of the research interlude and not separate from it. It helps make visible how identities are informed by multiple systems of meaning and can be shifted through awareness of those systems.

Moment Two

Moment two is from a study group transcript of junior high teachers. There are five teachers in the group. Prior to the moment identified below, Lara had been facilitating a discussion about how EB students are integrated into the sixth, seventh, and eighth grade teams. Lara asked whether the seventh and eighth grade teachers all instruct the same group of students. The teachers respond and begin to explain that they "all have the same core of students" but the "ESL" students are not divided among equally among the three grades of teachers, although each team is comprised of 130 students. Lara asks if all ESL-classified students receive support in language acquisition together, and the teacher explains that the students are divided into ability levels for seventh and eighth grade. The next exchange involved Lara asking how sixth grade is different.

LINDA: But yes, we all have the same core of students [Lara: okay] so our team is made up of our 130 kids and we all have that except that I do not have all of the ESL students because I am English . . .

LARA: and they go to ESL when everybody is?

LINDA: Right. We have a breakdown of ESL beginning, intermediate, and advanced so

LARA: And so, they stay with you?
LINDA: Yeah, right.
[Unintelligible]
LARA: So how does sixth grade differ?
WENDY: (unclear) About the same. We have an ESL teacher attached to our team. I came with nothing and they said, "Oh, you are going to the gifted and the ESL".
[Difficult to hear individual voices because of laughter etc.]
LINDA: They are new teachers so they take what is open and this is very hard for some people to do like in our with seventh and eighth grade. Every other team in this building is either all seventh grade or all eighth grade. Whereas we are juggling two curriculums and people don't want to do that. They want to be able to teach the same thing five times a day. Sixth grade they don't have that same setup because it is set up on more of an elementary type, um, curriculum level as far as how they teach but still nobody really wants to deal with these non-English speaking students so the new teachers get them.
STUDY GROUP PARTICIPANTS: [Laughter]

Linda responds that the sixth-grade team has a designated ESL teacher. At this point an explanation about how the sixth grade differs from the seventh and eighth grade teams ensues. Discursively, the construction of a deficit perspective was articulated in the statement, "but still nobody really wants to deal with these non-English speaking students so the new teachers get them," which is followed by laughter from the study group members. It is important to note that the shift from "ESL" that was used earlier to "non-English speaking" is significant because it more explicitly reframes the students based on what they cannot do. Further, the claim that new teachers "get" the "non-English speaking students" also suggests a traditional power structure in the school whereby new teachers, who traditionally have the least capital in a building, are assigned the students that "nobody really wants to deal with." The group laughter that follows this comment can be interpreted as validation of the teacher's statements (Attardo, 2015), and as a paralinguistic feature of the transcription, it signifies an emotional response to the discussion (Chafe, 2007). Pausing the study group conversation just after the group's laughter and implementing a research interlude approach to replay this moment is potentially productive for reframing deficit discourse about EB students.

The group's laughter provides an opportune moment to step in using role play and other process drama tools to reimagine moment two. Following Bakhtin (1984), who argued "Our everyday speech is full of other people's words: with some of them we completely merge our own voice, forgetting whose they are," (p. 195) we theorize laughter in this transcript as double-voiced discourse. The laughter expressed by the group merges the individuals' responses into an emotional expression. And while we cannot know for certain that all of the participants in the study group affirmed a deficit view of learning, the merging of individual's words into collective laughter suggests this as a possible interpretation. Viewed this way, laughter opens space for us to ask "what if," replay the moment, and inquire into how teacher identities are constructed moment by moment. In reimagining and replaying moment two, the research becomes a dialogic data generating activity (Norris, 2009) because stepping into role generates collaboratively produced discourse among the participants.

What follows is moment two reimagined. As with moment one, we use italics to show the drama work and include stage directions to show physical movement and repositioning of participants.

Moment Two Reimagined

As researcher/facilitators, we physically step into the study group conversation. This shifts our position to being in the middle of the exchange and signals that we are participants in the moment as well. Our language is invitational, and we use phrases such as "what if . . ." or "I wonder how" to suggest possibilities for renegotiation of perspectives.

LINDA: They are new teachers so they take what is open and this is very hard for some people to do like in our with seventh and eighth grade. Every other team in this building is either all seventh grade or all eighth grade. Whereas we are juggling two curriculums and people don't want to do that. They want to be able to teach the same thing five times a day. Sixth grade they don't have that same setup because it is set up on more of an elementary type, um curriculum level as far as how they teach but still nobody really wants to deal with these non-English speaking students so the new teachers get them.

STUDY GROUP PARTICIPANTS: [Laughter]

TOM: We were all new teachers once. And, I know for me, that first year was not always easy. I worked hard to balance my enthusiasm of wanting to be successful with learning the ins and outs of working in that school. I made mistakes, learned practical lessons about how to access resources, how to plan lessons that worked, and when to let go of the lessons that flopped. I remember that first month I was so tired at the end of the day. But I kept showing up, and I was fortunate to have experienced teachers working beside me who helped me grow and slowly improve. I invite each of you to think back to when you were a new teacher. Remember that first day? First week? Month? What were some of the emotions you felt? What did you worry about?

We work with silence and ask that no one speak aloud for 30 to 60 seconds. This allows study group members to travel back into their memories and call up those emotions and anxieties associated with that time.

TOM: Lara, would you come sit in the center of our group? [to the group:] Imagine this figure is you as that new teacher. If you could speak to yourself in the past, I wonder what the you in the present would say to your new teacher self in the past. When you're ready, speak to this figure as if it were you. What would you like to tell her or him? After each comment, I am going to ask Lara to smile or laugh softly.

Moving back and forth in time during the research interlude is valuable because playing with time allows us to play with identities. In this case, asking a more experienced, present teacher self to speak to a past new teacher self initiates a dialogic relationship between identities who occupy different spaces in time. This even the case to the novice teachers in the audience who may only be speaking to their selves from weeks or months previously. Speaking to a new teacher self in the past from the present might seem trivial, so facilitator modelling as a participant in the group would be important to show potential insights. Study group participants could provide practical advice, encourage perseverance, even warn their past selves what should be avoided.

Predicting exactly what would be said is difficult. However, to model, after about a minute, Tom would speak to his new teacher self.

TOM: You should respectfully stand up for your principles when you know you are right. This seems scary now, but, I know I gave in sometimes when I shouldn't have. Compromise is always desirable, but remaining opposed is okay. Also, language choices you make to speak to students during instruction and other interactions are so critical. Harsh comments cut, impatient statements belittle. These will derail curiosity and come back to haunt you. Looking back, you should laugh more. It really helps.

Lara [Tilts up her head and smiles or laughs]

The smile or laugh that Lara provides, and lifting of her gaze, are important, and we would ask the participants to interpret her response in response to Tom's comments to tease out how nuances of meaning are communicated in small gestures or sounds. We expect that other participants from the study group will enter into dialogue with their new teacher selves at this point in the process. In the research interlude, we are striving to soften traditional boundaries between new teachers who "get" the EB students that no one else really wants to teach and who more experienced teachers who have more capital therefore do not. We recognize that research interludes do not erase power differentials and successful teaching experience should be acknowledged. However, the tactic of Tom and Lara stepping into the role makes the abstract idea of new teachers' experiences more concrete and personal.

As with moment one, we would debrief and discuss how the participants were accessing their new teacher memories to explore how memories shape our present identities with a goal of discovering five or six themes pertaining to being a new teacher that emerged. After these were identified, tableau work would begin. Tableaus are silent frozen moments that signify concepts, emotions, or experiences. Participants are invited to arrange themselves to represent fear for example without using words. We would ask a sub group of participants create a tableau that shows us one of the themes pertaining to new teachers and then freeze and hold their arrangement for a short period of time. The tableau becomes a text that can be interpreted and revised. We reimagine moment two with tableau work below.

> We ask three of the participants to choose one of the themes, plan a tableau, and then present it to the rest of the group. Once they are ready, the count is one, two, three, and they are asked to "freeze" and hold their positions while the rest of us interpret the tableau text they create.
>
> Questions that help facilitate interpretation.
>
> - What do you see happening?
> - What aspects of new teacher identity is the group showing us?
>
> After a few minutes, we shift one of the figures in the tableau by asking an individual participant to raise or drop her arms, face away or inward toward the others, step back away, or similar positional changes, and the interpretation of the text changes for us as interpretants.
>
> Questions to facilitate re-interpretation
>
> - How has this tableau changed?
> - What aspects of teacher identity are they showing us now?

In this part of the research interlude we are generating data to help us think differently about deficit discourses. That new teacher referred to in the conversation has now moved closer to us, and we remember being that person in our pasts and generate new discourse about those previous identities. As study group participants, we are action researchers exploring teacher identities by dramatically investigating how deficit discourses can be shifted toward more relational and asset-based views of learning. Edmiston and Wilhem (1996) theorized action research with teachers as a mode of drama as research that could examine "how their actions change, change in the classroom context, and effect the relationships between people" (p. 95). The participants in this study group could analyze data generated by the two segments of the research interlude for reimagining moment two, Lara in role as the figure of new teacher, and the tableau. Analyzing this new layer of data could help us see and revise (see anew) our previous new teacher identities and better understand how we have become the teachers we are now and the teachers we desire to be.

In the reimagining of both moments, process drama is used to create spaces within professional development where members of the study group can reflect on how discourses shape and inform our teacher identities moment by moment. Further, we can recognize that identities are dynamic and can be re-authored through working in role and applying other tools. As such, we can understand possibilities for reframing professional development as identity work rather than technical training. Overall, a research interlude is a potentially powerful inquiry method to bring to teacher professional development. In the next section, we describe guidelines and practices for using this approach.

Research Interludes in Professional Development

Like process drama, research interludes do not require training as an actor or actress. What it does require is what Coleridge (1907) called the "willing suspension of disbelief," and what Edmiston (2003, 2014) has argued is the ability to ask "What if" to imaginatively explore other possibilities to understand social interactions. In research interludes, imagination is a research tool to help generate alternative data and make sense of social interactions within teacher study groups for professional development. Imagination in research interludes helps us visualize how situations could be "otherwise" (Enciso, 2017, p. 29) and push our thinking beyond overly simplistic understandings of phenomena. For example, in moment one, the teacher uses the term "disadvantaged families," which implies the opposite as an unstated norm—families with advantages—against which immigrant families are positioned.

However, when we use research interludes within a process drama frame to imaginatively step into role as members of an immigrant family, affordances of that family are recognized. Facilitating research interludes requires becoming familiar with specific practices in order to shift teacher study groups away from technical training to engaging in identity work. In this next section, we describe these practices.

The Practices of Research Interludes

Bolton (1996) argues that using dramatic structures in research is not an easy task and urges caution when involving teachers in systematic inquiry. It would be easy to tell teachers in a study group, "Now, you are researchers investigating identity," but that is not how research interludes work. A key aspect of this approach is developing details about roles that you want study group participants to take on and building trust with participants. This is vital to using research interludes in professional development.

Research interludes draw on action research and reflective practice, particularly as they have been applied within a dramatic context (Norris, 2016; Erel, Reynolds, & Kaptani, 2017). Action research involves participants systematically investigating their own practice with the intention of improving it. When process drama informs action research, imagination is foregrounded and becomes central to the inquiry process. In process drama, the teacher or facilitator is not separate from the process of creating a drama world (O'Neill, 1995), but rather is central to the process. Research interludes position teachers as co-researchers and as central to the process of researching teacher identities in the study group.

Learning to recognize moments of discomfort in which deficit or other problematic discourses are being produced, moments of understanding, awareness, epiphanies about professional identity, or other significant developments as teachers work in study groups requires some experience using process drama. However, we all grow as teachers and researchers from doing the work of instruction and inquiry. Actively listening to the discussion, focusing on language, and noticing body movements and positioning are all important for determining when to stop the discussion, examine the dialogue, and replay moments as part of identity research.

We recognize that it takes some skill and practice to bring research interludes into professional development, and we advocate for drama work as central to teacher preparation and professional development in the last chapter of this book. To conclude this chapter, we briefly describe three important elements of using research interludes: (1) developing role details and building trust; (2) positioning teachers as co-action researchers; and (3) identifying moments that warrant intervention.

Developing Role Details and Building Trust

Developing details for roles pertinent to research interludes in study groups and building trust work together. We recommend the following practices.

- At the beginning of the study group meeting engage in a discussion of what research interludes are and how they will be used as part of professional development.
- Use warm up activities, such as stating your name in a way that siginfys an aspect of your personality, or standing in a small circle and clapping hands, or other gestures and then inviting others in the circle to add other movements of gestures to create a rhythm for the circle, to build trust among the group.

Positioning Teachers as Co-action Researchers

To position teachers as co-action researchers in the study group requires some initial roleplaying that is safe enough so that teachers will it. We recommend the following.

- Beginning in the Middle—In this situation we work in role as researchers involved in a project that has been going on for a while. Making lists of what tools we might need, creating a social history of the group, and identifying our findings and successes would be important so that we can feel like researchers.
- Discussing action research by debriefing after the work in role so that the fictional informs the real.

Identifying Moments that Warrant Intervention

Identifying moments of tension like those described in moments one and two earlier in this chapter will initially be the work of facilitators. However, as the study group works together over time, the hope is that participants as co-action researchers would identity moments of tension as well. We recommend the following.

- As the study group discussion flows, videorecord it to capture the discourses produced.
- Review the discussion with the group, stoping at key points, and ask participants to "think aloud" with the group about their interpretation of what was going on in the group.

These recommendations are designed to set up a community of trust and willingness to ask what if, think imaginatively, and invite study group participants into spaces with us where we can explore who we are as teachers and who we would like to be. However, while we view processes within research interludes as playful, we also understand them as a serious research endeavors that could redefine relationships among data, imaginative play, analysis, as well as researcher and participant relationships (Crumpler, Handsfield, & Dean, 2011). Redefining these relationships among researcher, participants, data generation, and analysis, and asking about our own complicity in the production of deficit views of learners and communities has been studied by others in our field (Alvermann & Hagood, 2000; Eakle, 2007; Leander & Rowe, 2006). We believe research interludes enrich this conversation and provide new practices to study the complexities of teacher identity work.

In the final chapter, we argue for reimagining research on teacher identity from a dramatic frame. We present two scenes of research using transcript data from study group discussions from the project. Based on these scenes, we show how tools and structures of process drama we have highlighted throughout this book open new vistas into studying teacher identities.

References

Acton, R., & Glasgow, P. (2015). Teacher wellbeing in neoliberal contexts: A review of the literature. *Australian Journal of Teacher Education*, 40(8), 6.

Alvermann, D. E., & Hagood, M. C. (2000). Critical media literacy: Research, theory, and practice in "New Times". *The Journal of Educational Research, 93*(3), 193–205.

Attardo, S. (2015). Humor and laughter. In *The handbook of discourse analysis* (pp. 168–188). Chichester, England: Wiley.

Avalos, B. (2011). Teacher professional development in teaching and teacher education over ten years. *Teaching and Teacher Education, 27*(1), 10–20.

Bakhtin, M. M. (1984). *Problems of Dostoevsky's poetics* (C. Emerson, Trans.). Minneapolis, MN: University of Minnesota Press.

Branscombe, M., & Schneider, J. J. (2013). Embodied discourse: Using tableau to explore preservice teachers' reflections and activist stances. *Journal of Language and Literacy Education, 9*(1), 95–113.

Britzman, D. P. (2012). *Practice makes practice: A critical study of learning to teach.* New York, NY: Suny Press.

Butler, L. B., & Schnellert, L. (2012). Collaborative inquiry in teacher professional development. *Teaching and Teacher Education, 28*(8), 1206–1220.

Chafe, W. L. (2007). *The importance of not being earnest: The feeling behind laughter and humor* (Vol. 3). Amsterdam, the Netherlands: John Benjamins Publishing.

Chan, K. W., & Elliott, R. G. (2004). Relational analysis of personal epistemology and conceptions about teaching and learning. *Teaching and Teacher Education, 20*(8), 817–831.

Coleridge, S. J. (1817, 1907). *Biographia Literaria* (J. Shawcross, Ed., 2 Vols.). Oxford, UK: Oxford University Press.

Crumpler, T., Handsfield, L., & Dean, T. (2011). Constructing difference differently in language and literacy professional development. *Research in the Teaching of English, 46*(1), 55–91. (Research supported by Spencer Foundation.)

de finna, A., Schiffrin, D., & Bamberg, M. (2006). *Discourse and identity.* Cambridge, UK: Cambridge University Press.

Denzin, N. K. (2003). *Performance ethnography: Critical pedagogy and the politics of culture.* Thousand Oaks, CA: Sage.

Eakle, A. J. (2007). Literacy spaces of a Christian faith-based school. *Reading Research Quarterly, 42*(4), 472–510.

Edmiston, B. (2003). What's my position? Role, frame and positioning when using process drama. *Research in Drama Education, 8*(2), 221–230.

Edmiston, B., & Wilhelm, J. (1996). Playing in different keys: Research notes for action researchers and reflective drama practitioners. *Researching drama and arts education: Paradigms and possibilities.* London: Falmer Press, 85–96.

Enciso, P. E. (2017). Stories lost and found: Mobilizing imagination in literacy research and practice. *Literacy Research: Theory, Method, and Practice, 66*(1), 29–52.

Endacott, J. L., Wright, G. P., Goering, C. Z., Collet, V. S., Denny, G. S., & Davis, J. J. (2015). Robots teaching other little robots: Neoliberalism, CCSS, and teacher professionalism. *Review of Education, Pedagogy, and Cultural Studies, 37*(5), 414–437.

Erel, U., Reynolds, T., & Kaptani, E. (2017). Participatory theatre for transformative social research. *Qualitative Research, 17*(3), 302–312.

Greer, C. (2006) The discursive construction of teacher identities. In A. de finna, D. Schiffrin, & M. Bamberg (Eds.), *Discourse and identity* (pp. 188–213). Cambridge, UK: Cambridge University Press.

Hall, D., & McGinity, R. (2015). Conceptualizing teacher professional identity in neoliberal times: Resistance, compliance and reform. *education policy analysis archives, 23*, 88.

Hollins, E. R. (2015). *Rethinking field experiences in preservice teacher preparation: Meeting new challenges for accountability.* New York, NY: Routledge.

Kennedy, M. M. (2016). How does professional development improve teaching?. *Review of Educational Research, 86*(4), 945–980.

Kershaw, B. (1992). *The politics of performance.* London: Routledge.

Leander, K. M., & Rowe, D. W. (2006). Mapping literacy spaces in motion: A rhizomatic analysis of a classroom literacy performance. *Reading Research Quarterly, 41*(4), 428–460.

Leu, D. J., Lankshear, C., Knobel M., & Corio, J. (2014). Central issues in new literacies and new literacies research. In *Handbook of research on new literacies* (pp. 19–40). New York, NY: Routledge.

Little, J. W. (1993). Teachers' professional development in a climate of educational reform. *Educational Evaluation and Policy Analysis, 15*(2), 129–151.

Lortie, D. C. (2002). *Schoolteacher: A sociological study.* Chicago, IL: Chicago University Press.

Mockler, N. (2012). Teacher professional learning in a neoliberal age: Audit, professionalism and identity. *Australian Journal of Teacher Education, 38*(10), n10.

Moll, L. C., Amanti, C., Neff, D., & Gonzalez, N. (1992). Funds of knowledge for teaching: Using a qualitative approach to connect homes and classrooms. *Theory into Practice, 31*(2), 132–141.

Norris, J. (2009). *Playbuilding as qualitative research: A participatory arts-based approach.* New York, NY: Routledge.

Norris, J. (2016). Drama as research: Realizing the potential of drama in education as a research methodology. *Youth Theatre Journal, 30*(2), 122–135.

Rodenburg, P. (1993). *The Need for Words: Voice and the text.* London: Methuen Drama.

Sondel, B., Kretchmar, K., & Hadley Dunn, A. (2019). "Who Do These People Want Teaching Their Children?" White Saviorism, Colorblind Racism, and Anti-Blackness in "No Excuses" Charter Schools. Urban Education. https://doi.org/10.1177/0042085919842618

Stanley, A. M. (2011). Professional development within collaborative teacher study groups: Pitfalls and promises. *Arts Education Policy Review, 112*, 71–78.

Vangrieken, K., Meredith, C., Packer, T., & Kyndt, E. (2017). Teacher communities as a context for professional development: A systematic review. *Teaching and Teacher Education, 61*, 47–59.

· 7 ·
REIMAGINING TEACHER IDENTITY RESEARCH—A DRAMATIC APPROACH

In this current educational climate, which privileges autonomous ideologies of teaching, learning, and identity (Street, 1995), teaching is situated a-temporally and a-spatially. In other words, teaching is too often viewed instrumentally as a set of skills to be mastered that can be applied in any context. One result is that instructional practices are often presented in a decontextualized fashion and conceived primarily as "best practices" (Duke & Del Nero, 2011) that translate across timescales and space-times of classrooms, schools, and districts with minimal attention to how teacher identities interlace with classroom pedagogies and teacher development.

Of course, we understand that there are some teaching practices that, based on research in literacy teaching and learning, are more effective than others. For example, the all-too-familiar practice of "round robin reading" (Ash, Kuhn, & Walpole, 2008) is ineffective for promoting comprehension and oral reading fluency (Rasinksi & Nageldinger, 2016). However, a view of instruction that ignores the importance of teacher identity development positions teachers as technicians who need to merely learn sets of teaching strategies and apply them in whatever classrooms they find themselves. We wonder, for example, how teacher identity development relates to a teacher's decision to use round robin reading as an instructional practice, despite the lack of research evidence supporting the practice. What are the discourses (personal, professional, institutional) and relations of power shaping a teacher's choices to implement a teaching strategy that is widely criticized in the professional and research literature? Contexts and the discourses of schooling and identity that we have analyzed and described throughout this book are critical for understanding complex processes of teacher development. Ignoring them inhibits both preservice and practicing teachers from recognizing the dynamic nature of identity work and from potentially gaining insights and agency into their own ongoing professional development.

Throughout the preceding chapters, we drew on theories of space and time, in particular the work of Bakhtin (1986), to argue that, like languages, teacher identities are dialogic; indeed, they are practices rather than *things*. We foreshadowed using practices informed by process drama to encourage teachers to systematically inquire into traditional and new identities. This inquiry is situated in a qualitative approach of interpretive and performative research (Denzin, 1997, 2003) and positions process drama practices such as working in role, tableau, research interludes, and others as research tools to generate, analyze, and interpret data about identity development. Dialogically, we argue for positioning preservice and inservice teachers as researchers of and informants regarding their own professional identity development (Edmiston & Wilhelm, 1998) and believe a "productive tension" (Smagorinsky et al., 2004) is created that helps participants disrupt binary thinking. We use dramatic tools to help teachers recognize these tensions, create opportunities to push past them, and think differently about identity.

Building on work in our own teacher education program, we offer dramatic sequences in this chapter that invite preservice and inservice teachers to critically examine their own professional identities and systematically inquire into how these identities are constructed and shift in both small moments and longer timespaces. These sequences are based on process drama as a research method to explore teacher identities in preservice instruction and professional development. In this chapter we return to the concept of research interludes (Crumpler, Handsfield, & Dean, 2011) and other dramatic tools as tactics (de Certeau, 1984) to pause conversations among preservice or inservice teachers, "replay" moments of identity construction, and analyze how these moments could be reimagined. Research interludes allow for what we term ongoing active repositioning," which moves beyond member checking to "recognize and open space for playing with and redistribute relations of power which are part of all research" (Crumpler, Handsfield, & Dean, 2011, p. 79). This approach will allow for reimagining teacher identity research with an emphasis on reflexivity and participants as co-constructors of data (Hunt, Crumpler, & Handsfield, 2015).

We begin with a synthesis of scholarship in process drama as a research method. Then, we present two "research scenes" (Norris, 2000) of identity work (one for preservice and one for inservice teachers) developed from data we generated during our project.

Process Drama as an Approach to Research

Drama as a research method and is not new and has been described by important scholars in drama education (Bolton, 1996; Carroll, Anderson, & Cameron, 2006; Edmiston & Wilhelm, 1996; Neelands, 1990; Norris, 2000, 2017; Raphael & O' Mara, 2002, Taylor, 1996). Taylor (1996), drawing on Britzman (1991), summarized the potential for process drama to discover theory in practice. He argued "The field setting becomes the site wherein understandings are shaped, and the bases for curriculum action developed, in other words, the field is the direct site of theorizing" (p. 5). The field could be university classrooms where preservice teachers are educated, or schools where inservice teachers work. However, the field can also be the *drama world* (O'Neill, 1995) created by participants as they use the imaginary to explore the real and develop multiple perspectives on identity development (Edmiston, 2014). Edmiston and Wilhelm (1998) contended that "imagining the world through others' eyes is essential if we are to understand some of the complexities of other people, times, and places" (p. 99). We extend this idea to show how analyzing and reimagining teachers' own identities through their own and others' eyes helps them understand the complexities of their professional growth.

Recent scholarship has investigated how drama can be utilized to investigate teacher identity work in inservice and preservice preparation, second language instruction and classroom settings (Branscombe & Schneider, 2018; Cook-Sather, 2006; Dutton & Rushton, 2018; Piazzoli, 2012; Powers & Duffy, 2016). Together, these studies spurred our thinking as we stepped back to complete this book and reimagine how dramatic tools and structures could help us open theoretical and pedagogical windows into studying both preservice and inservice identity development with participants.

One of the key insights from our research is the importance of small moments of interactions in classrooms. In those moments, preservice and inservice teachers can scale jump (Lempert, 2012) from novice to experienced teacher and recruit other discourses, such as motherhood, to mediate multiple ideologies and positionings in their work. We also recognize that identity work occurs across longer time scales (Lemke, 2000) as well, such as the duration from teacher education course work through student teaching. We wondered how we might prompt teachers to notice and examine the complexities of their work in different time scales and position both preservice and inservice participants as co-investigators along with us to look deeply into identity development.

Gavin Bolton (1996) saw the promise and challenge of process drama for research over two decades ago. He recognized the potential of participants as co-researchers in process drama Bolton (1996), pushed researchers to build on reflection in action (Schon, 2017), and consider the methodological challenges of involving participants in process drama in systematic research. Bolton also argued that assigning participants as researchers similar to assigning preservice teachers into groups as part of teaching or inservice teachers into groups as part of professional development is not enough. In other words, Bolton recognized that participants must *identify* as researchers through framing the intellectual work of learning in which they are engaged. This is not easy.

For us, process drama offers a way to theoretically frame scenes of research (O'Neill, 1996) and mobilize investigative methods (Edmiston, 2016) to explore the complexities of preservice and inservice identity work. Our goal is to provide careful, detailed description of research methods that can be used by other researchers who seek new strategies to shift their research on teacher identity toward drama-oriented practices. If we examine identity work in this way, we must address relations of difference and power in teacher education, including race and language. Recent researchers have noted the importance of this work (Lensmire, et al.) and suggested using play building and other qualitative strategies to investigate constructions of "Whiteness" with secondary students (Tanner, 2016). We extend this scholarship to preservice and inservice teachers by using process drama with teacher candidates and inservice teachers. In the excerpts and redramatization of them in chapter 6 and in this chapter, we see the power of whiteness emerging through deficit discourses. The next section provides background and details for two research scenes.

Research Scenes

Similar to research interludes in professional development, discussed in the previous chapter, research scenes use process drama as a research approach and are facilitated by a teacher-researcher who is also a participant in the scene. As we have conceptualized them, research scenes are dialogic in that they involve creation of multiple voices and perspectives to examine issues from diverse perspectives and move participants into other roles and timespaces. Scene One focuses on data from a preservice teacher literacy memoir, and Tom facilitates the scene. Scene Two includes data from one of the study group discussions of inservice teachers and Lara facilitates this scene.

Before we introduce the scenes, Table 7.1 defines some terms from process drama that we use as research tools in each scene (Bolton, 1979, 1992: Edmiston, 2014; O'Neill, 1995) and can be used to investigate teacher identities. We also include the research purposes and the type of data generated so that the potential of using this approach is evident.

Scene One Overview

We draw on Norris' more recent scholarship (2009) about what he calls "play building" (p. 21) in qualitative research to develop these research scenes and show how collaboratively, educators, teachers, and preservice teachers can generate, analyze, and interpret data. Conceptualizing research scenes to explore identity illustrates the value of our approach and allows us to demonstrate tactics to play with time and space as we examine preservice and inservice teacher identity work with participants. In the first research scene, we begin by describing the framing so that the preservice teachers are positioned as researchers with social history, not just arbitrarily assigned the role.

This scene stages an excerpt from an assignment collected in phase one of our project that was often used in the first of our institution's literacy methods classes, literacy memoirs. The literacy memoir was the initial assignment in the course, which introduced preservice teachers to expanding understandings of literacy and literacy practices, language development, and how children become literate in classroom and community contexts. Instructors introduced preservice teachers to language cueing systems, concepts of multimodality, print and digital literacies, children's literature, as well as other aspects of language and literacy development, and they completed observations of literacy practices in diverse community contexts.

Table 7.1: Process Terms as Research Tools.

Term	Definition	Research Purpose	Data Generated
Drama World	Context generated as a result of participant's interactions with the real and imaginary	To create another field for inquiry into teacher identity	Interactions in which identities are created through the imaginary informing the real
In role	Teachers, teacher interns, and teacher educators in role as someone other than themselves	To explore multiple perspectives and viewpoints in a research scene	Interactions of participants taking on another identity
Tableau	Silent, frozen moments in which teachers and teacher interns, teacher educators arrange themselves in ways that signal meaning	To create meaning and interpretation of a modality other than linguistic	Interactions that are gestural, open to multiple interpretations, and embody identity development
Research Interlude	Research interludes are moments of discomfort in which the facilitator steps into the discussion, stops the discourse, and invites participants to replay the moment in order to explore other perspectives	To construct opportunities to critically examine how particular discourses can position participants in certain roles, signal deficit thinking or other contentious views.	Participants Coconstructing data with researchers as identities are shifted through replaying moments of interaction
Ongoing active repositioning	During research interludes, the facilitator of a research scene repositions participants to examine issues of power in research work	To use imaginative play to create a space in which issues of power can explored that is safe for participants.	Interactions that show how issues of power are situated in identity development
Social History	Building a history of participants connections to a community or enterprise to deepen investment in creating the drama world	Creates opportunities for deeper buy in to working in role rather than just assigning roles to participants	Reflection about how participants play with time as they construct identities in role

Table 7.1: *Continued*

Term	Definition	Research Purpose	Data Generated
Tapping In	Facilitator of research scene "taps" lightly on the shoulder of a participant in a tableau and asks others to speculate aloud what the participant is thinking.	To invite participants to collaboratively construct an "inner voice" of an individual	Interactions of how participants chorally articulate the identity of an individual
Debriefing	Participants step out of role and are themselves again to talk about how they were making decisions in role	To work at the metacognitive level of analysis and invite participants to articulate what affordances they drew on while in role.	Reflective accounts about what resources or meaning systems participants draw on to work in role.

The literacy memoir assignment invited preservice teachers to compose a narrative describing an important aspect or moment of their development as literate individuals. Many teacher candidates wrote about reading with a mother or grandmother, or how a favorite teacher had changed their view of reading or showed them the pleasure of reading a new genre such as poetry. Some memoirs included dialogue in which preservice teachers recounted conversations with parents or other family members about choosing books to read or recreated interior monologues reporting their own thinking about book choices or memorable experiences.

We use the literacy memoir as both pretext (the genesis for the dramatic work) and as data to interpret. The beginning of the scene describes classroom instruction with a group of preservice teachers, positions them as researchers, and introduces a memoir written by a preservice teacher, Janice. Then, there is discussion in which Tom poses questions about definitions of literacy teaching implied by the memoir, and leads the group into a discussion about identities suggested by the memoir.

Using tools of process drama, Tom moves the group into a series of role plays, and tableau work designed to challenge preservice teachers to investigate aspects of Janice's identity as well as their own, and invite preservice teachers into other timespaces as a part of collaborative research. Janice is a fictional character and the dialogue among the preservice teachers is imagined and created to show the possibilities of our approach for research into teacher identities. As noted in the previous chapter, process drama requires that the individual facilitating the dramatic work be a participant as well. Therefore, it is impossible to predetermine the exact direction of the scene because improvisational decisions are made based on what unfolds at the moment, and how the participants respond (O'Neill, 1995). The "script" below is used to show possibilities for collaborative inquiry, but it is not written to be reproduced exactly, and every research scene will be different. We would videorecord the scene and involve preservice teachers in interpretation as another layer of data generation (Crumpler, Handsfield, & Dean, 2011).

Research Scene One—Preservice Literacy Memoir

In the Classroom

The literacy methods class is composed of 30 preservice teachers, all of whom are white and female. This is a typical demographic in our courses and not unlike other predominantly white teacher education institutions. The preservice teachers have been introduced to process drama and participated in dramatic work earlier in the semester. Further, they have been briefed ahead of time about the use of drama work as research and agreed to be involved process drama activities as a facet of the course. Our work takes place over two classroom meetings. The next section demonstrates our framing, or positioning, of the preservice teachers as researchers within the scene.

Researching Identity With Literacy Memoir—Day 1

> Tom: Good morning. Today we have some data to look at. It's an excerpt from a literacy memoir from a preservice teacher. I have made copies for each of you. As co-researchers who have worked together for a while now, I wonder if we could reaffirm what strategies and skills we will need to analyze this piece of data.
>
> Teacher Candidate 1: Reading really closely, making inferences, identifying themes, that kind of thing?
>
> Tom: Right, those types of analytical skills will be vital. Anything else?

Teacher Candidate 2: I think research is about testing hypotheses. It's what scientists do.

Tom: You are right. That is one kind of research. Our research is more about exploring ideas, but we will be working collaboratively, like scientists do.

Teacher Candidate 3: Listening to each other will be important. Maybe collaborating too.

Tom: Good. Yes, those are important. Thank you. Before we start, I would like to move back in time to a few hours before this meeting. I would like you to think about what actions you were doing to prepare for our research together today. When you are ready, position yourself somewhere in the room and imagine yourself doing that action—whatever it is.

- The purpose of this framing activity is to invite preservice teachers to identify as researchers. After everyone has moved around the room and is engaged in their action, Tom asks one of the class members to freeze and hold their position for a about ten seconds. The group observes the person and speculates on what action they are doing and how it might help prepare for research.

Tom: Alright, now our research meeting is about to begin. Please bring your chair into the circle in the middle of our research office. I need your expertise today to analyze and interpret this literacy memoir in terms of what it suggests to us about how the writer understands teaching literacy. Here is the excerpt from the memoir written by Janice. I have copies for each of you, and I will project it up on the Smart Board as well.

"Okay everyone, we are going to get started. Everyone find a comfortable place on the carpet." It was the same time every morning and happened about the same way.
 "Quote from beginning of book."
 As we all sat attentively, I watched and listened as she read. Something about the way the words came out made every child in the class freeze and take in every word she said. She sat in her white rocking chair, as we all found comfortable seats on the beanbags, small chairs around the outside of the carpet, or the red carpet. I always sat in front so I was able to really get into the book without being distracted by my peers. I sat and enjoyed her reading to us. It was favorite time of everyday in the 1st grade.
 Mrs. LaMagna was my first-grade teacher, and I can remember vividly the times when she read to my class each day. The book I can best recall is The Boxcar Children. I loved the series of books all through my elementary years, and still do to this day.

Tom: After you have read through these data, turn to the researcher sitting next to you and talk with her about what you notice in this text and any initial themes you have identified.

- Sharing in partners allows the preservice teachers in role as researchers to rehearse their ideas and interpretations.

Tom: Let's hear from researchers—what did you talk about with your partner? As you tell me what you noticed, I will list your ideas on the Smart Board.

- At this point in the scene, tableau work (silent moments in which individuals position themselves to represent a theme) would be used as a tool to enhance interpretive thinking through creation of embodied texts. Recent research (Branscombe and Schneider, 2018) used tableau and other dramatic structures to explore how preservice teachers conceptualized their future pedagogical practices and solved instructional dilemmas. In this research scene, we use tableau for three purposes. First, tableau work provides a way to demonstrate multiple interpretations of a text. Second, the interpretations themselves become another layer of data to analyze. Third, videorecording allows us to view the tableaus as a group to debrief and reflect on how gesture and body movements signal meaning.

Tom: I would like to begin tableau work in which we create tableaus in groups of four. Choose one of the themes we have generated and develop a tableau to represent the theme. As your co-researchers, we will interpret the text you create.

- During the tableaus, I ask the group to interpret what each one is signifying. Then, I would ask individual members in the tableau to shift their position (turn and face a different direction, raise or drop their arms, sit or stand, etc.) and then ask the group to reinterpret what they see. This aspect of the research demonstrates how small gestural changes can shift meaning. At the end of the tableau work I ask the group to come back together as a class to debrief about decisions they were making on a metacognitive level. In other words, what meaning systems (personal, professional, cultural) were individuals accessing as they composed their tableaus? This would end the first day of our research.

Scene One—Day 2

Tom: Let's begin by returning to the memoir we analyzed yesterday and focus on the teacher, Mrs. LaMagna. Based on Janice's narrative, how would you characterize her as a teacher, and what in the memoir suggested this to you?

- The excerpt from Janice's memoir presents a classroom where the first graders are mesmerized by the teacher's read aloud. Her memories are "vivid." She sat in a rocking chair like a favorite grandmother. As the facilitator, I want the preservice teachers to interpret this description and begin to move into investigating identity. We would discuss how they were understanding Janice's view of Mrs. LaMagna and then facilitate a discussion that attempts to tease out their perceptions of her identity. This is important for the next phase of this research scene in which I step into role as the teacher with the preservice teachers as my audience. Entering the realm of "what if" (Norris, 2000, p. 41), I would ask the preservice teachers, "what if you could talk with Mrs. LaMagna in the second day of the research scene? I wonder what you would ask her." Also, at this point, I want use the idea of another spacetime. Therefore, I enter into the role of Mrs. LaMagna as the experienced teacher who is now teaching in a new school that is much more diverse. In role as Mrs. LaMagna, I am not completely comfortable teaching first graders that do not look like me. What follows is fictional account of how the conversation could go.

Tom: Well good morning all. It is so great to be here, and thanks for inviting me to your class this morning. I am Mrs. LaMagna, a first grade teacher at Brown Elementary. I just started there after 15 years at my previous school. I didn't want to leave, but the district transferred me, and I am making the best of it. It is so great to see all of these young people who want to be teachers. I am glad Dr. Crumpler left us alone here so that we can talk candidly about teaching. Maybe the best way to start is for you to ask me questions.

Student 1: You said you are "making the best of it." Can you tell me more what you mean?

Tom (in role): Well, the students are very different that's for sure. In my previous school the students all were polite, listened, and I never had a problem. Parents cared more too. At Brown, some days, it is a zoo. So many students are late, they come unprepared, and I have been teaching for 25 years now; I know how to teach a child to read. But some of these students come from homes where there are few or no books and literacy is not valued. Don't get me wrong, I do my best to make sure all of them are learning. It's challenge though, but I do my best for the students, and make a difference in their lives.

Student 2: How do you know literacy is not valued? Have you visited their homes? I remember we talked about the value of visiting student homes and learning the community in our class.

Tom (in role): A good idea of course but not practical for two reasons. Many of these students live in neighborhoods that are not safe. And second, a lot of the parents are not fluent speakers of English. For me those are roadblocks that *I* cannot get around. I am *always* available to meet with families after school though.

Student 2's question to Mrs. LaMagna disrupts the frame of Whiteness mentioned earlier in this chapter. Mrs. LaMagna's response dismisses the question with faint praise and then recites stereotypical complaints about unsafe neighborhoods, and lack of English proficiency among parents. She concludes with emphasizing her availability if parents are willing to meet on her terms. Moments like this one, analytically re-imagined within a process drama-based approach to investigating teacher identity, open possibilities for change.

- One of the primary reasons to videorecord these interactions is so that we can pause them and use research interludes to analyze how within small moments of interaction, identities are being constructed. After an exchange like the one above, it would be useful to use a research interlude to stop, evaluate how identity was being performed, and replay this moment to explore other possibilities. Inviting the preservice teachers to review the language and gestures of my performance as it is replayed frame by frame would show how identities are performed moment by moment.
- It is important for Mrs. LaManga to not be merely a straw figure to easily discredit. From a research perspective, we are trying to create a productive tension so that complex issues about identity can be examined, reconstructed, and re-performed differently. To complete research scene one, I would invite preservice teachers to step into role as colleagues of Mrs. LaManga. I would build a social history by asking them to work in pairs, and discuss how long they had been at Brown elementary, what grade they were teaching and what they had heard or knew about Mrs. LaMagna as a teacher. Then, I would come back into role as assistant principal Jones to talk with them about her.
- Finally, we would step out of role and, as ourselves again, debrief about what meaning systems they were drawing when they were in role as teachers at Brown Elementary. Importantly, we would connect these to broader ideologies of teaching, learning, and literacy, including deficit discourses, and concepts such as funds of knowledge.

Framing Research Scene Two—*Inservice Teachers*

In this second scene, we imagine working with a group of inservice teachers who are interested in identity. In our project all but one of the teachers who participated was white, and all but two were female. This reflected the demographics of the school district we worked in as described in Chapter 2. In research scene two, we draw on these demographics to imagine a professional development workshop of thirty teachers who have indicated an interest inquiring into teacher identity and how it impacts literacy instruction. There is a range of teaching experience among the group from four to fifteen years in the classroom.

The following transcript data is from a discussion group with middle school inservice teachers at Prairie Central. Working as the facilitator, Lara invites the group to analyze these data using tools of process drama during a professional development workshop. This excerpt includes exchanges between Linda, Penny, and Lara. Lara creates a social history of the group by welcoming them into a role of expertise as teachers who expressed interest in collaborative research.

Research Scene Two-One Day Workshop

Lara: Welcome to the research project on teacher identity and thank you for agreeing to work on this important project. I know how valuable your time is, and I am excited to begin this work with you today that focuses on understanding the role teacher identity has in supporting effective instruction. I have piece of data that I would like us to analyze together. It is a transcript of a discussion about working with multilingual students students. I was actually a part of this discussion, and tried to clarify for the group the questions that were being asked.

- At this point in the transcript data, the study group was talking about experiences and opportunities the district had provided them to work with EB students. Linda asks the group to focus on "experiences, opportunities, and philosophy," Penny responds with questions, and then Lara comments to focus the discussion.

Linda: So, any of those three topics. If you want to start piggybacking off of each other, then for a few minutes [Bell rings] I will try to take [Intercom voices] some notes.

	Then I'll shut up and let you do what you came here to do. So experiences, opportunities, and philosophy are kind of the three areas.
Penny:	What? Experiences?
Lara:	Experiences, what opportunities? You know what has the district offered you? How did you come to know what you know? And what do they offer you now in the way of developmental growth in terms of EB students, and then philosophically how do you feel about what you are doing? And it does not have to be in that order; just begin with whatever is on the top of your head and I might even jump in with some thoughts too.
Penny:	Well, I think the big thing is the training because there really has been none. It has all been trial and error. I mean we were asked if we wanted when we first started three years ago if we wanted to be on the ESL team, and a group of us got together. It is not the same group today as it was then. It has changed a little bit, but we got together and said, "Well what do you think?" We have to teach seventh and eighth grade so we have two grade curriculums to cover. Hum—but we would have these ESL students—whatever that is [H: laughter] and so it might make our classes a little less crowded than some of the other team's classes seem to be, and a [bell rings and intercom: (unintelligible)] (unclear) so we went "oh, okay, we are going to do it" and so for the first two years we didn't have the ESL teacher attached to our team. She just came as often as she could and she was beating her head against a brick wall because none of us had any formal training, so we knew nothing about what we were doing and, uh, so this year has been the best because she is attached to our team and she can guide us and help us and so she gives us little mini seminars during our team times and, uh, but the training has fallen on her. We don't have any formal training [P: that's not her job] No, that's not her job but because she feels so strongly about it and we all would like to know how to help them a little better and so she has taken over the role of trainer and, so we use some of our team time listening to her. She has given us booklets and put together notebooks for us and strategies and all kinds of things.
Linda:	How much time do you have with her in the course of a week or a day, or is she permanently assigned to your classroom all the time, or does she go to other buildings or?
Penny:	No, this year she is permanently attached to our team, which is the first year we have had that. She normally had to bounce between sixth and other teams because she also had to teach Spanish for a while and, a, so she had a class she had to teach. And this year she is strictly assigned to us which is really nice and very beneficial for us and for the students too because we get to know them a little better and she can give us insight into them. And a, so I think that it has helped a lot but so far as meeting with her on her agenda half a class period once a week, if that.
Lara:	As you read through this transcript data, what themes did you notice what jumped out at you?

- If teachers are reluctant to identify themes, Lara will volunteer some examples

Lara: One of the themes that I noticed was lack of district support for teaching EB students in Penny's comments. Did others notice this too? I would like to use process drama to unpack this and delve more deeply into that idea so we can analyze it together. When we think about district support what ideas are associated with it?

Inservice Teacher 1: Access to resources, curricular materials, maybe demonstration lessons?

Inservice Teacher 2: RESOURCES is right. How about an aid our classrooms that is fluent in Spanish? And we need more PD about working with English learners in Middle school.

Lara: What about Penny's comment in the transcript about the ESL teacher being "strictly assigned to us"? She saw that as beneficial, didn't she? What if you could talk someone who could make decisions and recommendations—an Assistant Superintendent for example—about what is working for teaching EB learners and what is needed to improve instruction? I wonder what questions you would ask. Could each of you write down one question you would ask if you could talk to her?

- At this point in the scene Lara steps into role as an Assistant Superintendent

Lara (In role): Welcome to today's meeting about how to more effectively teach second language learners. Many of you know me. I am the assistant superintendent in our district, Debbie Jones. Superintendent Green asked me to invite you all here today. You were invited to this meeting because you have been identified as excellent teachers and we value your input. She understands there are concerns about teaching second language learners. I am here to listen your concerns and report back to her so that decisions can be made.

Inservice Teacher 3: My question is once you listen to our concerns and take them back to Green, will anything change?

Lara (In role): Well, I cannot promise anything at this point, but please share your ideas and concerns with me and I will make sure Superintendent Green is aware of them. Of course, she has to assess the costs of any potential changes.

- It is important that Lara is representing the Superintendent and defers final decision making to her. This drama structure is important because it creates tension and multiple potential perspectives in the scene in regards to the power differential being created. In role as the Assistant Superintendent Jones, Lara deflects questions and defers to Superintendent Green. This opens possibilities for participants

to navigate issues of power and rehearse speaking truth to power (Novinger & Compton-Lilly, 2005), by which we mean speaking in role having been positioned as "excellent teachers."
- Lara could at some point appear in role as Superintendent Green and present a different view that contradicts Jones's version.

Inservice Teacher 4: Can we hire more bilingual teachers? I think that would solve a lot of problems?

Lara (In role): Well, I am so glad you brought that up. It's a priority for Dr. Green. You may have heard she met with all the building principals two weeks ago to discuss this very issue.

Inservice Teacher 5: Can you tell us the outcome of that meeting? What decisions were made?

Lara (In role): I can tell you this. Dr. Green came away from that meeting much more aware of the challenges facing the schools throughout the district. I know she is looking into what is best for the district given our current list of priorities.

- At this moment in the discussion, Lara stops the discussion and uses the dramatic structure of research interlude to replay the discussion to explore other interpretive possibilities.
- Among the possibilities of interest is scaling practices. Lara introduces parents in role into this research scene and creates an opportunity for teachers to speak in role as parents. This dramatic move introduces a different discourse and scale of accountability because parents are part of the conversation.
- In Chapter 5, we described how Camille uses her experiences as a mother during student teaching to scale jump when she is in Jean's classroom. When Lara steps back into role, there are new voices of parents brought into the scene and new opportunities for different conversations at a different scalar level.

Lara: I want to use another structure, a research interlude, to replay the discussion you were having with Jones. In this research interlude, I am going to step back into role as Jones. However, I would like to introduce a parent's perspective into this research scene to see what types of questions and concerns a parent might have. I would like to invite four of you to take on the roles of parents whose children are in the schools. I will repeat my last comment and then I will acknowledge that there are parents here today, and give you an opportunity to speak.

Lara (In Role): I can tell you this. Dr. Green came away from that meeting much more aware of the challenges facing the schools throughout the district. I know she is looking into what is best for the district given our current list of priorities.

Lara (In Role): I know we have a group of parents here today as well, and I want to thank them for taking their time to come to our meeting today.

- The goal of this research interlude is to introduce other perspectives into the discussion and complicate the situation. Lara had talked to four of the teachers before the research scene began and asked them to become parents of students later in the scene.
- The parents might praise, criticize, or have a mixed interpretation of what was happening in the district in terms of second language instruction. Whatever their responses, it repositions Lara (in role as Jones) into a different space and scale of accountability—speaking to parents.
- After the research interlude, Lara debriefs with the group and invites the group to generate some themes or ideas about they noticed in the research scene during their interactions. After listing these, the teachers can work in groups of five to create tableaus to embody the themes they have identified.
- To move the research scene to another scale—a district level conversation, Lara divides the group into pairs and invites them to develop a dialogue in role as Green and Jones two days later after this meeting. One teacher takes on the role of Jones and the other Green. Lara creates social history with simple stage directions that place the two the district office. They have worked together for two years now, and generally have a good working relationship. Volunteers are invited to perform their dialogue for the group.

As we stated earlier in the chapter, examining "whiteness" and how it informs discourses of teaching, schooling, and other social interactions connected to education is vital.

The Potential for Process Drama for Identity Research with Preservice Teachers and Inservice Teachers

In this section, we discuss the generative possibilities for a process drama approach, who benefits and how, and the risks and challenges of for inviting preservice and inservice teachers to participate in collaborative research on teacher identities. Berry's (2002) work on using the dramatic arts inspired our thinking about the potential of process drama for this research. She argues for the value of "the ludic imagination" (p. 132) by which she means imagination informed by play but also dramatic work in which "We must be willing to interrogate and dismantle modern cultural constructions and be unafraid to find out about ourselves and others" (p. 132). Teacher identity is a cultural construction that, as we have argued in this book, is informed by dichotomous terms like novice and expert and historically positioned by discourses of motherhood and nurturing that discursively construct teacher identity as static and linear and predictable. We recognize the importance of classroom experience for teacher identity development, and we have also demonstrated the dynamic, complex nature of teacher identities. We have provided examples from our research that illustrate how those identities are created, recreated, and shift in moments of instructional and professional interactions.

Process drama is a generative approach to teacher identity research because it provides opportunities to co-construct and analyze data with participants (Hunt, Crumpler & Handsfield, 2015) this way, the traditional positions of researcher and participants are shifted toward a more collaborative relationship. We recognize that relationships of power still exist in this approach; however, as participants become both co-constructors and analyzers of data, these relationships are redefined in ways that push these traditions toward one that is more collegial in nature. Redefined in this way, teacher candidates become makers of knowledge (Cochran-Smith, 2005) and more active participants in examining their own identities and begin to dismantle and reimagine the traditional constructions of teacher identity.

However, there are challenges that accompany using a dramatic approach to research on teacher identities. The facilitator of research scenes is also a participant in creating the drama world through their interactions with teacher candidates and inservice teachers. Therefore, the individual facilitating research scenes loses the ability to be in complete control of how ideas are taken up, replayed, and interpreted. Edmiston (2013) identified the tension that arises in facilitating performances with learners because while "dramatic performances extend the possibilities of performative learning. . .and ideas that might have remained unshared may be made visible for others" (p. 51), participants must also feel emotionally safe to work in role, develop tableaus, and participate in other process drama activities. Bolton (2007) argued for using drama games and warm up exercises as important for creating a relaxing environment in which participants felt comfortable enough to take a risk like stepping into role as someone else. These activities are not separate from the research scene but are an integral part of it because they initiate building a context through creating trust. Working with teacher candidates and inservice teachers to examine identity in a research scene has interpretive potential that we have shown in this chapter and throughout this book.

The potential of process drama for helping better understand teacher identity and how it can inform teacher education is promising. O'Neill (1995) argued that process drama's power resides its "demand that we discover other versions of ourselves in the roles we play or watch other actors playing." For a while, "We slip the bonds of our identities and participate in other forms of existence" (p. 151). Identities are dynamic and situated in the discourses in which we participate. Preservice and inservice teachers can "slip the social bonds" and identities that have been ascribed to them and that they have created for themselves, analyze them, and learn that understanding identity more deeply is integral to becoming a teacher. Based on this learning, the complexities of teacher identity become more visible and offer an affordance for more creative education of all teachers.

References

Ash, G. E., Kuhn, M. R., & Walpole, S. (2008). Analyzing "inconsistencies" in practice: Teachers' continued use of round robin reading. *Reading & Writing Quarterly, 25*(1), 87–103.

Berry, K. S. (2002). *The dramatic arts and cultural studies: Educating against the grain.* New York, NY: Routledge.

Bolton, G. M. (1992). *New perspectives on classroom drama.* New York, NY: Simon and Schuster Education.

Bolton, G. (1996). Afterword: Drama as research. *Researching drama and arts education: Paradigms and possibilities.* London: The Falmer Press, 187–194.

Bolton, G. (2007). A history of drama education: A search for substance. In *International handbook of research in arts education* (pp. 45–66). Dordrecht: Springer.

Branscombe, M., & Schneider, J. J. (2018). Accessing teacher candidates' pedagogical intentions and imagined teaching futures through drama and arts-based structures. *Action in Teacher Education, 40*(1), 19–37.

Carroll, J., Anderson, M., & Cameron, D. (2006). *Real players?: Drama, technology and education.* Stoke on Trent: Trentham Books.

Cochran-Smith, M. (2005). Teacher educators as researchers: Multiple perspectives. *Teaching and Teacher Education, 21*(2), 219–225.

Cook-Sather, A. (2006). Newly betwixt and between: Revising liminality in the context of a teacher preparation program. *Anthropology & Education Quarterly, 37*(2), 110–127.

Crumpler, T. P., Handsfield, L. J., & Dean, T. R. (2011). Constructing difference differently in language and literacy professional development. *Research in the Teaching of English, 46*(1) 55–91.

Denzin, N. K. (1997). *Interpretive ethnography: Ethnographic practices for the 21st century.* Thousand Oaks, CA: Sage.

Denzin, N. K. (2003). *Performance ethnography: Critical pedagogy and the politics of culture.* Thousand Oaks, CA: Sage.

Duke, N. K., & Del Nero, J. R. (2011). *Best practices in literacy instruction.* New York, NY: Guilford.

Dutton, J., & Rushton, K. (2018). Confirming identity using drama pedagogy: English teachers' creative response to high-stakes literacy testing. *English in Australia, 53*(1), 5.

Edmiston, B. (2013). *Transforming teaching and learning with active and dramatic approaches: Engaging students across the curriculum.* New York, NY: Routledge.

Edmiston, B. (2016). Promoting teachers' ideological becoming: Using dramatic inquiry in teacher education. *Literacy Research: Theory, Method, and Practice, 65*(1), 332–347.

Edmiston, B., & Wilhelm, J. (1996). Playing in different keys: Research notes for action researchers and reflective drama practitioners. *Researching drama and arts education: Paradigms and possibilities.* London: The Falmer Press, 85–96.

Hunt, C. S., Crumpler, T. P., & Handsfield, L. J. (2016). "Do you want an idea of what they're doing?" Transgressive data generation and analysis within a bilingual writers workshop. *International Journal of Qualitative Studies in Education, 29*(3), 399–425.

Lemke, J. L. (2000). Across the scales of time: Artifacts, activities, and meanings in ecosocial systems. *Mind, Culture, and Activity, 7*(4), 273–290.

Lempert, M. (2012). Interaction rescaled: How monastic debate became a diasporic pedagogy. *Anthropology & Education Quarterly, 43*(2), 138–156.

Lensmire, T. McManimon, S., Tierney, J. D., Lee-Nichols, M., Casey, Z., Lensmire, A., & Davis, B. (2013). McIntosh as Synecdoche: How teacher education's focus on white privilege undermines antiracism. *Harvard Educational Review, 83*(3), 410–431.

Neelands, J. (1990). *Structuring drama work: A handbook of available forms in theatre and drama.* Cambridge, UK: Cambridge University Press.

Norris, J. (2000). Drama as research: Realizing the potential of drama in education as a research methodology. *Youth Theatre Journal, 14*(1), 40–51.

Norris, J. (2009). *Playbuilding as qualitative research: The collective creation of dramatic representation.* Walnut Creek, CA: Left Coast Press.

Novinger, S., & Compton-Lilly, C. (2005). Telling our stories: Speaking truth to power. *Language Arts, 82*(3), 195–203.

O'Neill, C. (1996). Into the labyrinth: Theory and research in drama. *Researching drama and arts education: paradigms and possibilities,* London: The Falmer Press, 135–146.

O'Neill, C. (1995). *Drama worlds: A framework for process drama.* Portsmouth, NH: Heinemann.

Piazzoli, E. (2012). Engage or entertain? The nature of teacher/participant collaboration in process drama for additional language teaching. *Scenario, 2012*(02), 28–46.

Powers, B., & Duffy, P. B. (2016). Making invisible intersectionality visible through theater of the oppressed in teacher education. *Journal of Teacher Education, 67*(1), 61–73.

Raphael, J., & O'Mara, J. (2002). A challenge, a threat and a promise: Drama as professional development for teacher educators. *Critical Studies in Education, 43*(2), 77–86.

Rasinski, T. & Nageldinger, J. K. (2015). *The fluency factor: Authentic instruction and assessment for reading success in the common core classroom.* New York: Teachers College Press.

Schön, D. A. (1983, 2017). *The reflective practitioner: How professionals think in action.* New York, NY: Routledge.

Smagorinsky, P., Cook, L. S., Moore, C., Jackson, A. Y., & Fry, P. G. (2004). Tensions in learning to teach: Accommodation and the development of a teaching identity. *Journal of teacher education, 55*(1), 8–24.

Street, B. (1995). *Social literacies: critical approaches to literacy.* London, England: Longman.

Tanner, S.J. (2016) Accounting for whiteness through collaborative fiction. *Research in Drama Education: The Journal of Applied Theatre and Performance, 21*(2), 183–195.

INDEX

A

action research, 158, 159
adjacent timescales, 16
alternative assessments, 57
alternative identity trajectories,
    possibilities for, 82
assembly moves, in representational field, 44
authoritative discourse, 19, 84

B

Bakhtin, M. M., xiv, 12–13, 15, 17, 19, 21,
    26, 56, 82, 92, 93, 120, 142, 146, 151,
    155, 166
    See also chronotopes
Ball, A. F., 18–19
basal reading series, 38, 57, 60, 61, 94
becoming, identity as, 55–56
    See also Isabel's story (identity as
    becoming)

Berry, K. S., 25, 147, 148, 182
Biklen, S. K., 118
Blommaert, J., 17, 59, 92, 120
Bloome, D., 121
body movements, 34, 42, 43, 44–46, 81, 82,
    93–94, 121–122, 148, 160
    See also physical mobilities/movement
body positioning, 96, 120
Bolton, G. M., 22, 113, 159, 168, 183
Bourdieu, P., 35, 119
Britzman, D. P., 20, 135
Broadacre, 37–38
Brown, M. S., 119
Buchholz, B. A., 18, 20

C

Cafaro, F., 122
Camille's story (multiple identities), 11, 117
    mediating identities as a student teacher,
    124

multiple identity positioning, 122
multi-voiced identities, 120
ongoing active positioning, 135
popular culture and literacy instruction, 133, 139–140
positioning, 134
as a student teacher, 122–124
tactical positioning, 130
teacher identity of motherhood, 122
Canagarajah, S., 93
Carpenter, B., 60
chronotopes, 12, 32, 43, 120, 125, 134
application, 13
of becoming as identity. *See* Isabel's story (identity as becoming)
definition of, 17, 19, 92
and dramatic view of teacher identities, 12–13
historical and momentary agency, 17
quality, 13
and scales, 15
and scales, in literacy research, 18
and scaling practices as strategies and tactics, 17
and sociolinguistic scales, 15, 92
timescales, 15
as tying and untying of narrative, 15
clandestine interactions, 94, 111
clandestine mobilities, 112
classroom interactions, of students, 17, 19, 61, 135, 171
clock time, 12
co-action researchers, positioning teachers as, 160
Cochran-Smith, M., xiv
code/meaning dualism, 59
Coleridge, S. J., 159
collaborative instructional approaches, 33
Collins, J., 59
communicative competence, 59, 75
communicative repertoire, 81
comprehension instruction, 61, 78
Compton-Lilly, C., 18, 19
conceptualization of identity, 20–21

construction and reconstruction of identity, 12
contextualization cues, 46, 121
Conway, P. F., 20
Courtney, R., 24
cross-timescale relations, 19
Crumpler, T., 55

D

Danielson, C., 2
data
analysis of, 42
generation of, 41
debriefing, 153, 157
de Certeau, M., 17, 18, 35, 56
decontextualized language skills, 59
decontextualized word meanings, 74
De Costa, P. I., 93
Denzin, N. K., 148
dialogic model, 33, 166
and discursive turn, 34
dialogic relationships, 24, 142, 152
dialogue and interaction, 33
difference, identity as, xv
digital and multimodal literacy practices, integration of, 35
digital technologies, new, 95
digital turn, 32, 36, 34
discourse analysis, 33
discursive positioning
and repositioning, 4, 15
and scaling, difference between, 93
discursive turn, 32, 33, 36
dominant discourses, 35
double voiced discourse, 146, 152, 155
drama
and teacher identities, across timespaces, 21–24
dramatic approach, xvi, 2
See also process drama
dramatic inquiry, 24
dramatic positioning, 25, 113, 134

dramatic sequences, 167
drama worlds, 21, 24
dual immersion program, 58
Durkin, D., 61
dynamic, identities as, 26

E

eclipse motion, mobility literacy, 103–109
Edmiston, B., 24, 113, 134, 158, 159, 167, 183
Elbaz-Luwisch, F., 120
emotions
    in coaching interactions, 24
    and process drama, 24
    in relationship to agency and power, 24
    and teacher identities, 24
Estola, E., 120
event
    conclusion of, 75
    framing of, 64
everyday practices
    in cultural production, 17
    and power, 18

F

Foucault, M., 17, 20
framing activity, 173
framing of event. *See* event, framing of
Freedman, S. W., 18–19

G

Galman, S., 119
Gee, J. P., 26
Godley, A., 60
Gonzalez, L. E., 119
Goodwin, C., 44, 122
graphic organizers, 95
Green, J., 45–46, 121

Greenblatt, S., 26
Griffith, A. I., 120
group work, 57
    See also teacher study groups

H

Halverson, E., 18, 19
Handsfield, L., 55
Harré, R., xv, 25
Heathcote, D., 113
historical and momentary agency, 17
Hobson, A. J., 20
holistic code instruction, 59
Hunt, C. S., 24

I

identity awareness, and teacher development, 2
identity becomings, 91
identity construction, and timescales, 13
ideological becoming, xiv, 13, 19
independent silent reading, 94
indeterminacy, 71, 82, 84, 81
indexical meanings, in body movements, 44, 122
Initiate-Respond-Evaluate (IRE) exchanges, xvi, 71, 134
instructional sequence, and popular culture, 12
instrumentalism, 143
interaction unit (IU), 64
interaction units (IU), 46
internally persuasive discourses, 19
Isabel's story (identity as becoming), 57, 56
    all-English instruction, 58
    alternative identity trajectories, possibilities for, 82
    basal reading series, 61
    classroom research context, 83
    comprehension strategy instruction, 61

dual positioning, 65–71
English as a Second Language (ESL) instruction, 58
event conclusion, 75
framing of the event, 64
indeterminancy, 81
instructional approach, 57
literature discussion, 62–63, 60
meaning-based education, 60
positioning, 77, 83
and positioning and participation, 83
reshaping identities, 81
standardization, 59
strategic reading, 61
tactics, 84, 81
theorizing word meaning, 71
Transitional Bilingual Education (TBE), 58
isolated and direct code instruction, 59

J

Jackson, A. Y., 118, 125
Johnston, B., 20

K

Kennedy, M., 144
Knobel, M., 34

L

Landeros, M., 118
Langenhove, L., xv, 25
language and literacy, 33, 55
language shifts, and globalization, 17
Lankshear, C., 34
Lasky, S., 20
LeBlanc, R. J., 92
Lemke, J. L., 13, 16
Leonard, R., 90

linguistic code, 59
linguistic competence, 59
linguistic modeling, 33
linguistic turn, 33
literacy instruction, 5, 6
and integrating new teaching practices, 6
and learning tricks of the trade, 32
literacy memoirs, 169–171
inservice teachers, 177
preservice teachers, 172
literacy practices, shifts in, 5
literature discussion, 57, 62–64, 84, 60
Luke, A., xv, 4, 13, 23
Lyons, L., 122

M

making, in process drama, 22
"mantle of the expert" concept, 113
May, V., 118
McIntyre, J., 20
mechanistic models of language acquisition and assessment, 59
mediating identities, as a student teacher, 124
microethnographic discourse analysis, 43–46, 118
Mills, K. A., 34
mobile infinity of tactics, 18
mobile literacies, 18, 89
and identities, 90, 112
moved across the classroom space, 122
paradox of, 90
and scalar analysis, 93
See also Paula's story (mobilities)
mobility in troubleshooting encounters, 98
eclipse motion, 103–109
physical mobilities and collaboration, 98–103
stable designs, 103
technology consultants, 110–112
Mockler, N., 144

Moje, E., xv, 4, 13, 23
moments of interactions, 12, 17, 20, 23, 117, 120, 149–158, 168
Morgan, B., 20
motherhood
   identities, and teachers identities, 118
   as mediating identity, 120
   mothering as discursive practice, 120
   mothering as protective practice, 119
   and nontraditional preservice teachers and, 118
   as scale in language practices, 120
multilingualism, 36, 95
multiliteracies, 35, 36
multimodal literacies and language arts instruction, 6
multiple identities, 117
   nontraditional preservice teachers and motherhood, 118
   research practices, 121
   See also Camille's story (multiple identities)
multiple ideologies, 53
multi-voiced identities, 120
Murphy, R., 20

N

narratives, xv, 4
   dramatization of. See dramatic approach
   identity as, xv
narrative time, 12
nature of text and language, 21
New London Group, 34
Nielsen, A., 119
No Child Left Behind (NCLB), 59
Norris, J., 169

O

off script, 83
O'Neill, C., xvii, 22, 24, 183

ongoing active positioning, 135
O'Toole, J., 23, 147, 148

P

participation frameworks, 44, 122
Paula's story (mobilities), 89, 94, 124
   digital technology incorporation, 95
   digital technology incorporation, 95
   discourses of learning in, 124
   mobile practices, 91
   and mobilities, 95–96
   mobilities, cultivation of, 96
   mobilities and identities, 112
   positioning, 98
   stability and mobility in troubleshooting encounters, 98
   teacher participant, 90
   translingual mobilities, 96
   upscaling, 102–103
   writing, structuring of, 95
   on writing curriculum, 94
performance of identity, 26
permeable curricula, 84
Phillips, N., 90, 111
physical mobilities/movement, 98, 112, 151
   See also body movements
play building, 169
popular culture literacies, 52–53, 95
   literacy instruction, 11–12, 16
   and motivation, 123
   tactic messages, 52
position, identity as, xv, 4, 13
positionality, 26
   and emotions, 24
   as identity, 23
   teachers as shape shifters, 25
positioning, 83, 149
   and identity, xv, 4
   multiple positioning, 81, 120
   and repositioning, 25
   theory, xiv
positioning diamond, xv

positioning triangle, xv
power, 18, 135
power relations, 4, 34, 42, 44, 53, 89, 92, 102, 113, 119, 130, 147, 151
practice-based models, 35
practice turn, 32, 36, 35
procedure versus interpretation, 83
process drama, xvii, 2, 4, 134, 142, 147, 158, 159, 166, 172, 182, 167
   benefits, 183
   challenges, 183
   and chronotopes, 13
   and dramatic structures, 14, 15
   and emotions, 24
   framework, 26
   as a generative approach, 182
   and identity construction, 23
   and literacy instruction, 22
   and play with time, 23
   positioning and repositioning, 25
   and possibilities for teacher identity development, 21
   power factors of, 22
   and scaling practices, 113
   and teachers as co-learners, 22
   uses of, 14
professional development
   research interludes in, 158
   and teacher study group, 144
professional identities, 3
professional learning communities, 35

and action research and reflective practice, 159
debriefing, 153
developing role details and building trust, 160
identifying moments of tension, 161
imagination in, 159
as instances for data generation and analysis, 147
positioning teachers as co-action researchers, 160
and power relationships, 147
practices of, 159
in professional development, 158
and re-authoring a text, 148
and renegotiation process, 147
and scaling practices, 147
use of gesture and body movements, 148
research project, phases of, 5–6
research questions, 36
research scenes, 169
   inservice literacy memoir, 177
   preservice literacy memoir, 172
research settings, 36
reshaping identities, 81
Roberts, J., 122
Rogoff, B., 113
role details, and research interlude, 160
role playing, 147, 172
round robin reading, 166
Rutherford, V., 20

R

Radinsky, J., 44, 122
reading and writing workshop, 84
recursive coding process, 43
replay, and process drama, 23
repositioning, 4, 15, 25, 151
representational fields, 122
   and embodied actions, 44
research activities and participants, 38
research interludes, 23, 142, 143, 151, 152, 154, , 146, 156–158, 167, 176

S

scaled configurations, 93
scales, and chronotopes, 15, 93
   in literacy research, 18
   sociolinguistic scale, 16
   timescales, 15
scales/scaling, 89, 113, 122
   and discursive positioning, difference beween, 93
   higher scales, 93
   lower scales, 93

and mobility, 93
motherhood as, 120
scale jumping, 93
as strategies and tactics, 17
See also sociolinguistic scales
second career teacher, 118
semiotic mediation, 33
semiotics, and discourse, 34
shape shifters, 26
shape shifting
and meaning, 26
and social class, 26
and teacher identity, 23
sharing in partners, 174
shifting of identities, 32, 91, 102, 106, 109, 118
Slate, J. R., 119
Slembrouck, S., 59
Slocum-Bradley, N., xv
Smith, A., 90, 111
Smith, D. E., 120
social-communicative repertoire, 79
social positioning, 74
social practices, 16
social turn, 33
sociolinguistic scales, 16, 91
chronotopes, 15
See also scales/scaling
space-time intersections, 20
See also chronotopes
Spanish–English transitional bilingual education (TBE) program, 37–38
spatiotemporal concept, history as, 17
standardization, chronotope of, 57, 59
standardized test preparation, 60
Sterponi, L., 82, 94, 111
Stornaiuolo, A., 90, 92, 111
storylines, 35
strategic reading, 57, 75–78, 81
chronotope of, 61
repertoire, 79
strategies, definition of, 17
students' writing practices, 90
Sumara, D. J., 60

T

tableau work, 157, 172, 174
tactical negotiations, 94, 113
tactics, 84, 81
definition of, 18
mobile infinity of, 18
teacher evaluation, 2
teacher identities
boundless futures, 26
boundless pasts, 26
complexities, 13
development of, 1, 166
as dramaturgic, 20–21 (*See also* process drama)
performances in classroom research context, 83
and positioning. *See* positioning
scholarship on, 20
teacher study groups, 141
definition of, 142
guidelines for work team meetings, 145
and professional development, 144
and research interlude, 146
working with, 149
Teach for America, 35
teaching and motherhood, as embodied activities, 120
technology consultants, and mobilities, 110–112
textual discussion, 84
theoretical turns, 32
digital turn, 34
discursive turn, 33
practice turn, 35
theorizing word meanings, 71
time, playing with, 13
time and purpose, cycle of, 33
timescales
adjacent timescales, 16
and chronotopes, 15
and identity, 12
nested characteristics, 16
shifting across, 15

transitional bilingual education (TBE) program, 57, 58, 96
translingual mobilities, 96
troubleshooting encounters, stability and mobility in, 98
trust building, and research interlude, 160

U

use moves, in representational field, 44

V

Varghese, M., 20
video games, 11, 52

Vygotskian theories of semiotic mediation, 33

W

Wallat, C., 45–46, 121
Werner, C., 60
"what if" approach, 14, 24, 152, 155, 159
Wilhelm, J., 158, 167
Wortham, S., 18, 19

Z

Zembylas, M., 20, 24